The decline of transit

# The decline of transit

*Urban transportation in German and U.S. cities, 1900–1970*

GLENN YAGO
*State University of New York, Stony Brook*

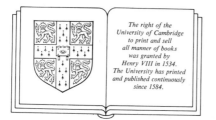

The right of the
University of Cambridge
to print and sell
all manner of books
was granted by
Henry VIII in 1534.
The University has printed
and published continuously
since 1584.

CAMBRIDGE UNIVERSITY PRESS

Cambridge
London   New York   New Rochelle
Melbourne   Sydney

*For Newman Zelinsky*

Published by the Press Syndicate of the University of Cambridge
The Pitt Building, Trumpington Street, Cambridge CB2 1RP
32 East 57th Street, New York, NY 10022, USA
296 Beaconsfield Parade, Middle Park, Melbourne 3206, Australia

© Cambridge University Press 1984

First published 1984

Printed in the United States of America

*Library of Congress Cataloging in Publication Data*
Yago, Glenn.
The decline of transit.
Includes bibliographical references and index.
1. Urban transportation – United States – History –
20th century. 2. Urban transportation policy – United
States – History – 20th century. 3. Urban transportation
– Germany (West) – History – 20th century. 4. Urban
transportation policy – Germany (West) – History – 20th
century. I. Title.
HE305.Y33   1984   388.4'0943   83–7297
ISBN 0 521 25633 X

# Contents

v

# Preface

Transportation captured and shaped Americans' vision of themselves and their country. The image of the railways and the open road reaches deep into our national memory. Physical and geographic mobility often substituted for social mobility – from the westward movement of the nineteenth century to the northern urban migrations of the twenties and thirties to the sunbelt flights of today. The romanticism of the railways and the animism of "Cougars," "Mustangs," and "Broncos" symbolize our collective identification with and sometimes alienation from a sense of place and a means of motion.

Today, most Americans live, breathe, and walk within the sight and sound of heavy traffic. Cars, keys, style changes, repair bills, and gasoline prices are so omnipresent in our lives that we have almost ceased to think about them. Transportation, deeply ingrained in our culture, is transparent; its impact on our daily lives is invisible and inevitable, beyond our vision of what can and could change our cities and our lives.

We confront the phenomenal cost of our urban transportation system – oil shortages, rising auto prices, highway repair costs, transit budget crises, mass unemployment in the automobile and tire industries, and rising environmental and highway safety problems. Less tangible, but no less real, are the effects upon community life. The division of urban space resulted in the isolation of the workplace from community life, the invisibility of the elderly and the young, and the erosion of social cohesion that preserved socially mixed and stable neighborhoods. Patterns of residential segregation by groups within classes (ethnic, racial, or age) drained community life

vii

of political vitality. Community interests are now perceived as separate from workplace concerns; the primacy of private over public life weakens political participation; and the socialization of children isolated from diverse income, age, and social groups reinforces the privacy of consciousness. The decline of mass transit narrows the range of urban experiences, isolating communities and workplaces and insulating urban travelers from the world between. These costs of the decline of transit are really a shorthand for the impact of transportation on ordinary lives.

The urban transportation policy question is usually posed in fragments: How must our means of travel change in the face of energy scarcity? How can we solve the fiscal crisis of transit? How can we improve the accessibility of jobs and services to the poor, elderly, young, women, and handicapped? How can we improve transportation productivity? These questions strongly challenge our past policies and suggest that a reassessment is in order. National policy prescribes bailouts, tax credits, and massive federal subsidies for the auto industry, while Americans are chided for their "love affair with the automobile." Consumers are urged to forgo car travel for a transit alternative that does not exist. The impossibility of rail development is countered by arguments of the energy limits of auto dependency. The options and accounts are contradictory and muddled.

First we must know what happened – the calculated abuses of political and economic power, the well-intentioned, although flawed, designs of planners and policymakers, and the structural changes in technology and the economy. This research hopes to link fragmentary questions and to sort out diverse issues in our urban transportation past by merging quantitative and historical methods in a comparative analysis of German and U.S. cities.

The years of research have produced many debts. I would like to thank Bradford C. Snell, whose work introduced for the first time consideration of economic institutional impact on transportation, for his cooperation and encouragement. I would also like to thank Maurice Zeitlin, Michael Aiken, Manuel Castells, Yudit Jung, David Kramer, Aage Sorenson, Erik

Wright, Leonard Weiss, Franklin Wilson, and my colleagues at the Social Organization Colloquium of the University of Wisconsin–Madison and the Sociology Workshop at the State University of New York at Stony Brook. My colleague and companion, Yudit Jung, deserves special thanks for her support and patience during trying times. I would like to thank L. J. and Sylvia Yago for their help and Noah and Gideon Yago for their good cheer. Also, I would like to thank the Data Programming and Library Service of the University of Wisconsin, the Madison Area Computing Center, the National Archives in Washington D.C. and Chicago, the Library of Congress, the Chicago Historical Society, General Motors Institute Alumni Foundation's Collection of Industrial History, the U.S. Department of Transportation Library, the American Public Transit Association Library, the Frankfurt Stadtarchiv, the Frankfurter Historisches Museum, and the Bundesarchiv. Frank Smith, my editor at Cambridge University Press, along with Helen Greenberg, the copyeditor, contributed immensely to this book. I am also grateful to Steve Fraser for initially encouraging interest in the manuscript. Thanks are also due to Ralph Nader, David Vladeck, and the Freedom of Information Clearinghouse, for helping me gain access to Antitrust Division and FBI files that had not been destroyed for "lack of historical significance." The American Public Transit Association, Highway Action Coalition, Department of Justice, and Federal Bureau of Investigation were also helpful, as were employees of other government agencies, law offices, and large corporations who undoubtedly would prefer to remain unnamed.

The Fund for Investigative Journalism, the Social Organization Research Committee, and the Graduate School of the University of Wisconsin–Madison supported this research. Many people helped; any mistakes are my own.

Glenn Yago

*October 1983*
*Port Jefferson, New York*

# 1

# Introduction

After World War II, most urban analysts greeted highway transportaion as a solution to urban congestion. Increasingly, mass transit was considered marginal to urban travel, limited to older, densely populated cities. Accordingly, policy decisions limited subsidization to transit in favor of the construction of highways.

Mass transit's decline was consistent with theories about urban change: Urbanization, housing, and industrial location patterns resulted from successive changes in the technology of transportation. Electrical traction first expanded transit's role but simultaneously dispersed urban residents, who came to prefer the automobile; changing consumer tastes reinforced this pattern. The most obvious factors associated with transit's decline – population, economic, and consumption changes – became central to theories accounting for it.

The prolonged energy crisis, beginning in 1973, shattered most accounts about the role of transit, which was suddenly promoted as central to energy-efficient and rational land use. If transit was now possible and desirable in new, automobile-oriented, low-density cities – whether Los Angeles, Frankfurt, or Tokyo – why had it declined in the first place? Why had researchers from fields as diverse as geography, sociology, economics, political science, and urban planning argued for decades that the population, income, and spatial characteristics of cities impossibly constrained mass transit services, thereby promoting motorization by federal, state, and local planners?

Heretofore, changes in urban spatial structure, consumer preferences, transportation policy, and business were explained in terms of technological developments that organized human activity and structured social life in our cities. Population and the supply of urban land grew as cities participated increasingly in the interregional economics made possible by technological advances in transportation (Berry and Garrison, 1958; Berry 1958; Berry and Horton, 1970).[1] These successive changes, in which new innovations overcame old spatial boundaries, characterized urban growth – the pedestrian, streetcar, or automobile city, the suburb, exurb, or agglomoration. The resulting size and density characteristics of cities thus predisposed them to "optimal" transportation solutions through both individual choice and the policies that reinforced them.[2]

Further elaboration of this theory in geographical, sociological, and historical studies came when economists focused upon how firms and urban residents choose to minimize their costs. Assuming rational choice, their econometric models postulated a trade-off between land and travel costs (for industry and individual alike) as changes in transportation technology increased access to cheaper land.[3] Historical decisions and institutional changes affecting urban services were considered irrelevant; current market costs of travel or land could explain urban changes "without reference to the heritage of the past" (Muth, 1969:47).

But what if cities were more than empty maps willed by railroads, highways, suburban developments, and office buildings whose location was determined by the last generation of technology and, in turn, structured the next group of market choices? How might the shared or conflicting interests of individuals and groups, and the results of their actions and policies, shape technology and, perhaps, limit it? Could the demographer's analysis of urban population characteristics or the cartographer's view of economic activities shaped by geography account for all the processes causing transit to decline?

The present research connects unexplored changes in the politics and the economy of the transportation industry and government policy, both at the national and local levels, to previously observed technological developments, urban growth, and consumer behavior. Which economic and social factors create transportation policy, the decision-making environment of consumers, and the spatial expansion of cities that diminish public transit? Why does the balance between public and private transportation vary within urban systems and between nations? How do state and economic policies operate to produce so many different outcomes?

In earlier research, the emphasis on technology, urban space, and/or consumer behavior resulted from studies within single nations. Such studies were unable to isolate variations in social, economic, and political structure highlighted by comparative analysis. The purpose of comparative analysis is to "manipulate groups of cases to control sources of variation in order to make causal inferences" (Skocpol and Sommers, 1980:182).[4] This process is acccomplished at various levels of analysis (both statistically and through comparative case studies) addressed to specific issues: the shared pattern of transit decline, the different rates of decline between societies, and the decline within them.

Although automobile transportation is ubiquitous, as are urban processes of metropolitanization, suburbanization, and industrial decentralization, the patterns of mass transit decline are by no means uniform. Comparative analysis identifies those factors in transit decline common to industrial societies, yet also isolates unique features within each society that account for differences in the rates of decline. By contrasting cases, analytically focused generalizations about sources of variation between urban societies and the political and economic factors favorable or unfavorable to motorization and transit decline can be made. Finally, local case studies within those societies illustrate the mechanisms of these macrosocial processes.

The study that follows compares urban transportation history in Germany and the United States since 1900, combining cross-national comparisons, cross-sectional analyses within countries at different points in time, and local case studies to present quantitative and qualitative historical evidence of how corporate power and state policy control urban development. As the most dynamic and powerful economies of their respective hemispheres in the twentieth century, Germany and the

3

United States are uniquely suited for comparative analysis of transit change.[5] Although the processes of capital accumulation and economic growth in these industrial societies are putatively similar, the composition of growth industries, the timing of economic concentration, and the process of state formation differed substantially. In both countries, transportation investment, first in railways and later in automobiles, was crucial to expanding industrial investment and output. Wildly changing forms of state intervention in the economy also occurred in both countries after the turn of the century. The similarities and differences of the two societies, and their political and economic institutions, allow the construction of a multilevel research design to explore the decline in transit in both societies and the differing dimensions and rates of urban transportation change.

## Structural conditions affecting transportation decline

Chapter 2 introduces and compares subtle changes in urban structure and corporate power that may precede changes in urban transportation systems. In that chapter, the shared pattern of transit decline is elaborated by measuring the location and composition (diversity or specificity) of economic production in a city, changing city functions (administrative, commercial/financial, and manufacturing), and regional and national differences in the growth of corporate power. Data for the largest German and U.S. cities in 1900 and 1970 are presented. Structural factors in these two sets of cities are discussed, and the following changes are compared: (1) ecological factors – physical characteristics of the city, and population size and density; (2) the position of the city in the national urban system; (3) the economic structure of the city as indicated by its pattern of industrial employment; and (4) the structure and role of corporations, as indicated by the number of corporate headquarters, their industrial composition, and their influence on transportation planning.

Descriptive data on transit decline and panel data analysis of German and U.S. cities address the following questions:

4

How did the different rates of capitalist development in Germany and the United States, reflected in their urban systems (indicated by differing rates of economic concentration, the composition of growth industries, and metropolitanization), result in transportation change? Did the scope and timing of corporate presence affect local transit decline? Was the diversity or specificity of corporate interests a factor? How do these complex relationships reveal why transportation-producing or consuming industries become dominant influences in transportation policy?

## National transportaion policy

Although Chapter 2 presents quantitative evidence on the structural conditions of transit decline, it cannot explicate the mechanisms involved. Historical evidence is necessary to link the analysis of macrosocial structural forces at both national and local levels with the mechanisms of corporate strategy and state planning policies.

Chapters 3 and 4 look at changes in economic growth, corporate structure and strategy, political institutions, and policy organizations at the national level that constrain transportation choice. Marxian and neo-Weberian theorists have argued in recent years that economic concentration and political centralization are the primary processes governing social and technological change. This claim will be examined by contrasting the timing and nature of economic concentration and political centralization, which condition the development and structure of transportation interests in Germany and the United States.

In the United States, the companies that produced transportation equipment and services favoring automobile use dominated transportation policy earlier than in Germany. Until the Great Depression, corporate strategy was sufficient to undermine public transportation. However, during the economic crises in the Depression and the post–World War II period, greater state intervention occurred to accommodate automobile expansion. German economic concentration occurred earlier in industries that consumed, rather than produced, trans-

portation services (coal, steel, mining, and other heavy industries), allowing diverse transportation interests (particularly
railroads) to survive longer. The emergence of the German
automobile coalition (including the growing oil and rubber
industries), however, led to the promotion of state policies
encouraging motorization. How did this change in industrial
interests alter the pace and direction of transportation
changes?

To understand transit decline, we must examine the strategies of companies and coalitions involved in transportation
production, the history and orientation of national transportation policy, and the conflicts within government and industry
over specific transportation proposals. How did industrial coalitions around transportation issues emerge from the different methods of capital accumulation in Germany and the
United States? How did these coalitions impinge upon state
policy, blocking alternative transportation technologies? What
are the organizations, political institutions, and historical conditions that turn corporate interests into state policy? What
characteristics of government (e.g., political fragmentation
and centralization of political authority) facilitate or hinder the
emergence of transportation policies?

## Local transportation politics

The urban structures and historical processes elaborated in the
earlier chapters are illustrated in Chapters 5 and 6, where case
studies of Frankfurt and Chicago are presented. These cities
were selected because as major growth centers, they have
served comparable functions in their respective national systems. This comparison demonstrates the macrosocial processes operating at the cross-sectional and national levels.
This examination of two cities with similar production structures and national standing links the national processes of
corporate strategy and state policy to local transportation
politics.

Local histories reveal how changes in transportation systems are related to changes in local political organization and
economic structure. Public participation in transportation deci-

sions, the bureaucratization of transportation planning, and the insulation of local corporate interests from public opposition are all examinied. The class composition of cities and their neighborhoods changes, thereby shifting spatially linked political interests and the constituencies mobilized in transportation conflicts. As urban government becomes increasingly centralized, local control decreases. This local decline in an environment of growing corporate power concentrated in specific industries nationwide affects transportation policy.

To illustrate this process, conflicts by transit workers and consumers over strikes, routes, rates, public control, and highway construction; changes in urban transportation planning and local government organization; and the link between urban planning and transit decline are all presented in these chapters. Class-linked organizations, interests, and decisions contributing to local transportation politics are identified.

The case studies address the following questions: How did changes in the urban economy affect transportation development? What was the interplay between economic changes in the city and corporate involvement in transportation planning? Did the organization of local government facilitate corporate intervention? If so, which organizational forms permitted penetration of special interests? What business associations, civic groups, or policy organizations provided the forum for corporate interests to develop and popularize their position? How did communities with less voice in local government organize around transportation issues? Which factors blocked the transportation alternatives formulated by conflicting or competing class interests?

## 2

# Twentieth-century mass transit in German and U.S. cities

Why did mass transit decline? Which processes, common to German and U.S. history, account for the shared pattern of decline in public transportation? The automobile is the easiest and most misleading answer and moreover under-scores the primacy of technical explanations of social change. As we shall see, increased car ownership did not always mean decreased use of transit. At times, the two modes coexisted peacefully; at other times not. What accounts for the variation between nations and cities in the rate of transit decline?

In this chapter, we consider data on U.S. and German cities and their transit systems before and after the rise of the automobile. The aim of this quantitative analysis is not to provide a definitive theory of what determined mass transit and its decline (such time-series data are not available) but to explore systematically and to approximate the structural factors of cities affecting transit's role.

This chapter presents a correlational and multiple-regression analysis of the largest U.S. and German cities in 1900 and 1970 to explore and identify urban structural processes of transit decline. The statistically minded reader should examine Appendix 1 for details about the data and procedures used. First, however, we should consider the extent of transit decline in Germany and the United States over this time period. These nationally aggregated figures describe the broad contours of urban transportation change. Next, the focus shifts to city-level data examining intercity variations of that process. The analysis concentrates on four sets of characteristics and their relationship to transit ridership and its decline: the level

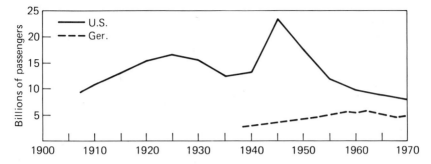

Figure 2.1. Decline of total public transit ridership in the United States and Germany, 1900–70. (Sources: for United States: American Public Transit Association, *Transit Fact Book, 1975–76;* data for 1907–40 are from Wilfred Owen, *The Metropolitan Transportation Problem* rev. ed. 1965; for Germany: Jahrbücher des Deutsches Reich, 1920–71.)

of urbanization (i.e., ecological characteristics of the city), the location of the city in its national urban system, the industrial structure of the city, and the presence and composition of corporate power.

The results of this exploratory analysis suggest the complex interaction of ecological and politicoeconomic characteristics of urban structure that produce transit change. How strong is the relationship between any of these factors and public transit? How are the observed relationships changed when controlled for by historically antecedent factors? What can these statistical observations tell us about urban structure and its impact upon public transportation?

**The extent of transit decline**

Figures 2.1 and 2.2 show the changes in public transportation in Germany and the United States over the past decades. Since 1900, public transportation has declined in both countries. Although the data comparing transportation development and use in their respective cities since the turn of the century are incomplete, several observations can be made on

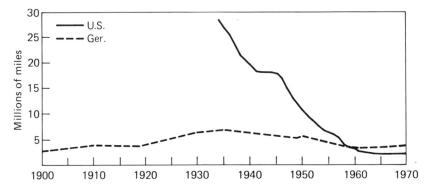

Figure 2.2. Decline of rail transit in the United States and Germany, 1900–70. (Sources: for United States: *Historical Statistics of the United States,* U.S. Census Bureau, 1975; for Germany: *Statistiches Jahrbücher des Deutsches Reich, 1920–71.*)

the basis of national data. Transit ridership in the United States began to decline immediately before World War I and stagnated throughout the twenties. This decline was hastened by the rapidly rising transit failures of the thirties. The decline leveled off during World War II, but ridership fell sharply and consistently afterward.

The impact of the automobile in Germany is evident in the decline of rail transit that began during the thirties and continued after World War II. (Aggregated ridership data for all transit modes for the prewar period are unavailable.) Although overall ridership increased gradually during the reconstruction period (1945–59), all transit modes suffered a decline that persisted until 1970. This decline was hastened by the substitution of buses for rail lines, producing an overall reduction in ridership.[1]

Since the 1930s, the use of the automobile has risen dramatically in both Germany and the United States.[2] Nevertheless, the relationship between public and private transportation has been neither constant nor continuous. However, both countries have seen fluctuations in the decline of mass transit, and there have been differences in the national experience. Germany's decline in mass transit came later and less suddenly than in the United States.

In the thirty largest German cities for which data were available, and which are in what is now West Germany, public transit ridership peaked later than it did in the United States. The greatest period of transit growth occurred during the Weimar period and peaked in 1929. From 1900 to 1970, average ridership in transit increased by about 210 percent, from 67.7 to 209.5 passengers per inhabitant. However, nationally aggregated figures show a decline of 27 percent by 1970, whereas the decrease in our sample of largest cities was only 16 percent. This indicates that the heaviest decline in mass transit occurred in middle-sized and small cities. During the same period, the automobile swept the country. In 1920, 422,000 private automobiles were registered, compared to 13,168,000 in 1970 (Krämer-Badoni et al., 1971: Tables I, II; 11, 16).

These shifting fortunes of mass transit reflect the massive "municipal industrialization" of infrastructural services by local governments between 1900 and 1929 (McKay, 1976). Transit decline between 1929 and 1970 indicates the impact of growing motorization policies of the Nazi and post–World War II periods.

Transit ridership in the United States peaked rather early, in 1908, and declined nationally by about 75 percent by 1970. In the thirty-one major metropolitan centers for which the best data were available, the decline was over 82 percent. This indicates that the pattern of decline was more uniform among cities of all sizes in the United States than in Germany. By 1970, U.S. operating deficits were about $2 billion annually, and nearly 90 percent of all operating systems that had existed before World War II had gone bankrupt and were municipalized. The reduction in passengers per inhabitant, from 205.8 in 1900 to 44.58 in 1970, is consistent with the massive reduction of transit service. From 1915 to 1957, 815 transit operating companies abandoned 18,082.54 miles of electrical rail service, which were not replaced by bus service (ATA Files, memorandum, New York City, November 18, 1958). Details on such abandonments in our sample cities are given in Appendix 1.[3]

What accounts for both the overall similarity between the two countries and the different rate of decline? By disaggregating national data and observing the magnitude of mass transit in cities and its change over time, the roles of different urban characteristics can be weighed and assessed.

In the following sections, we will consider the effects of urbanization, urban industrial structures, the place of cities in their national urban system, and corporate presence. For each effect, we shall examine the role of these characteristics upon the level of mass transit ridership in 1900 and 1970, and upon the rate of decline over that period.

## The effect of urbanization

Heretofore, it was thought that mass transit was determined by spatial (or ecological) characteristics describing the degree of urbanization of a city. Ecological research argued that the time of urbanization (a city's age) and its population structure (size and density) determined the level of transit services. Market scale and operating costs benefit from large populations and high density. The physical structure and settlement pattern of older cities were likely to be relatively dense, optimizing the access and efficiency of public transportation. Urban analysis in both the United States (Hawley, 1950; Schnore, 1968) and Germany (Lösch 1952; Christaller, 1966; Iblher, 1970; Klemmer, 1971; Weber, 1928) viewed transportation infrastructure as the outcome of its spatial location and population characteristics.

This argument is also the basis for conventional explanations of European and U.S. differences in mass transit. High national population density in Germany compared with the United States is considered to result from preindustrial and early industrial settlement patterns. The density and age of German cities allegedly account for their more advanced transport systems (Adams, 1981; Dunn, 1981). The same argument is used, of course, to explain intercity variations within countries–with older industrial cities more predisposed to transit than newer, low-density cities.

A closer look suggests that this argument oversimplifies the social processes of transit change. Although U.S. population density in all urbanized areas is half that of Germany, the population size and density per capita of the largest U.S. cities are only slightly greater than those of the top German cities in our sample. The greater proliferation of small and medium-sized cities in the U.S. national urban system, *not* vast differences between German and U.S. major metropolitan centers where mass transit is most important, misleads researchers to state that ecological characteristics determine the level of public transportation. For example, Hamburg and Los Angeles have similar population densities and totally dissimilar transportation systems – the former with a balance of auto, rail, and bus systems, the latter largely auto dependent.

The statement that urban size, age, and density determine the demand for transit services is widely repeated in sociological and planning studies of U.S. cities (Schnore, 1965; Kain, 1967; Council on Municipal Performance, 1975; Guest and Cluett, 1976; Legitt, 1974; Mamon and Marshall, 1975). The large correlation and multiple regression coefficients between these characteristics suggest spurious relations between them and mass transit; statistically, this indicates "multicollinearity," that is, that theoretically unspecified (and therefore unmeasured) variables inflate the effect of these characteristics on mass transit.[4] This suggests that characteristics causally prior to urbanization exist, and that by identifying and controlling for them, the observed relationship between ecological structure and transit would be reduced and more variance between cities would be explained.

In order to eliminate the problems of multicollinearity of these ecological variables and statistical problems of small sample size in both national groups of cities, factor analysis was used to reduce these measures to a single measure of the concentration and distribution of population in German and U.S. cities in 1900 and 1970. Many urban variables were included in this index, although they differed slightly due to time period and country – population size, population density, number of industrial establishments, rank of the city on a scale of national dominance (Abrahamson and DuBick, 1977: Table 3, p. 763), city age, value added in manufacturing, total retail sales, and volume of wholesale trade. In both countries,

13

similar patterns of population and spatial structural change occurred; mean population size doubled, and density declined by more than 50 percent in the sampled cities.

For German cities at the turn of the century, a high level of urbanization was strongly associated (.56) with extensive transit ridership and accounts for 29 percent of the variation between urban transit systems. However, when we control for other characteristics of urban structure, the impact of urbanization disappears and the amount of variance explained by a model including political and economic factors increases by 48 percent. Pre–twentieth century patterns of urbanization neither promoted nor inhibited mass transit system development. As we shall discuss later, the role of the big-city mayor in encouraging and accommodating industrial expansion was crucial to infrastructural development in cities (Hoffman, 1974).

By 1970, German cities had undergone cataclysmic changes associated with Nazism, war, and the "economic miracle" of the Federal Republic. Mass transit in the thirty largest German cities recovered from wartime destruction but never achieved the level of ridership of the Weimar period. Urbanization characteristics had an independent effect upon public transportation in 1970, illustrating how the cities' ecological structure was historically derived from the political and economic conditions of an earlier period. Population and density characteristics developed simultaneously with twentieth-century industrialization centrally linked to pro-rail industrial consumers of transit services. This interpretation is consistent with historical evidence discussed in later chapters. Urban spatial structure conducive to higher levels of public transportation in 1970 is the legacy of urbanization linked to capital accumulation and national urban system development during the earlier part of the twentieth century.

The above results relate to the role of urbanization under static conditions; focusing upon transit change as measured by declining ridership is a separate theoretical issue. To the casual observer, German urban dwellers enjoy more transit services than do their U.S. counterparts. This observation, although obviously true, obscures processes in both countries that have taken a toll on mass transit; it also obscures processes operative in one nation, but not the other, that slowed the decline. In Germany, as we shall see later, those processes were muted by support of mass transit by business leaders historically tied to rail transit and municipal social democratic policies. Nevertheless, despite the various countertendencies to transit decline, the role of mass transit was transformed and greatly changed by transportation policies. Did urbanization create spatial structures that promoted the demand for transit services and reduced mass transit's decline? Did larger, strongly urbanized centers experience less decline than lower-density, smaller cities? Was the degree of urbanization the salient feature of a city that reduced transit decline? According to our results, urbanization played no significant role in affecting the pattern of transit change in German cities.

In 1900 in the United States, ecological characteristics of cities measured in the urbanization index had a highly significant, positive impact upon the level of public transportation, accounting for much of the variation between pre–World War I cities. However, as in Germany, controlling for other urban structural characteristics reduces the impact of the urbanization index to zero; the variance in transit systems explained nearly doubles. The urbanization index serves as a proxy for generic processes of political and economic change that influenced urban spatial form.[5]

In 1970, U.S. urbanization factors had an increased impact on public transportation. The political and economic processes of the earlier period predisposed city development toward the spatial distribution of economic activity in residential, industrial, and commercial areas that supported mass transit. Urbanization became the central factor through which other structural effects of the city upon public transport are mediated. Rather than a proxy, urbanization was now an intervening variable between other determinants of mass transit. The spatial and population structures of the city were the result of its earlier position in the national urban system and its current role as a coordinating center requiring some level, although a greatly reduced one, of mass transit.

15

## The effects of urban centrality

Public transportation needs are defined, in part, by the role of the locality in the larger national system of cities. Cities have different functions in the organization of production, consumption, and distribution in broader regional economies. Geographers and sociologists have long noticed how these distributions of functions result in a stratification of cities (Duncan et al., 1960; Duncan and Lieberson, 1970; Pred, 1974; Berry, 1978; Preston, 1978). The position of a city within an urban hierarchy shifts with changes in market expansion and the location of growth centers in changing waves of economic development (Alonso and Meredich, 1970).

The more central a city is within the national urban system, the greater are the demands upon it to coordinate regional activities and control economic development. Consequently, the role of tertiary industries increases in those cities in order to coordinate agricultural and manufacturing activities in the broader region. In these cities, service employment, trade, and transportation are attracted from the hinterlands to a cental place where sufficient service infrastructures, including mass transit, are provided. Transit is necessary to expand the boundaries of urban settlement, absorb migrants to the cities, and spatially distribute economic activity.

The effects of centrality upon urban transportation are specific to the types of industrial activity that dominate a city and a nation during a given economic period. The more diversified the national industrial structure, the more likely the transportation system is to include and preserve mass transit. On the other hand, if the city exists in an economic environment strongly linked to auto–oil–rubber growth industries, highway transportation is more likely to be the preferred solution to regional integration of urban and hinterland activites.

Because of the small sample used in this study and the large size of the cities within it, it was impossible to use some of the potential measures of urban centrality used by others (Aiken and Bachrach, 1976; Preston, 1978; Newton, 1979). Most studies of urban centrality have large samples representing a wide distribution of city sizes and types. This allows the researcher to capture broader variations of central place functions between regional cities. Nevertheless, all previous studies have used the level of tertiary sector employment in the urban labor force as a dimension of the city's coordination function in the national system. The proportion of tertiary activities in a city indicates its functional specialization in servicing economic expansion. Higher demands for service, trade, and transportation reflect the city's position and function within the national urban system. This characteristic of urban labor force provides an approximation of the complex coordinating and integration functions of central places within the national urban system.

The role of tertiary sector employment, and thereby the centrality function of the largest German and U.S. cities for their regional economies, increased similarly between 1900 and 1970. The number of people employed in personal, business, government, educational, trade, and transportation services increased from 28.1 to 50.2 percent in Germany and from 32.1 to 51.8 percent in the United States.

Before the automobile era, the impact of urban centrality upon public transportation appears to have been quite strong. The concentration of central service, trade, and transportation functions during the height of German industrialization and regional economic expansion created structural demands for urban and regional circulation that were satisfied by growing mass transit.[6] Urban migration and work-related and commercial travel were all facilitated by transit developments. Also, in the United States, urban centrality before World War I was tied to a diversified industrial base requiring mass transit for spatial expansion. By 1970, urban centrality had no significant impact upon mass transit or its decline. This finding can be interpreted in two ways: (1) with the reestablishment of the national urban system in a divided Germany after World War II, tertiary employment varied less between the cities in our sample; or (2) tertiary employment after the war was too limited a measure, since the relevant centrality function is not national economic coordination but international integration. By the 1970s, Germany had achieved a dominant economic position in the European Economic Community. City functions characterizing integration and domination of the European market might have more relevance in explaining an infrastructural development such as transit. In any case, a more refined measure appears to be needed.

The growth of the service sector and its role in coordinating urban activities also do not play a significant, direct role in the United States. However, by affecting the form of urbanization, urban centrality of an earlier era indirectly affects the city's ecological structure, which in turn shapes and limits mass transit. The situation in the United States illustrates the possible role of urban centrality, in a specific economic context, in advancing transit decline. The more central a city was in the national urban system by 1970, the greater the level of transit decline. By 1970, corporate groups dominating cities and the national economy were closely linked to highway transportation. This more specific, economically concentrated corporate power differed substantially from the diversified and competitive corporate presence in U.S. cities in 1900, which encouraged transit development through urban centrality.

## The effects of urban industrial structure

Urban sociologists have long argued that the structure of local economic activities affects urban public policy (Mills, 1946; Crenson, 1971; Green, 1976; Friedland, 1981). Local economic activity organizes markets and spatially structures social interaction (Fischer, 1976). The distribution of commercial and residential neighborhoods and social activities is believed to facilitate or hinder political responses by city dwellers to social and political changes. It is also believed to direct flows of daily traffic patterns in ways amenable to public or private modes of transportation. These processes are assumed to be linked to the structure of economic activity in a city. Categorizing cities by their industrial activities allows us to identify the period of economic growth associated with the city's expansion, the city's integration with nationally important economic sectors, and the link between spatial patterns and different periods of economic growth (e.g., centralized versus decentralized manufacturing locations).

18

We are particularly interested in the impact of automobile, oil, and rubber industries – the major growth industries of twentieth-century U.S. and German economies – upon local economic activity and public transportation. The role of these growth industries is believed to have had an important influence on the types of transit systems that emerged and survived. In cities with relatively diversified economies the dependence of industries and consumers upon mass transit would encourage its continuation. Where local industry was specifically linked to transportation equipment-producing industries (e.g., automobile, tire, oil) through employment, branch managers, and employees, a political constituency and an economic market for highway transportation were assured. These newer industries, which were more likely to locate on the urban periphery, were important in structuring the urban market for automobile consumption and in mobilizing political support for highway building.

Unlike U.S. cities, German cities were formed before the industrial period. Nevertheless, German cities and the national urban system were fashioned by Germany's belated industrialization (Kölmann, 1976; Rüleke, 1977). Increased investment by German banks in heavy industry at the end of the nineteenth century initiated massive metropolitan growth that was sustained by the movement of workers to urban industrial centers. The increased industrial demand for labor, I will argue, resulted in more public transit to aid work-related travel and channeled explosive growth toward the urban periphery.

In these leading industrial centers, German social democracy found its strongest political base. The urban working class demanded more transit service as a central goal of local policy. Thus, demands by both business and labor contributed to Germany's level of transit service and its survival. After World War II, as Kindelberger (1967) has shown, investment and labor were concentrated in key growth industries: automobile and rubber manufacturing, oil processing, and construction. This later specialization of industrial and urban growth in transportation-producing industries might harm mass transit.

To test these arguments, it is necessary to measure the specialization or diversity of urban industrial employment in relation to old and new capital growth sectors (steel–electricity–mining or auto–oil–rubber) and industrial complexes. This measure shows the relationship of the local economy to national forces in order to ascertain the linkage between them and with mass transit. In Germany, no auto–oil–rubber sector really existed in 1900. Therefore, we measured the level of the older industrial group in 1900 and 1970 and found that it had increased slightly, from 27.3 percent to 36.7 percent in 1970. Thus, the old industrial sector survived and grew during this period.

However, the old sector's growth was far outstripped by explosive gains in the auto–oil–rubber group that started in the 1930s and accelerated after World War II.[7] By 1970, that sector accounted for 42.1 percent of the industrial employment in our sample German cities. In the United States, growth in the highway share of local industry had increased by over 360 percent.

The hypothesized relation between old industrial employment and transit is confirmed in German cities before World War I. Cities whose industrial labor force was concentrated in those core sectors of German industrialization – iron, steel, electrical manufacturing, mining, and other heavy industries – had more transit service than other cities. Because of class competition for urban residential space, business leaders attempted to resettle workers in suburbs where work-related travel would be subsidized by local and central governments. Additionally, as we shall discuss later, the steel–electrical–mining industries had the most unionized and politicized workers in Germany. This urban working class pushed for transit services as part of an expansion of all urban services.

For 1970, the evidence is clearer still. The finding that local industry is specialized and helps to shape the urban transportation system is particularly well demonstrated in German cities. The composition of the industrial labor force reflects both the structural requirements for work-related travel and the political base that can be mobilized to support specific transportation solutions. In cities with a higher concentration of workers in the older heavy industries, public transit is significantly more important. In contrast, in cities specializing in transportation-producing industries (auto–oil–rubber), public transportation significantly declines.

In accounting for the decline in transit, the specialization in automobile-related industries seems to play a role. In the United States, urbanization, industrialization, economic concentration, and specialization coincided, compromising the position of transit in American cities. As local economies became more dependent upon the prohighway industrial group, the decline in mass transit increased in both German and U.S. cities.[8] Cities economically tied to the dominant growth industries were more likely, it appears, to sacrifice transit to highway development in order to promote the consumption of locally produced goods, create employment, and strengthen their connection to national economic interests.

## The effects of corporate power

Social scientists have long investigated corporate intervention in local policies.[9] Previous studies emphasize the importance of the composition and economic concentration of industry in communities. Based upon observation of other policy areas, there are two ways in which we might expect corporate power to influence urban transportation systems. First, the concentration of major corporatons indicates that the city is the place where business strategies are coordinated and implemented, and where those strategies might affect local public policies when business interests are conveyed to public officials. Corporate policy can cover a wide range of issues, including, of course, transportation. Second, when national corporate power is linked to a particular set of industrial interests (e.g., auto–oil–rubber), local corporate representatives might intervene to pursue and protect business interests in regional planning projects.

Most previous urban and community power studies were case studies of this articulation of class power. In considering the effect of corporate power, corporate presence (as indicated by headquarters location) suggests the capacity to intervene, manipulate, and possibly control local transportation planning decisions. The ability to mobilize local support for its transportation interests might be linked to the corporation's presence at headquarters.[10] Thus, we might expect variation between urban transit systems to depend upon the distribution of corporate power and its role in local politics. The mechanisms of this process can be demonstrated only through an examination of the historical record.

Although German industry was highly concentrated late in the last century, it was composed of diverse industrial interests that fought over transportation policies.[11] The early cartelization of heavy industry and its connections to mining and banking created a powerful lobby by the end of the century that supported rail transportation between cities to subsidize lower prices and within cities to provide access to cheap labor. Thus, the older base of corporate power in Germany reflects the interests of industries requiring and promoting mass transit between and within cities.

However, the rise of automobile, rubber, and oil-processing firms in Germany during the thirties and after World War II could be expected to weaken public transportation. The decline that finally did occur by 1970 might be largely attributable to the recent link between German capitalism and highway transportation. Over the past century, highly concentrated elements of German industry competed for hegemony. These clashes influenced urban transportation policies as corporate power shifted to include growth sectors of autos, oil, and rubber. The mean number of top corporate headquarters in German cities increased from 1.6 to 10.9 from the period before World War I to 1970. But the smaller rate of transit decline in Germany, compared to the United States, can be imputed to the longer survival of competing industrial and consumer interest groups and their institutionalization.

The organization of corporate power in the United States took a different form. Since the turn of the century, the structure and composition of U.S. business shifted from competition and diversity to oligopolies linked to major growth industries, primarily automobile, oil, and rubber manufacturing (Weiss, 1962; Duncan and Lieberson, 1970; Evans, 1972). The mean number of corporate headquarters in the largest U.S. cities increased by about 19 percent between 1900 and 1970. Economic concentration and the rise of highway-linked growth industries, two coinciding processes not present in Germany, greatly weakened mass transit in U.S. cities.

How did corporate power influence mass transit? The statistical evidence is strongest when we examine mass transit in German cities in 1970 and its decline until that time. By 1970, the auto–oil–rubber industrial group had become one of the most influential business blocs in German politics. Highway building stimulated economic expansion both under the Nazis and during the postwar period. The pro-highway industrial group became rapidly concentrated and competed heavily with older industries over economic issues. The regression analysis indicates that by 1970 corporate power had weakened mass transit ridership; when we consider only the auto-linked industrial corporations, the negative impact is even greater. In terms of transit decline, this finding is even more dramatic. With economic growth dominated by automobile interests, transit decline in German cities depended entirely on local corporate power. The results, although not definitive, suggest that the political power of local corporations encouraged transit decline.[12]

In the United States, multiple regression analysis indicates that corporate effects vary with the composition of business power and competitive conditions of different historical periods. During the pre-auto era, corporate power was linked with an increase in public transportation. This finding is consistent with an analysis of the diversification of corporate power before World War I, when the auto–oil–rubber group was scarcely represented among the top U.S. corporations (Navin, 1970). The rapid expansion of mass transit at the time is associated with the rise of the coal–steel–electricity group, the major growth industries at the time. The electrification and expansion of transit pushed back the borders of cities; the use of electricity increased dramatically both domestically and in transit.

Although corporate power appears to have had no significant direct effect upon 1970 transit usage, it acted indirectly

23

through the historically derived demographic structure of the city. Nevertheless, it appeared to accelerate the pace of decline between 1900 and 1970. By 1970, the corporate groups predominant in U.S. cities and the national economy were closely linked with highway planning. This monopolistic corporate power differs substantially from the diversified and competitive economy of U.S. cities at the turn of the century. Concentrated corporate power may have furthered highway solutions to transportation problems at the expense of transit ridership, thereby maximizing the interests of transportation-producing firms.

## The effects of corporate and state intervention

In considering mass transit decline from 1900 to 1970 in the United States, attempt was made to measure corporate and state intervention in transit planning. Although such efforts oversimplify the processes involved and are difficult to interpret, they do approximate the impact of these interventions, which will be described more fully later.[13] Both intervention measures had little statistical significance, but the *direction* of their impact – with corporations increasing and municipalization decreasing the pace of decline – is worth noting.

As later historical evidence demonstrates, corporations furthered transit decline. For study purposes, corporate intervention was noted if the transit company of a city had been bought by National City Lines (the transit operating company created by the auto–oil–rubber firms to dismantle electrical transit) or if the local system participated with those firms in noncompetitive supply contracts for bus conversion, which led to reduced transit service. More than half of the largest U.S. cities met one of these criteria for corporate intervention. Although other tie-in arrangements could not be categorized, this finding supports later historical evidence presented in Chapter 4.

Did public ownership of mass transit inhibit its decline? In order to answer this question, we categorized cities according to whether or not they were controlled by public corporations. Apparently, public ownership did lessen the rate of decline in the largest cities.[14] Where municipalization occurred, transit declined less.

A closer look at this process suggests conditions under which public ownership reduced transit decline. If municipalization occurred when transit was a popular issue in local politics, as in the Populist era, a tradition of transit service was institutionalized locally. However, when failing private transit operators were simply bailed out, public takeovers probably had little impact. This interpretation is suggested when we examine transit decline in the handful of cities municipalized under popular pressure prior to 1945 (New York, San Francisco, Cleveland, and Detroit). In those cases, mass transit declined less than the mean of other large U.S. cities.

## Conclusions

Traditionally, social scientists have focused on spatial and population characteristics of cities to account for variation between transit systems. Theoretically, this explanation concentrates upon the most proximate, visible, and easily measurable dimensions of urban structure. But in some cases, when we compared data on German and U.S. cities with nearly identical population size, density, age, and other ecological characteristics, we found little more difference than among random cities. Urbanization, when it seemed to play a role, had a strong historical component – that is, how it was developed and shaped by the political and economic conditions of earlier eras. How, then, can we explain variations in the level and decline of transit among cities with similar population and physical structures?

This comparison of German and U.S. cities over the past century introduces dimensions of urban structure previously ignored. To measure and assess the role of these dimensions is a complex undertaking, and this study is only exploratory. We suggest that the difference in transit between Germany and the United States and between the largest cities in those two countries can be traced largely to the following characteristics: the position of the city within its national urban system; the link between the local economy and national economic interests; the industrial composition, level of economic concentration, and presence of corporate power; and the influence of these factors upon urbanization.

By examining sets of cities in these two countries over the past century, this study reveals aspects of cities that are causally prior to the ecological structure of cities shaped by technology. This chapter has explored possible indicators of the political, economic, and social structure of cities, but the measurement of these theoretical categories is by no means complete. Many potentially relevant variables – plant locations of top corporations, industrial trade associations, financial organizations, real estate market data, and so forth – are missing given the limitations of our data. No information is available about the changing economic, ecological, or transportation structure of cities at this level of detail between 1900 and 1970, or of transportation market changes that might have affected them.

Although we can account for some of the variation between cities in their levels of transit service and the transit decline common to countries, quantitative analysis cannot identify the mechanisms involved or the historical and socioeconomic forces that activated them. Partially, this problem results from the limits of measurable data on transportation systems and politicoeconomic characteristics of cities during the process of decline, rather than from our before/after statistical snapshots of the largest cities in both countries. The lack of intervening data makes it difficult to construct a causal model, but the material available is suggestive. However, it is also possible that the decline of transit may not be explainable by the characteristics of the cities involved.

Our statistical models deal primarily with factors that structure the demand for transit services; neglected are all the factors beyond the city limits that affect localities and the national industries that supply transportation. Although an attempt is made to identify national linkages between localities, the national urban system, corporate power, and the industrial structure of employment, these city traits are really only proxies, albeit statistically stable ones, for complex historical forces that produced these relations.

Identifying quantitative variables from both ecological theory, which is implicitly functionalist, and political economic theory, which is based on differential power, clarifies more about transit change than either theory alone. Earlier sociological research on transportation used static cross-sectional data to make what is fundamentally a longitudinal argument. By introducing these panel data before and after motorization, this research embeds ecological processes in a broader historical context.

In short, the research in this chapter poses the following questions: What were the major powerful forces in Germany and the United States during the period under consideration, especially forces with direct interest in transportation? Given such a distribution of power and interests, what transportation outcomes could be expected? It follows that one of the emergent power blocs has been the automobile–oil–rubber complex. Transit decline can be expected to be most severe where that complex is strongest – and as the results indicate, it is.

This type of macro-panel study is a fertile methodology that offers the possibility of both quantitative rigor and historical sensitivity. The research taps aspects of cities causally prior to what has heretofore been considered as the technologically derived ecological structure of cities. The research explores possible indicators of political, economic, and ecological aspects of cities, but the measurement of those theoretical categories is by no means complete, as noted above.

Because of methodological limitations we must move beyond quantitative analysis to examine historical processes at the national level. These processes better define the social origins and mechanisms that produced transit decline in Germany and the United States, explain the great variations in the rate of decline, and further illustrate their operation in local case histories.

**3**

# The formation of national transportation policy: the case of Germany

## German economic background

By the end of the first wave of industrialization in 1873, Germany under Bismarck had established the legal framework, the interurban transportation system of railroads and shipping, and other infrastructural supports for economic growth and market expansion and organization. Unlike other capitalist economies in the nineteenth century, Germany showed increased industrial and financial concentration from the very beginning.[1] Moreover, the largest monopoly firms were more vertically integrated and diversified than was big business in the United States, Great Britain, or France. The amount of family control over these businesses was clearer and more significant than it was in other capitalist countries (Sombart, 1954:447; Kocka and Siegrist, 1978:36–49).[2]

Aside from economic concentration and monopoly present in early German industrial structure, the nature of the dominant firms was critical to transportation policy formation. German industrialization, which rested on heavy industry, mining, railroads, and electro-machinery, produced a group of capitalists whose power dominated until the close of the Weimar period (Brady, 1934:129–34; Kocka, 1973; Abraham, 1981). The strong control over the economy exercised by a comparatively small industrial group, combined with centralized state power, resulted in an exceedingly narrow definition of transportation policy.

Another economic element mitigating the effects of early suburbanization, which in the United States often made rail lines less lucrative and thereby opened the way for automotive transport, was the strong concentration of land owner-ship. The land speculation and suburban settlements that were possible largely through decentralized landholdings in the United States were prevented in Germany, where land was concentrated primarily in agricultural hands. Urban ex-pansion in Germany was largely dependent upon the annexa-tion of surrounding villages, and not upon settlements or housing booms involving open lands that surrounded major cities (Dickinson, 1961; Hartog, 1965; Emrich, 1974).[3] There-fore, the reduced speculation in German land and housing markets contributed less significantly to capital accumulation than in the United States.

The absence of economic growth and concentration in the auto industry that might have given rise to earlier motoriza-tion attempts in Germany cannot be explained solely by that country's highly concentrated, politically powerful heavy in-dustries. The earlier rise of the automobile sector in the United States, and later growth in Germany as well, required assembly-line techniques and mechanized production to re-duce unit costs, thereby permitting mass production and consumption.

The slower implementation of full-scale mechanization in the German auto industry, compared to the United States, helps explain the differences in transit development between the two countries. Both the type and the extent of mechanization dif-fered as a result of class relations in the German factory system (Maier, 1970; Roth, 1975). Mechanization began there in the simpler tasks of production to assist skilled laborers and im-prove their production (Gideon, 1948:38). These same craft workers resisted any extension of mechanization to more com-plex tasks that might compromise their job autonomy and secur-ity (Roth, 1976). The existence of craft traditions and strong skilled labor unions in the German auto industry, which evolved out of the highly skilled bicycle industry, helped to delay implementation of the assembly line in Germany (War-ner, 1968:169). Thus, extensive mechanization and the assem-bly line, central to mass production in the auto industry, were resisted in Germany until the thirties. This suggests how class relations in production, by resisting full-scale mechanization, affected the speed of corporate growth and concentration in the auto sector.

This combination of forces led to a stalemate in urban transportation policy between industrial groups. The economic domination by railroad interests – namely heavy industries and mining – created clear partiality toward rail transport, and a reluctance to change the production of transportation equipment – particularly the automobile. German capitalists resisted the economy based on consumer demands that characterized U.S. economic growth. Their investments were oriented instead to increased production of capital goods.

American industry, based on the concept of lowering production costs through mechanization and increasing profits by forging an internal mass consumption market, was rejected in Germany. For German capitalists, consumer goods industries were merely a diversion from their traditionally export-oriented market of capital goods (Hartwich, 1967; Maier, 1975; Davis, 1978; Aglietta, 1979). The technology and organizational innovations of U.S. industry were considered adaptable; high wages and mass markets were not. Economic concentration and mechanization were the mainsprings of German rationalization. This selective rationalization and resistance to mass marketing and production reinforced the power of the old industrial groups, whose stranglehold on market innovations was broken only by the Nazis.

The stalemate between transportation equipment producers and transportation consumers in traditional sectors of German industry was manifested in the lack of capital available to the nascent German automobile industry for expansion (Klapper, 1910:17–20; Pflug, 1929:256–7). Given the lack of supporting industries such as petroleum and rubber production, which were abundant in the United States (Kocka and Siegrist, 1978:36), the German automobile industry developed only a limited luxury market for automobiles.[4] In 1929, the *Vossische Zeitung* (14 March, "What the Banks Scorned") exposed the German banks' refusal to give the Opel family more capital for expansion, and efforts by other groups to establish an automobile trust.

The subdual of the automobile industry and its impact on

transportation policy was broken with the penetration of U.S. capital into Germany during the Weimar period, and later under fascism. With no German capital, Adam Opel AG and numerous other German firms obtained U.S. capital under the Dawes plan (Link, 1970). Investments by General Motors (GM), Standard Oil, Dupont, U.S. Lines, and other industrial, banking, and transportation firms were common. With new foreign capital for new industries, the prominence of automobile related industries in public policy formation became apparent.[5]

The GM takeover of Opel was the turning point in the history of the German automobile industry, and was typical of the activities of the earliest and still most powerful U.S. multinational firms. The GM strategy regarding foreign acquisitions was, in the words of GM Overseas President James Mooney, "to get in quickly where the Huckleberries were thickest" (*Fortune*, November 1945:36). GM believed that through Germany it could dominate the European market using the same strategy that had been applied in the United States:

General Motors' analysis of the European economic situation justifies the conclusions that Germany has effected during the past few years great industrial progress. It is believed that insofar as the automotive industry is concerned, Germany's present position is now somewhat analogous to that of the U.S. at the beginning of the development of the industry. A great expansion therefore appears to be certain. (*General Motors World*, April 1921:1)

Mooney, also president of the American Manufacturers' Export Association, commended the aid of the Dawes Commission in allowing such investment to occur (speech to Export Managers' Club, *Detroit News*, March 25, 1928). By 1933 Opel had become the largest auto manufacturer in Germany.

## German political background

The nationalization of the German railroads in 1879 was an early recognition of the state's responsibility to meet the infrastructural needs of business. It has often been noted in German historiography that limited reforms (such as those instituted under Stein-Hardenberg and, later, Bismarck) led to the centralization and rationalization of state bureaucratic power, which made German absolutism compatible with the emergence of capitalism. The state became the structure through which the often shaky coalition of industrial, financial, and agricultural capital operated. Centralized government insulated this coalition from the pressures of the middle and lower classes, and it tended to solidify the economic and political support for state power in upper-class German society.

The focus on local government in Germany was to improve cities as loci for capital production, distribution, and exchange, just as it was in the United States during its reform period. Urban expansion had to be orderly, insulated from erratic speculative development that might raise questions about the legitimacy of such growth. Thus, building codes, land use ordinances, and urban planning were integrated in municipal government by the late nineteenth century. Attempts by less powerful speculators to enter and grow in the interstices of the urban economy were deterred by the expanding functions of city government and the centralization of landholdings on the urban periphery. "Municipal industrialism," the expansion of municipal ownership and control over infrastructural investment in social services, became widespread.[6] Urban mass transit was electrified almost completely by the city governments (McKay, 1976), and since this work was done by municipalized public transit firms, transportation fares declined during the first decades of the twentieth century. The declining rates, enhanced by state subsidization, had enormous effects upon the growth of public transportation, housing, and other public expenditures (Desai, 1969).

Social measures in general and public transportation in particular benefited during the period following the 1918–19 revolutionary upheavals in German cities (Rebentisch, 1975). However, the increasing costs of public transportation due to rising material and labor costs, the reluctance of progressive city governments to raise transit rates, the growing fiscal crisis of German cities, and the parliamentary stalemate within the central government created a transportation policy impasse that was broken only under fascism.

This early institutionalization of public support for rail transit greatly strengthened public transportation and ensured the continuing role of rail transit in Germany. Central railroad nationalization, municipalization of local systems during a period of increasing ridership, and public demands for transportation service during the Weimar period left historical traditions of rail traffic that were preserved in spite of the motorization strategies of Nazi and post–World War II Germany.

What occurred during the twenties–the identification of transit as an economic issue by an increasingly politicized urban working class–will be illustrated in greater detail in the case history of Frankfurt. The rise of transit in local politics, along with the established role of urban planning in city government, which assigned a central role to transit, created unified pressure to make urban issues such as transit subject to state control and regulation. This process is central to explaining the differences in magnitude and rate of decline in transit between Germany and the United States.

## German national transportation policy and the decline of public transit

German national transportation policy excluded highway transportation prior to 1933. Until then, transportation policy meant rail policy. Rail-related industrial capital's interests were advanced by state fiscal, trade, budgetary, and regulatory measures.

### Fiscal measures

As early as 1906, the Reich Stamp Tax Law mandated the taxation of automobiles to provide general revenue. On April 8, 1922, that tax was expanded to cover higher engine size, and was raised again in 1927. In addition to this excise tax, a 15 percent tax was levied on automobiles. The Reichfinanzhof (tax ministry) allowed income tax deductions for the journey to work *solely* for public transit-related travel. These fiscal measures promoted public and discouraged private transportation. Moreover, they were part of the SPD's (Sozialdemokratische Partei Deutschlands–Social Democratic Party) fiscal strategy of subsidizing public services. This policy coincided with the desire of older industries to maintain adequate public rail transportation to facilitate urban growth and physical mobility to urban workplaces.

## Trade policy

The automobile was sacrificed to foreign competition in order to protect the market for established German products. Again, this policy reflects the failure of the automobile industry to place its own trade priorities on the agenda of German capital during the twenties.

## Budgetary measures

Paragraph 13 of the Fiscal Equalization Law of 1927 prohibited the use of automobile tax revenues for construction of public roads. Those revenues went into a general fund used for social services and other expenditures, including the public railroads. This law represented a convergence of the interests of the rail-related industrialists and the leftist political parties that opposed pro-automobile measures up to the early thirties (the Social Democrats changed their position; the Communists did not). Indeed, by 1931, city officials and business powers lobbying for more road construction were fearful that the left would block them (Magistratsratmitglied Dr. Heun to Kurt Batsek, 14 March 1931, FSA 3461/BD. 1; Kaftan, 1956).

## Regulatory measures

Regulation was critical to both commodity and personal transportation. The early nationalization of German railroads was designed to lower the cost of transporting coal in order to make German coal more competitive. Municipalization of urban public transit was based primarily upon the desire to decrease and subsidize the cost of transporting labor (Rowe, 1906). By the 1920's, rail-related interests had succeeded in binding together the rate structure of rail and motor carrier traffic (through the so-called Schenker contracts), thus insulating the rails from the potential threat of motor shipping. Rising rail transportation costs (and the rising state deficits resulting from rail subsidization) raised questions about the wisdom of rail dependency in the minds of some German capitalists. With support from older industrial circles, the Reichsbahn sought to buy up smaller trucking lines and exact heavy tolls from trucking firms connected with rail shipping. Further, with support from some elements within the DIHT (Deutscher Industrie u. Handelstag – German National Chamber of Industry and Commerce), the Reichsbahn asked the government to establish a rail monopoly over motor truck traffic.

Businessmen discussed policy measures and became part of a general Schiene/Strasse (rail/street) debate within German industry. Which mode of transportation should be actively subsidized by the state? Was German industry too dependent upon railroads? Which mode could provide lower short-term costs in fiscally tight times?[7]

German policy placed the automobile industry in a weak position. It is easy to see how this policy frustrated the industrialists interested in promoting new transportation alternatives. Nevertheless, economic conditions were shifting to make motorization more politically viable.[8] The influx of U.S. capital, the purchase of Opel by GM (Fleischer [Opel] to Hitler, 23.10.1936, BA, R43/753), and the rising costs of commodity and personal transportation all led to the emergence of a motorization lobby in Germany.[9]

By 1929, the activities of the RDA (Reichverband der Automobilindustrie – Reich Association of the Automobile Industry), the HAFRABA (Verein für Vorbereitung der Autobahn Hansastädte–Frankfurt–Basel – Association for Promoting the Hansa Cities–Frankfurt–Basel Autobahn), and others were creating political support in German industry for a shift away from the exclusive use of railroads. By the end of the twenties, industry and trade associations were split between the traditional rail enthusiasts and those supporting motorization and highway building. It is evident from the German business press and the "Denkschriften" (policy papers) of those associations that any mode of transportation was supposed to be able to meet the needs of both transportation-consuming and transportation-producing industries. By helping to increase profits, a given transportation mode would maximize employment, be a countercyclical source of government spending (without competing with private capital), and assist capital accumulation in other important branches of industry (e.g., military industries).

With the Nazis' takeover of state power, a concerted attempt was made by auto-linked capitalists to break the resistance to the automobile by rail-related capitalists and state bureaucrats. A community of interest was established between the automobile industry and the German fascists who pursued a national transportation policy encouraging motorization.

### Fascism and national transportation policy

By February 1935, the motorization policy of German fascism was firmly established. In that year, the International Motor Transport Congress held its annual automobile exhibition in Berlin, and Adolf Hitler greeted it with a bombastic speech advocating further motorization. Such speeches became an annual occurrence after the first automobile exhibition at his Chancellery in 1933. It was not surprising that automobile industrialists met with Hitler. Louis Renault and Adolf Hitler had much to discuss.[10] In their long, rambling talk, Hitler noted repeatedly the importance of motorization, how it could serve the "primacy of the Reich idea," economic recovery, and increased employment, and why it would transform German society:

The endeavor of the National Socialist leadership is directed toward decentralizing the industrial working population from the production centers to the countryside. Factory work must be supplemented by field work. For the conveyance from living quarters to work quarters a cheaper means of transportation than heretofore available must be created. (21 February 1935, BA, R4311/748)

Motorization would serve both industry and the nation through the Nazi social policy of "rebuilding the German worker within the German State." By dispersing the working class to various settlements on the outskirts of major cities under the Nazi formula, suburbanization would ensure a measure of social peace and redefinition of classes in a nationalist framework. Through motorization, the building of highways, the construction of the "people's automobile," and the general improvements associated with these policies, fascism would provide physical and geographic mobility for a disciplined work force instead of social mobility.

This transportation policy did not go unopposed within fascist ranks. It was not until 1931, after a meeting with representatives of the German automobile industry, that Hitler himself adopted the call for full-scale motorization (Grottkopp, 1954). The Nazis' so-called left wing continued to oppose motorization. Gregor Strasser, a spokesman for that group, denounced Hitler's opportunism and opposed pro-auto measures as "at the best a rising of comfort and serving the satisfaction of luxury needs" (quoted in Kaftan, 1956:152). Ernst Röhm, head of the SA (Sturm Abteilung), also opposed such policies, as did his economic adviser, Erich Lubbert, a member of the Reichverkehrsrat (Reich Transportation Council) representing the streetcar associations. This faction of the Nazis spoke to the consumers of urban transportation who sympathized with the Nazis and those elements within the industrial associations who opposed motorization. In spite of this support, these elements were purged from the Nazi party and from the Reichsverkehrsrat by 1934; Strasser and Röhm were murdered, Lubbert imprisoned (BA, R11/1542).

Motorization, mobilization, and militarization of the society and the economy merged and became central to Hitler's economic and social policies. Motorization would stimulate the economy and create jobs. The society could be mobilized to create a highway transportation system that would unite the Reich. Motorization was important for creating a modern military, whose expansion would spur economic growth and instill social discipline. In short, motorization was simultaneously a military, ideological, and economic strategy in the Nazi drive to restructure German society.

General Staff member Oberstleutenant Nehring captured the Nazi policy succinctly when he wrote, "No military motorization without economic motorization . . . the interests of defense demands the motorization of the economy" (quoted in Müller, 1936:40–1). After some prodding by the RDA,

Transportation Minister Freiherr Eltz von Rubinach stated his wish to reverse the amounts invested in transportation (7.3 billion marks for railroads and 4.2 billion marks for the automobile industry): "You see from these figures that motor transportation is in second place in German transportation and requires doubling [capital investment] to overtake the railroads. I only ask how I, as Reich Transportation Minister, can establish the means to produce this result?" (*Berliner Börsen-Zeitung*, March 11, 1934).

This position was strongly cultivated by the automobile industry. On every transportation-related issue, the RDA and representatives of the International Motor Transport Congress (including Louis Renault and James Mooney of GM) met early and often with Hitler and his aides to formulate transportation policy.

Mooney was particularly active in aiding Hitler's motorization program. GM's global strategy of promoting the automobile involved collaboration with the Nazis. As president of the GM Overseas Corporation and head of the U.S. Manufacturers' Export Association, he did much between 1933 and 1939 to aid Hitler's program. As Snell (1974:A16–A33) has suggested, Mooney was probably crucial to GM's efforts to direct operations in Germany and to extract profits even after the war began. GM has vigorously denied this. Fragments of documents from the Reich Economic Ministry suggest that American Opel directors Cyrus R. Osborne and Elis S. Hoglund arranged for continued contacts shortly before and after the United States entered World War II. (Vermerk, Saager to Krohn, Confidential, 19 December 1941, Reichwirtschaftsministerium, BA, R7/3288).

Even more suggestive of such an arrangement was a letter from James B. Stewart, American chief counsel in Zurich, to Fletcher Warren of the State Department containing the following report:

Mr. Eduard Winter, formerly General Motors distributor in Berlin and at present this Company's representative in Paris, acts as courier in delivering communications from Mr. James D. Mooney, President of General Motors Overseas Corporation, to high German officials in Paris. Mr. Winter has a special passport which enables him to travel freely between occupied and unoccupied France. Mr. Mooney is known to be in sympathy with the German Government and the persons who supplied this information believe that the General Motors official is transmitting information of a confidential nature through Mr. Winter. (Stewart to Warren, February 5, 1941, released under a Freedom of Information request from the State Department)

Mooney's philosophy about business and politics is revealing. At the International Motor Exhibition in Berlin in 1933 he said:

The Management Mind in the Automobile Industry has always had a great contempt for politics. The point has been missed that although we, in the Automobile Industry, have continually dismissed politics and government as quite unworthy of the attention of serious-minded men like ourselves, politics and government have been continually increasing their interest in the Automobile. (Mooney, 1933:2)

In spite of his contempt for politics, Mooney deftly used it to promote GM interests by embracing the Nazi regime and participating in the America First Movement to keep the United States out of the war. This action was consistent with the politics of the Dupont family, who owned and controlled GM at the time, and who supported the Liberty League and the America First Movement. Mooney was also an early organizational theorist who wanted to see U.S. business run like the "Prussian military" he so admired and who called for "military efficiency" in business and society (Mooney, 1931).

To understand the motorization policy that eventually led to public transportation decline, we should examine the various regulatory, fiscal, and direct subsidizaton and investment policies that promoted the automobile under the Nazis.

### Regulation

During the first years of fascist rule, many of the legal barriers to motorization were swept away.[11] Requisite fees (registration, driver's license, and inspection) were set at "reasonable levels." Parking regulations, traffic controls, technical inspections of automobiles, and various other measures were used to rationalize motor traffic and increase the demand for automobiles (*Berliner Börsenzeitung*, October 10, 1935). These regulatory laws also provided for training and "motorization propaganda."[12] The authorization of driving schools, planned activities of the Hitler Jugend to encourage motor transport, and sports and educational activities of the NSKK (Nationalsozialistisches Kraftfahrkorps) were consciously designed to popularize motor travel.[13]

## Fiscal relief

"Fiscal relief for motor transportation" became the central slogan of transportation policy. Due to the active lobbying of the RDA in both the Economics and Transportation ministries, measures were quickly adopted that created a demand for automobiles. The goal, as James Mooney had indicated to the Germans in 1933, was "to make the masses articulate as buyers again" (Mooney, 1933:4). By March 1933, the excise tax had been removed from all new cars, lowering the price of automobiles by 10–15 percent. Used-car owners were also permitted to pay a one-time tax during 1933. In 1934, the daily trip to and from work by automobile was made tax deductible, as were auto purchases. Businesses were given incentives to replace old motor vehicles with new ones. The government gave bonuses to civil servants for buying new automobiles, and private employers were encouraged to do the same. Finally, tax incentives were provided for plant construction and expansion in the automobile industry (Reichsverkehrsministerium, February 13, 1935, BA, R78/1542; Hüfner, 1936:19; Müller, 1936:45; *Berliner Bösenzeitung*, November 11, 1935).

## Direct Measures

Trade policies greatly aided the growing automobile industry. Import tariffs were raised (1934), and at the same time, an export equalization fund was established to subsidize external export prices through internal demand. This was referred to as a "dumping premium," which was paid in order to narrow the difference between German and foreign auto prices. In 1935, the auto industry received 3.5 million marks through such subsidies. In addition, direct loans were granted to the automobile industry for plant expansion, and

40

various state banks bought up automobile stock (May 22, 1934, BA, R43/1468; Müller, 1936:46).

Military production in the automobile industry was also essential for its growth. Germany had suffered militarily during World War I due to its lack of motorization. This lesson did not go unnoticed by the German High Command, which pushed for the production of military vehicles of all types – trucks, motorcycles, and later, tanks. Government contracts to all major automobile manufacturers for military production were significant (Voigt, quoted in Krämer-Badoni et al., 1971:10).[14]

The state also intervened in research and development by subsidizing the construction, financing, and completion of all race cars. This policy at once aided automotive development and popularized motorization (Verband der Automobilindustrie, 1975; Link (Daimler–Benz) to Hitler, March 15, 1933, BA, R4311/748, BA, R43/753).[15]

Concerning the people's automobile project, however, the RDA and the automobile industry did a lot of foot-dragging. Although Hitler demanded coordination and cooperation from various manufacturers for building the "small car for the small man," manufacturers were unwilling to trade production secrets and build automobiles that would compete with their own products. In 1937, Opel tried to convince Hitler that they had already produced a Volksauto (Hopfinger, 1956:86). Hitler finally took the project away from the RDA and gave it, along with 110 million marks, to the DAF (Deutsche Arbeitsfront) to construct the car (Allmers to Lammers, February 8, 1936; Willuhn to Lammers, June 29, 1934; Memo of RVM Ministerialdirektor Hiller with RDA, April 2, 1934, BA, R4311/753; see also Nelson, 1965; Wiersch, 1974).

## Highway construction

Highway building as an employment policy did not originate with Hitler. As noted earlier, the industrial and financial interests, which advocated highway construction, preceded and survived fascism. The autobahn lobbying effort was an early example of corporate influence on transportation planning. HAFRABA, founded in 1926 under the direction of Willy Hof, and STUFISTRA (Studiengesellschaft für die Finanzierung des Deutschen Strassenbaus), established in 1928 under the business management of Dr. Otto Fischer, were the major highway lobbying organizations; the former was concerned with technical planning, and the latter concentrated upon financing highway construction.

Banks, business associations, and the construction and automobile industries supported these organizations. Hof later became head of GEZUVOR (Gesellschaft zur Vorbereitung der Autobahn) under the Nazis and a member of the "Frankfurter Kreis" of highway lobbyists after the war. Anton Wörner, a member of the construction firm Sager and Wörner, was a director of HAFRABA and later had one of his top engineers, Dr. Fritz Todt, appointed as Generaldirektor des deutschen Strassenwesens.

Fischer and Hof were both present at a cabinet meeting in March 1933 at which Hitler made the final decision on autobahn construction and prepared his May 1, 1933, Tempelhof speech concerning highways. In that major address, Hitler announced with great flourish the "work and bread" goals of his transportation policy: Through highway building he would unite the Reich, preserve Germany's military integrity, and further the expansion of a new "settlement policy" in German cities to make them "physically and biologically renewed" (*Die Strasse*, May 1, 1933). This policy was reflected in the discussions of the Deutsche Gemeindetag (Association of Cities), the Reich Office of Planning, and the SS–Reich Commissar for the Unification of the German People.

### The organization of transportation policy under fascism

Motorization policy during the Third Reich subordinated rail transit through the centralization of transportation planning organizations. Local autonomy was eliminated by fascist legislation, and the state bureaucracy ensured the smooth functioning of the motorization program.[16] That bureaucracy came to reflect the particular interests of the automobile industry by eliminating local planning units, by increasing coordination of industrial associations (such as the DIHT), and by enlarging the role of the NSDAP in forging transportation policies.[17]

After Hitler's motorization policies were established, the automobile industry made a concerted effort to reorganize and control policy making within the various ministries. While the EKA (Eisenbahn–Kraftverkehr Ausschuss–Rail/Motor Traffic Commission) of the DIHT had been the semiofficial advisory board to the RVM (Reichsverkehrsministerium–Transportation Ministry) prior to 1933, that ministry ordered a special Reich Transportation Council to be organized within the government. At the behest of Allmers, then head of the RDA, the Reichsverkehrsrat was to be made up of representatives of the top transportation industries (Hilland to Müchener, Industrie u. Handelskammer, March 20, 1934, BA, R11/1542). This move was viewed with suspicion by other industry representatives (in the DIHT), who saw it as an attempt by the auto industry to gain control of transportation policymaking. Allmers and Major Adolf Huhnlein, head of the NSKK, formed a coalition whereby the "motor industry renewed plans for a united front . . . in some ways as a forerunner of creating a unified Verkehrskammer" (BA, R11/1542, Hilland to Drucker, 10 November 1934).[18] Through the RDA, the automobile industry supplanted the general interest of capital in lower transportation costs (a spatial interest of corporate transportation consumers) by its own profitmaking interests in transportation production. The DIHT's worst fears came true with the composition of the Reichsverkehrsrat, which was heavily weighted with pro-automobile representatives (Mitgliederliste, August 1934, BA, R11/1540). With the aforementioned purge of rail representatives, the DIHT intrigued with the RVM to counteract the centralization of transportation planning that excluded other industrial interests.[19]

Nevertheless, although the RVM became convinced that the Chambers of Industry and Commerce (DIHT) should have some say in transportation planning, the Economics Ministry (RWM), which the RDA had more successfully penetrated, argued for further centralization. Increasingly, functions of transportation planning moved to the RWM, the RIM (Reichsinnenministerum), and the NSKK [Posse (RWM) to Willuhn,

18.11.38, BA, R4311/749a]. This concentration of planning in party and state agencies did not supersede the role of capital. The RDA was continually involved in these plans, supported various party organizations (e.g., the NSKK), and forged the economic measures that were to concentrate the automobile industry further (Swatek, 1972:133–44).

Through the motorization program, the automobile industry and related industries formulated and helped administer transportation policy. The rail/street debate was resolved by the systematic elimination of opposition (as in the case of Strasser, Lubbert, and Röhm) or through the cooptation of other industrial interests. Having eliminated local influence on policy, the automobile and related industries could more easily sway transportation policy by concentrating on the party that controlled the state. The auto industry was able, for example, to circumvent the rail-biased bureaucrats within the RVM.

Finally, the Nazi motorization program enabled the automobile industry to prove itself to be a viable transportation alternative for heavy industry. With state subsidies, street building, research and development, and motor shipping, the highway transportation sector could modernize, thus becoming competitive with other countries.

None of this could have occurred without the decisive intervention of fascism. The Nazi motorization program broke down all resistance by older industrial interests. The critical combination of the emerging automobile industry, with its vast potential for promoting growth and change in the German industrial structure, *and* the political, ideological, military, and economic goals of German fascism caused rail transit's decline. The state bureaucracy and the industrial coalition that promoted motorization during this critical period survived war and fascism to influence transportation policy in the Federal Republic of Germany. By 1939, the automobile industry, like other economic giants, had become highly concentrated, eliminating threatening technological and industrial competition and diversifying its production structure (Swatek, 1972:68–70).

However, in many ways, the auto-biased policies of the

Third Reich were unsuccessful. Growth and concentration within the auto industry did not provide sufficient transportation within and between German cities. By 1942, an emergency in public transportation was declared by the Secret Police. Ridership on public transportation had increased 300 percent, replacement parts for autos and trucks were lacking, and portions of the autobahn remained incomplete (Reichssicherheitsamt, 19.3.42, BA, R58/170; BA, R58/172). This failure of motorization was due to a contradiction in the economic policies of fascism. On the one hand, further capital accumulation was facilitated by investment in the auto industry. On the other hand, profits from that investment in civilian autos required more disposable income for workers. This contradicted the economic policy of keeping wages low under fascism.

## Postwar transportation policy

Kalecki (1972:100–1) was the first to note that "one of the basic functions of Nazism was to overcome the reluctance of big business to large-scale government economic intervention." Nowhere is this more apparent than in the case of transportation policy. The state's commitment to promote motorization was made during the Third Reich, and this intervention represented a substantive change "unparalleled in European transportation history" (Despicht, 1969:85). It gave the automobile industry and its allies a central role in the formulation of transportation policy. Although much transportation production was halted during and after the war, the structure of the automobile industry remained essentially untouched after twelve years of fascism and four years of half-hearted denazification by the Allies (Vogel and Weisz, 1976:902–4).

The restoration of the automobile industry and the reestablishment of its influence on transportation policy in favor of the private automobile occurred very early after World War II. The Wirtschafsgruppe Fahrzeugindustrie and the Hauptausschuss KFZ (Committee for Automobiles) continued after the war and aided the Allies in reconstructing and operating various automobile and truck factories. With the help of GM, by 1948 the RDA was reincarnated as the Verband-der-Automobil-industrie (VDA) and became a voice in Occupation economic policies.[20] Former Opel director and GM manager Elis S. Hoglund reappeared in Germany as a major in the U.S. occupational forces, directing the reconstitution of the automobile industry's trade association. Further, he arranged the appointment of former Opel plant director Heinz Nordhoff as head of the Volkswagen plant, and he was involved in other measures that enhanced the automobile industry. In fact, Hoglund was the U.S. officer placed in charge of the German automobile industry in May 1945 (Vorwig, 1970:24–5).

During the reconstruction period, the automobile industry became one of the primary growth industries in Germany. In lowering and rationalizing automotive production and associated labor costs, the industry stimulated other areas of the German economy. As per capita output recovered from the devastation of war, the automobile industry began to play a major role in both the industrial structure and its capitalist class (Wallich, 1955:23). The auto industry was uniquely placed to stimulate industrial growth since it was assured internal financing from its operations and capital from U.S. auto multinational corporations that were priming the pumps of the German auto market.[21]

During this period, a shift in the economy emerged that paralleled the shift from a steel–coal–electrical industrial complex to the auto–oil–rubber complex of production and capital accumulation that had occurred in the United States after World War I (Altvater et al., 1974:253–65). Automobiles became the second fastest-growing industry and represented a shift in the location of capital accumulation (Mertens, 1962:499, Table 2, 445; Busch, 1966:108). Growth and monopolization occccured simultaneously. In a manner similar to the growth of the automotive monopoly in the United States, a "shared monopoly" situation arose wherein the five largest firms controlled more than 70 percent of the market (Kilger, 1960:300).

The auto industry lobbied for a variety of measures concerning the reestablishment of the autobahn. Several factors led to continued automotive control over transportation policy: the trend in urbanization that created a demand for transportation services in outlying areas to bring labor and materials to major cities (Jürgensen, 1968:298); the use of street building expenditures as an instrument of fiscal policy (John, 1966; Sandhäger, 1967:23–65); and the centrality of the automobile industry as a growth industry in German recovery.

With both Christian Democratic and Social Democratic transportation ministers (Seebohm and later Leber), the emphasis on motorization persisted.[22] The consequence of this policy was to increase auto demand relative to transit demand. The number of journey-to-work trips by buses and cars rather than by rail increased (Weil, 1952:34–36, 91–95; Menke, 1975:43–52). Since 1965, however, when the SPD received the transportation ministry, motor fuel tax revenues for mass transit have increased. After 1969 and the rise of the SPD–FDP (Free Democratic Party) ruling coalition, the subsidization of transit was extended. In spite of this continuing support, however, the benefits of transit policy were vitiated by the activities of the highway lobby, which exchanged increased transit funding for a continued higher proportional federal subsidy for highway building.[23]

Transportation policy since the late sixties has been an arena of conflict between the competing interests of the working classes, larger cities, and union members working in transit and the automobile, trucking, construction, and oil industries over transportation problems associated with a growing economy.

## Conclusion

In this chapter, I have presented further evidence concerning the different patterns of transit development in Germany and the national role of transportation policy.

The environment of urban mass transit was defined by particular aspects of the economy and political institutions in Germany. There was an early concentration and monopolization of German firms based in coal and heavy industry. This industrial complex was highly dependent upon government subsidization of rail transportation for their products and for work-related travel of laborers. In addition, the effective resistance of German capital to mass production of consumer goods such as automobiles, which required higher wages to create a mass market, and the resistance of skilled German laborers to the introduction of the assembly line hindered the rise of the automobile industry. Transportation policy remained tied to rail transit and limited the financial support of the emerging automobile industry before 1933. These factors, together with the centralization of state power and the construction of local policy on public transit expansion, caused transportation policy to focus on ordering cities and regions for efficient capital accumulation.

As the railroads and street railroads weakened financially during the twenties, and U.S. capital invigorated the automotive industry, older industrial corporate power declined. Nazism broke remaining labor resistance to assembly-line techniques. Although spatial concerns still affected transportation policy, the profit strategy of the automotive sector dominated under fascism. The transportation producers who came to dominate transportation policy benefited by the increased centralization of state power over transportation. The ascendance of auto-related interests was facilitated by and, indeed, required a political structure that excluded competing policy alternatives in line with broader economic and local interests.

Although the spatial functions of transportation-consuming industries have continued to be served by rail subsidies in the post–World War II era, the advantage attained by the automobile industry has never been compromised. Once the motorization lobby became dominant through the intervention of individuals and trade associations in policymaking institutions, it biased both public and private investment toward motorization interests. Nationalization of the rail system, transit municipalization, and motorization were all policies that emerged from the contradictions between the timing and composition of economic concentration, the impact of class relations on corporate growth and concentration, and the institutionalization of govermental intervention in transit.

# 4

# The formation of national transportation policy: the case of the United States

It must be admitted that in the development of street railway systems and the corporations that control them in this country, the idea of public service has generally been incidental. The driving force, the motive that has negotiated franchises, consolidations, and mergers, has been for profit only. (Wilcox, 1919:34)

Reflecting on the beginning of the decline of the street railway system in the United States, Delos Wilcox, the country's most prominent transportation engineer at the time, recognized as early as 1919 that the profit motive lay behind the transit problems of his day. More than half a century later, Bradford C. Snell, Senate Antitrust Committee counsel, noted in his study of U.S. surface transportation that the highly monopolized, powerful automobile firms and their diversification into various areas of transportation manufacturing "may have retarded the development of mass transportation, and, as a consequence, may have generated a reliance on motor vehicles incompatible with metropolitan needs" (Snell, 1974:A47).

Both Wilcox and Snell recognized the underlying force that has led to the decline of public transportation in the United States. That force – the pursuit of profit by street railways, and, later, by automobile corporations and related industries – has harmed urban land use and energy and led to the disintegration of urban communities. Here we explore the development of national transportation policy in the United States: policy changes, corporate intervention in policy formation, and the influence of these state and corporate activities on the decline of public transportation. The goal of this chapter is to explain how the organization of urban transportation by cor-

49

porations has been the greatest hindrance to the successful development of urban transportation.

## United States: economic background affecting national transportation policy

Two major historical differences between the U.S. and German economy affect the more precipitous and earlier decline of public transportation in the United States: (1) the longer survival of competitive capitalism in the United States and (2) the earlier rise of an auto–oil–rubber industrial complex in that country as the basis of capital accumulation.[1]

Before World War I, U.S. capitalism was characterized by intraclass competition, rather than coalition. Although patterns of industrial development were apparent by the Civil War, the rise of corporations, the role of state intervention in providing the basis for economic consolidation, and the development of market infrastructure all occurred by the turn of the century, allowing the United States a more competitive manufacturing system with greater technical diversity (Averitt, 1968).[2] Corporate financing was internal, with banks entering the industrial stock market only in the late 1870s, *some forty years after German banks* began developing and controlling much of German industry. In this more competitive situation, the possibilites for innovative transportation technology arose more easily than in Germany. Whether in the more rapid electrification of streetcars or in the motorization of transportation, surplus-absorbing outlets for capital accumulation were created faster in the United States than in Germany.[3] Nor was there as much reliance upon existing corporate giants for technological innovation. The technical convergence of growth in automobile, oil, and rubber industries, as well as the internal expansion of cities during this period, made capital accumulation more dynamic and the realignment of industrial power more rapid.

The initial emergence of the auto–oil–rubber nexus as an industrial strategy for economic growth was the outcome of historical circumstances specific to the United States. Auto production began in earnest nearly a decade after the first mergers

50

in the petroleum, rubber, and steel industries began the process of monopolization (Kennedy, 1941:135; Bunting, 1972). Auto expansion and the new corporate strategies were financed by the largest U.S. banks during the twenties (Seltzer, 1928; Edwards, 1966; Chandler, 1968). These economic conditions provided a powerful base for motorization interests in financial-industrial integration, market expansion for basic industries (e.g., steel and oil), and the stimulation of consumer demand. Politically, the weaker involvement of government in accumulation at both local and national levels, together with the absence of organized labor and popular demands for transit services, allowed the unhindered pursuit of motorization as a corporate strategy for industrial expansion.

The unique circumstances in U.S. industrialization promoted the ascendency of the automobile sector and its related industries. By the end of the nineteenth century, the extension of the frontier was completed and the forging of a mass consumer market began. Primary sector industries (particularly energy and agriculture) intensified production, corporate mergers increased, and the influx of cheap immigrant labor permitted the deskilling and homogenization of the industrial workforce skills and production positions.

Nowhere was this combination of work process, industrial organization, and popular consumption changes dramatized more than in the auto industry, where "Fordism" was coined as a model for twentieth-century industrialization (Aglietta, 1979). The scarcity of skilled labor in the nineteenth century meant that early mechanization replaced complex, craft-dominated operations, unlike the situation in Germany, where the craft tradition protected autonomy over such skills. This established tradition of mechanization, along with the availability of unorganized, cheap immigrant labor, permitted the rapid introduction of assembly-line techniques. These labor process changes permitted greater profit, growth, and concentration in newly established growth industries. Davis (1978:223) describes the process:

The progressive transformation of the labor process was, of course, closely tied to the emergence of a new sector of consumer durable industries (auto, electrical appliances) at the end of the First World War. This new mass production was, in turn, the outgrowth of the vast centralization of capital accomplished by trust-building financing groups since the turn of the century.

## The growth period of public transportation in the United States

After the Civil War, the limitations of horse-drawn trolley systems became readily apparent (Ward, 1971:131–4). After an initial period of growth, the market for trolley systems became saturated; demand for this geographically limited transit technology was satisfied. Under these conditions, the electrification of trolley lines with lower per unit costs and increasing supply capability became desirable. More importantly, the electrification of urban transportation intersected with the electrical manufacturing industry, the most important growth industry of that early period (1888–1900).[4] Urban transportation became part of the universal growth in public utilities investment during this period.

Electrification meant growth. For most of the 1890–1918 period, urban transit ridership grew faster than urban population; investment in urban transportation more than quintupled (U.S. Bureau of the Census, 1905:6). The pace and timing of electrification correlate neither with population growth nor with traffic level changes in cities. We must look beyond urbanization to the organization and role of urban transit enterprises. Electrified streetcar networks pushed cities toward their peripheries and redistributed population and industry. Land speculators and transit owners nearly always spoke with one voice (and were sometimes the same person), encouraging this expansion (Wilcox, 1921:67–100; Cheape, 1980). Transit expansion was perceived by these financiers and investors as necessary to ensure the development of urban regions by private enterprise. Urban transportation was viewed by transit owners, city planners, and urban reformers alike as a "moral influence" in removing people from the deleterious environment of the inner cities (Tarr, 1973; MacShane, 1975; Warner, 1976; Cheape, 1980).[5]

Because of the increased costs of investment, electrification encouraged the consolidation and concentration of transit ownership. A conglomeration of landowning, public utility, and financial interests (e.g., "transit trusts" such as Yerkes in Chicago, Doherty on the East Coast, and Mellon) came to dominate public transportation.[6] Similarly, the private railroads also discouraged the growth of streetcar lines either by attempting to buy them or by developing competitive lines to divert commuter traffic. Rate wars and "linewrecking" were common, hampering fiscally sound urban transportation (Forbes, 1905:35). The resulting monopolization of street railways by land/public utility interests and steam railroads set the stage for electrical transportation's imminent decline (Report of New York Committee on Municipal Ownership of Street Railways, 1896:7–8).

Although the street railway building booms of 1890–1908 were well financed, transit monies were often pocketed through overcapitalization, corrupt accounting practices, or overextended transit lines that were unprofitable except, of course, for land speculation and investment. The combination of corruption and poor management resulted in a total credit collapse between 1916 and 1923, when more than one-third of the transit companies went bankrupt (Smerk, 1975:135). During this period, capital moved toward the more profitable, less politically problematic field of automobile investment. As one major transportation financier testified before the Federal Electrical Railway Commission (FERRC) in 1919, "we insiders are selling out just as fast as we can, and when ten years are up, you will not find your Uncle Dudley or any one of us that will own a share of stock or bond [in electrical transit]" (FERRC, 1920:1058).

The political activity of the producers and consumers of transportation services, as well as the cutthroat competition, discouraged investment in public transit. Between 1916 and 1920, the transit industry experienced the greatest number of strikes in its history (Kuhn, 1952:26–7). Labor costs in the transit industry increased faster than average wages (Schmidt, 1935). These higher labor costs, along with the wartime inflation affecting material costs, drove the ratio between operating cost and gross income of transit firms from 50 to 77 percent. As transit workers made gains through their trade unions and strikes, the profits of transit lines decreased.

During this early period, the right to operate public transportation was granted by local governments to private entrepreneurs. During the late nineteenth century, citizens and consumers formed popular movements to constrain transit operating companies through their local franchise charters. As a result, the power of those transit companies was curbed and, unintentionally, new entrants were barred from the public transportation market. Franchises often prescribed the types of equipment used, thus restricting innovation, and frequently they required line extensions, street maintenance, and street construction. Such practices usually served to benefit existing firms that were able to meet the costs. The use of streets by automobile owners also increased. Finally, flat rate fares in some franchises subsidized suburban development through inner city travel.

Attempts by transit trusts to circumvent or renegotiate franchise agreements led to overcrowding of passengers and the abandonment of lines. This situation eventually led to popular calls for public ownership. Between 1898 and 1920, virtually every major U.S. city was the scene of legal battles, referenda over rate hikes, public ownership campaigns, and investigations of transit corruption.[7] In this politically volatile climate, the corporate liberals of the National Civic Federation (NCF) intervened to consider the transit problem. As reported by August Belmont, owner of New York City's transit properties and president of the federation, the NCF's self-serving investigation determined that public ownership would be less efficient than adequate regulation (Jensen, 1956). But regulation for whom?

The resulting government policy was typical of urban reform during the corporate liberal period. Regulation removed the political struggle over transportation from the public sphere of city politics to the forums of appointed, business-oriented public utility and public service commissions at the state level. This was the first step in insulating transportation decisions from public pressures by the de facto disenfranchisement of the urban population. Transportation planning by appointed state-level organizations was very different from direct public participation in transportation policymaking that had existed up to this time.

Students of urban transportation have searched for a single cause for the origin of transit's decline, focusing upon corruption, poor business practices, the lack of technological innovation, overcrowded service, land use dispersion, and the rise of the automobile.[8] Although all of these factors played a role, they must be understood as part of a more general social change reflecting the shift from public to private transportation. This change involved more than the technological shift from rail to rubber-wheeled vehicles; it encompassed basic relations of labor and capital in the production of transportation equipment and labor's cost of job-related travel. By shifting from public to private transportation technology, business avoided rising labor and construction costs. Organizations of public transit workers could be left to attrition, and automobiles and streets could be built with unorganized and often (in the case of street construction) forced labor. Where private companies were obligated by public franchises to lay track, the federal government constructed roads. The costs of transportation infrastructure could thus be socialized. Secondly, the shift to private transportation would remove the volatile political issue of urban transportation. Consumer movements over rate hikes, public ownership, and transit corruption would cease. Finally, the shift from public to private transportation ensured the transfer of capital investment from an increasingly restrictive area to a more expansive one.

In these ways, the shift in production from public transit to private automobiles played a decisive role in the decline of transit and the rise of corporate power in the automotive sector. Public transit was, and is, largely a labor-intensive enterprise (about 80 percent of costs are for labor), with technical limits to mechanization and resistance by a highly organized labor force. Consolidation and economic concentration in transit were obstructed by work processes, the transit labor force, and the local or regional limits of transit service delivery. In contrast, the use of assembly-line techniques and continuous automation gave automobile manufacturers far greater control over labor costs, allowed them to set the price of the car without public interference (since a nationally produced and marketed mode of transportation replaced a locally regulated transit service), permitted national as opposed to local industry concentration, and consolidated corporate power in the private automotive sector.

### Corporate strategy and state policy: the fall of public transportation

Although the corporate abuse of the transit trusts, capital flight from public transportation, and the movement toward state regulation did much to start mass transportation's decline, it did not ensure its demise. During the twenties, when public transit stagnated, an ambiguous relationship between private and public transportation use in cities developed. Corporate capital interests, which were the basis of the automobile industry, found it increasingly hard to live with this ambiguity. After the initial rash of abandonments and receiverships following World War I, conditions stabilized. Receiverships fell from 9 to 7 percent annually and remained below 8 percent until the Depression. Moreover, the reduction in riders and track miles could be interpreted as the first rational shrinkage in railway networks to a more financially viable economic scale (Dewees, 1970:564–5). In addition, the decline in ridership may well have been the result of new, more honest accounting practices that became dominant through state regulation during the twenties.[9]

Perhaps the most important factor in the relationship between private and public transportation was the trend toward urban growth. If the ridership figures between 1918 and 1927 for major cities are disaggregated, we find an increase in ridership for some major cities (St. Louis saw a 3.1 percent gain in ridership; Chicago, 10.1 percent; New York City, 37 percent) (Barrett, 1976:418–19; Memo: The Effect of the Automobile on Patronage, APTA File No. 075.441). The idea that more autos resulted in less public transit, which is prominent in federal railway commission testimonials and among modern historians, seems a gross oversimplification. Decreases in public transportation occurred mostly in cities with less than 500,000 people. For all cities with more than 1 million people, the decrease was only 4 percent (Dewees, 1970:569).

There was an inverse relationship between automobile density and city size. In cities where bus and rail modernization was undertaken, traffic surveys showed public transit trips increasing at a higher rate than auto trips (25 compared to 17%) (*Transportation Journal*, 1940–5). A sharp decline in public transportation had been arrested. In spite of financial disasters and rising fares, rail transit was surviving and was cheaper than buses for urban transportation (St. Clair, 1981).[10]

The resiliency of public transportation, along with declines in the automobile market, produced a crisis for corporate strategists. From 1923 on, the new-car market had become saturated (Seltzer, 1928; Kennedy, 1941; Weiss, 1961). Alfred Sloan, Henry Ford, Charles W. Nash, the National Automobile Chamber of Commerce, and others agreed that a more rapid turnover of automobiles was required (Flink, 1975:145–52). GM led the way with strategies for style changes, extensive advertising, franchise distribution, and cheap financing. In spite of these changes, stabilization remained a threat to the automobile industry and those closely associated with it. The oil and rubber industries faced overproduction and falling prices; housing construction declined.[11] Corporations required long-range plans to neutralize public transportation and thereby promote demand. Early auto industrialists such as Billy Durant and Henry Ford were incapable of establishing the cross-industrial coalitions that would be necessary to accomplish such a task (Chandler, 1968; Flink, 1975).

The following scenario seems likely. The spectacular investment in street railways during boom years had "sunk" fixed capital costs (which by the twenties could be used at reduced expense), and this aided the mini-recovery of public transportation in major cities. Simultaneously, capital that was invested in street railways was devalued through lower productivity and use. Although the automobile industry attempted to overcome the old fixed capital investment in street railways with federally subsidized road investment (as new fixed capital investment), thereby facilitating automotive traffic, rail transit continued to limit the expansion of automobile and related industries, which were the centers of capital accumulation during this period. For this reason, American street railways were dismantled. The transportation technology that had first allowed the decentralization and expansion of cities ultimately inhibited that expansion. Continued urban growth was essential for cities to act as the loci of capital accumulation.

Ford was wrong. Inexpensive automobiles alone would not motorize the United States. By 1927, Chevrolet had overtaken Ford due to Sloan's product diversification, marketing, and auto-purchase financing (Chandler, 1968; Flink, 1976). But Sloan was also wrong. Refinements in automobile production and distribution were not enough. Competition from public carriers would not disappear. The stagnation of automobile demand, overproduction, the lack of "articulate consumers," and general indicators of economic crisis all required the automobile industry and its partners to develop a new corporate strategy: Urban rail transit was replaced by motor buses, which were to be replaced by cars.[12]

The fragmented nature of privately owned U.S. transit systems aided this corporate strategy in local transportation development. The lack of coordination between transit systems nationally and regionally allowed the isolation of key transit systems, their conversion to buses, and the subsequent decline of rail transit.

This "modernization" of public transportation substituted buses for electrical streetcars, which would be ineffective in counteracting the lure of the automobile. In 1925, GM purchased Yellow Truck and Coach Manufacturing, a firm founded by a former jitney owner, John Hertz. Former jitney operators such as Hertz (and later the Fitzgerald brothers, founders of National City Lines), were ideal small business allies for GM. They had run services parallel to streetcar lines, but had been regulated out of business. They could well benefit from the protection of size afforded by GM. Hertz, along with his top executives, John Ritchie and Col. G. A. Green, invigorated Yellow Truck and Coach under GM's control. They also maintained ownership ties with the Omnibus Corporation, Fifth Avenue Coach, and the Chicago

Motor Bus Corporation, creating the earliest strategy of conversion to buses. By means of their interlocking directorate with Fifth Avenue Coach, they converted the New York system to buses within eighteen months between 1935 and 1936, in spite of months of regulatory commission fights (R. A. Crist, undated; *Bus Transportation*, July 1953:54–5; Snell, 1974; "Yellow Truck and Coach," GM Pamphlet File G-230).

Simultaneously, by diversification into bus manufacturing, GM branched out into other forms of transit. Through its subsidiary, Motor Transit Corporation, GM became involved in the conversion of interurban lines by the formation of the Greyhound Corporation, being the sole supplier of its buses and owning a controlling stock interest until 1948. The tie between GM and Greyhound was not dissolved with its divestment of Greyhound stock. According to an FBI investigation, "[GM] had disposed of [Greyhound] by selling it to officers of General Motors Corporation and in this way continues to control Greyhound" (FBI Report, January 18, 1954).[13]

On June 29, 1932, through the executive committee of its subsidiary, Yellow Coach, GM introduced a proposal "for making investments in motorized transport systems with a view to stimulating more demand for more motor coaches" (Minutes of Yellow Truck and Coach Manufacturing Committee, executive committee, GM Trial Exhibit 1, NCL Civil Case). These investments were made through yet another company, United Cities Motor Transit (UCMT). As conversion proceeded, the American Transit Association (ATA), representing most transit operating companies, censured GM for forcing conversions through UCMT.

Less direct methods of controlling transit companies through supply contracts, interlocking directorates, and investments in other companies were less publicly visible. In 1936, National City Lines (NCL) was formed by GM, Yellow Coach, and former Greyhound executives. Between 1937 and 1940, NCL surveyed major transit operations throughout the country.[14] It then proceeded to purchase many of those lines and substituted buses for the existing streetcars. This conversion was financed by a scheme whereby NCL sold its stock to GM, Firestone Tire and Rubber, Phillips Petroleum, Standard

Oil of California, and Mack Manufacturing (1951 Trade Cases). These investors were then given sole supplier contracts for up to ten years with the acquired companies.

Even when NCL did not purchase a transit company, it established similar noncompetitive contracts with customers.[15] GM, for instance, would testify at substitution hearings on behalf of transit firms that they would finance bus purchases.[16] As one of the defense lawyers in the NCL antitrust case told me, "This was all part of a very reasonable corporate strategy to develop a market."[17] The decline of public transportation was accomplished, therefore, through acquisition of transit companies and/or the control of noncompetitive supplier contracts by means of conversion and resale (Snell, 1974).

The negotiations creating this corporate conspiracy are instructive in understanding the interests and actions behind bus conversion in the United States. Fortunately, documentary evidence of the discussions between the various parties planning to motorize urban transportation remains. Nearly all of the corporate executives involved recognized the potential problems of the "propriety and perhaps legality" of this investor–supplier arrangement (B. F. Stadley, secretary, Phillips Petroleum, to H. C. Grossman, vice-president, GM, October 11, 1943, quoted in Memo for the Attorney General, June 4, 1946, Department of Justice Files).

Aside from the written supply contracts and stock purchase exchanges, correspondence between the corporations indicates other "verbal understandings." H. S. Leonard, assistant treasurer of Firestone Tire and Rubber Company, wrote to Russell M. Riggins, treasurer of Phillips Petroleum, describing some of these negotiations (July 28, 1939, Department of Justice Files, Memo for the Attorney General, June 4, 1946):

I have been hob-nobbing with Roy Fitzgerald [National City Lines] and some of the others who are interested in our proposition. I also understood, as you advise, that General Motors and Mack Truck were in and also that Standard Oil of New Jersey and Standard Oil of California were in. Vic Palmer [Standard of California] was in New York when I was there, as well as Mr. Taylor of the Standard Oil of New Jersey . . . Everything seems to be going along very nicely and I do think we will probably all benefit by the arrangement.[18]

60

In some cases, stock purchases were made through nominees so as to avoid detection by the government regulatory agencies. In a letter dated December 13, 1939, B. W. Franklin, assistant secretary of NCL, wrote to GM Vice-President H. S. Grossman:

It is highly probable that your company will desire to take these blocks of stock in the name of nominees. By so doing you would avoid becoming a 10% holder of record of any class of our stock and hence would avoid the necessity of filing any contracts subsequently entered into between yourselves and our company with the S.E.C. and the two exchanges. (Quoted in J. R. O'Malley, Memorandum for the File, Department of Justice, NCL, December 3, 1946)

In the case of other corporations involved in the NCL arrangement, stock was held by employees as nominees. Standard Oil, for example, wished to avoid being identified with Pacific City Lines before the California Railroad Commission.

Aside from direct control over transit companies through NCL, the auto industry suppressed alternative transportation technology in other ways. Many individual transit operators, some of whom were former GM or NCL officials, converted to buses with the technical and financial assistance of GM and NCL. Similarly, exclusive contracts made without bids bypassed other transit equipment manufacturers.[19] These exclusive supplier contracts with the oil, rubber, and bus manufacturing companies were detrimental to the transit lines. Often, as the Federal Bureau of Investigation (FBI) discovered, the competitors of GM or Phillips Petroleum had lower prices. However, the oil and bus manufacturers offered financial arrangements that required no down payments. Although this arrangement was beneficial in the short run, the higher cost saddled transit companies with debt (FBI Field Report, Chicago, September 14, 1948, FBI Files, NCL). In other cases, conversions occurred in cities where private consultants, often with GM connections, recommended their approval on the basis of data supplied by GM and NCL.[20]

Subsequently, the Justice Department investigated the NCL arrangement, prosecuted the companies under antitrust laws, and won. The illegal stock ownership and supply contracts were dissolved by court order. However, it was a pyrrhic victory. After eight years of litigation, the guilty corporations were fined \$1,000 each for an arrangement that had yielded \$30–50 million. Corporate officers were fined \$1. If the punishment was less than crippling, neither was it effective in forcing the corporations to desist from monopolistic practices injurious to the nation's transit systems. When the FBI investigated the effects of the judgment, they found the auto–oil–rubber coalition still active. After one informant in the transit industry had been interviewed, the following report was filed detailing the behind-the-scenes involvement of GM in the transit industry:

He [the informant] said that he thought the government win in the National City Lines trial in Chicago had merely run them underground . . . [he] stated he felt the Government is merely playing around the fringes. He said he believed new legislation is necessary in order to combat the present situation. (FBI Field Report, Los Angeles, July 1, 1954, Motor Bus Industry Investigation, 60-438, FBI Files)

Ownership was abandoned as the means of controlling transit systems, and less direct means were used to further the motorization of transit. The most important new strategy was the use of either direct or indirect loans. The FBI discovered that both Standard Oil of California and Firestone had continued to "float loans in return for purchases" (FBI Field Report, Los Angeles, July 15, 1955, Motor Bus Industry Investigation). In East Lansing, "pressure was put on through banks and the city council to get GM coaches" (FBI Field Report, Philadelphia, January 18, 1954). There were numerous reports of transit operating companies that "experienced pressure through banking sources to change . . . to GM" (FBI Field Report, Cleveland, March 5, 1954, Motor Bus Industry Investigation). In Atlanta, Philadelphia, Dallas, Los Angeles, and elsewhere, GM successfully used business connections, stock ownership, and promises of deposits to pressure local banks into influencing local transit companies to purchase buses from GM (Motor Bus Investigation Fact Memo, Department of Justice, 1956).

In places where transit lines were municipally owned, GM induced public officials to adopt specifications that only GM could meet. This procedure, according to GM Vice-President

E. P. Crenshaw, "worked out in Cleveland, Boston, Detroit, Phoenix, and Chicago" (Motor Bus Investigation Fact Memo, Department of Justice, 1956). The FBI reported that the city council of St. Petersburg, Florida, had

> passed a resolution changing to buses . . . it was rumored that these councilmen and the city manager received gifts to influence this decision . . . [and] that transition [was] undertaken without regard to the financial condition of the city, in spite of the fact that street cars provided adequate facilities and were financially remunerative. (FBI Field Report, Miami, Florida, October 31, 1947, 60-145, NCL Investigation, FBI Files)

Finally, NCL came to dominate the transit trade association, the ATA. Voting in the association was based upon operating revenue. NCL, with $100 million in annual revenue, became the largest transit operator in the country and therefore the largest voter in the ATA. The evidence suggests that NCL successfully suppressed opposition to bus conversions using its dominant position within the ATA.[21] ATA members also had an agreement that no member could compete to provide transit service where a fellow member already held a franchise (FBI Field Report, New York, December 12, 1955, Motor Bus Industry Investigation). The Justice Department discovered that the Administrative Committee – the Manufacturers Division of the ATA – was the instrument through which GM suggested self-serving policies. Assistant Attorney General Stanley Barnes wrote to FBI Director J. Edgar Hoover that "many of the national and regional officers of ATA are persons known to be particularly cooperative with General Motors" (Barnes to Hoover, October 2, 1955, Department of Justice Files, 60-107-42). GM pressured ATA officers whom they had supported in their bids for high positions in the ATA (FBI Investigation GM-Bus Antitrust, 1954).

Bus conversions did not go unopposed. Other transportation equipment producers, such as Dr. Thomas Conway (president of the Cincinnati and Lake Erie Railroad), the Brill Company, Westinghouse, and other streetcar lines opposed conversions. Throughout the thirties, Conway called meetings to defend rail lines and to popularize the use of the lightweight aluminum Presidential Command Cars (PCC), which would reduce operating costs.[22] However, the attempts of equipment producers and users to inform civic associations, city governments, and transit groups concerning the use of modernized streetcar equipment were suppressed by GM and its allied companies.

Conversions were opposed as numerous stockholder suits were filed against transit companies. The injunctions argued that expensive conversions would place the companies in jeopardy.[23] Although these initial injunctions were never upheld, their arguments were validated; numerous companies collapsed under the debt of bus modernization and were municipalized.

Opposition to conversions also came from consumer and civic organizations and, less frequently, from local governments. Throughout California, community groups opposed the conversion to buses and the accompanying increase in fares (FBI Field Report, San Francisco, October 7, 1948, 60-263, NCL Investigation). In one case, the city of Oakland conducted a survey and contracted another survey with a planning firm showing that "the city of Oakland, because of its topography and location needs a variety of types of transit, such as buses, street cars and trolley buses, and interurban trains, rather than a complete motor bus system as conducted by the Key System since it was taken over by NCL." (FBI Field Report, October 12, 1948, 60-268).

Many riders were not enthusiastic about buses, which were more foul-smelling, noisier, less comfortable, and slower than rail transit. The Oakland study, which was the only known impact study on bus conversion, indicated that because of the smaller conveying capacity of buses, the number of riders actually decreased each year. Testimony at Public Utility Commissions and city-level boards of public transportation centered on these charges.[24] At such hearings, local GM representatives were ready with expert testimony. Pro-rail representatives emphasized that rail transit would prevent further congestion, expedite local service at transfer points, provide more efficient use of street space, provide faster service, and carry more passengers. GM testimony typically ensured cheaper fares and financing which were mysteriously available for bus conversions and absent for rail modernization.

Finally, there was the often ambiguous response to conversions by organized transit labor. The consequences of bus conversion were clear. Between 1945 and 1968, transit employment decreased 57 percent.[25] This consequence was noted only by officials of the Transport Workers Union-Congress of Industrial Organizations (TWU-CIO) and a few rank-and-file members. By 1939, the TWU saw conversions as "another blow . . . struck against the TWU" (TWU Convention Proceedings, 1939:52). However, even the TWU was seduced by the contemporary vision of the future when it stated that "no union can set itself against progress" (TWU, 1939:52). The leaders of other unions also discouraged questions about the conversion process.

Often, NCL entered a situation in which labor neogtiations threatened an already shaky transit operation. Usually, as the transfer of ownership occurred, the union would suspend negotiations. The international representative frequently would be sent from the Amalagmated Association of Street Electrical Railway and Motor Coach Employees of America-American Federation of Labor (AFL) to assuage rank-and-file fears about conversions. In St. Louis, the international representative told the members: "We know that behind the Fitzgerald brothers is a tire company, gasoline companies, and oil companies. What effect they, as a holding company, will have on the St. Louis situation, I cannot say." The following exchange then occurred:

Another member of the union, apparently a motorman employed by the Public Service Company, asked the international representative: "Don't they [NCL] always displace streetcars with buses?" The union leader replied that he knows "in many instances the Fitzgeralds have brought up old streetcar companies and replaced their equipment with buses and always reduced the fare and in many instances increased wages." (*St. Louis Star Times,* October 22, 1940:1)

While NCL and GM operatives were subverting rail transit systems throughout the country, they offered transit labor a temporary sweetheart arrangement: short-time wage increases in return for long-term job attrition. This arrangement was facilitated by inadequate trade union discussion, research, and strategy.

Figure 4.1. Beginning in the early 1930s, automobile, oil, and rubber industries promoted their products through corporate strategies and state policies that eliminated competition from other transportation technologies. This scene from Los Angeles's Henry Ford Avenue is from 1946. (Photographer unknown. From the collection of William A. Myers.)

Figure 4.2. This scene of now unfamiliar rail/highway coexistence is from Los Angeles's Cahuenga Expressway, circa 1946. Some early highway plans included right-of-ways for rail transit. This survived in a few cities (e.g., Chicago) but political pressure from the highway lobby at local, state, and federal levels resulted in the elimination and paving over of most rail right-of-ways. The possibility of mixed and intermodal transportation planning was thereby largely eliminated. (Photograph by Donald Duke. From the collection of William A. Myers.)

Figure 4.3. By the early 1950s, electrical transit was largely abandoned and most private transit operators were bankrupt. Motorization of transit led to higher costs and reduced service in U.S. cities. Automobile, rubber, and oil companies faced Federal investigation and prosecution for market manipulations that contributed to the elimination of rail transit. This 1959 photo shows Pacific Electric and Los Angeles Transit cars at a junkyard at Terminal Island.

The strategy of the corporate car coalition was highly successful. Every possible dimension of the transit industry was integrated into the automobile–rubber–oil complex.[26] Since future demand could be assured only insofar as future supply was secured, the coalition sought to eliminate technological competition from other modes. This corporate strategy was accomodated by emerging state transportation policies.

## State policy: the gradual shift toward automobilization

Current state intervention into transportation policy dates back to World War I. Although no single American policy measure during the pre–World War II era paralleled the major impact of Nazi Germany's motorization policies, many measures established the institutional framework supporting automobilization. Transportation policy was an element in such larger policy areas as national defense, public service, economic recovery, and urban planning.[27]

Although road building was certainly part of transportation policy in the World War I period, the relatively low level of highway construction reflects the ambivalence of state policy on transportation issues. Years of agitation by motorists, bicyclists, and farmers culminated in 1916 with the Federal Highway Assistance Act (the so-called Good Roads Act, named after the movement that had sponsored it), which reaffirmed and supported road building with the help of federal engineers (NA, RG30, General Correspondence, File 420).

State intervention during this period was critical in decreasing the time and cost involved in conveying goods to market and people to work (NA, RG 3, Box 414, General Correspondence, File 13). Street railways were supported with federally aided line extensions. But state subsidization was for construction costs only. Line extensions, although useful for the factories involved, were not financially sound. Streetcar companies were locked into serving these costly and often failing lines through existing franchise agreements.

Other more indirect measures taken at this time inhibited public transit, perhaps unintentionally. Restrictive franchise agreements forced streetcar companies to bear heavy tax burdens. In 1917–18, rail taxes used in road building reached $225 million (FERRC, 1920:425). Similarly, regulatory statutes created an oppresive environment for rail transit. Bus companies often required less stringent public franchises or none at all, and were thereby exempt from various taxation and impost arrangements since they did not need exclusive access to rights of way. State regulatory policies and the beginning of highway building offset (with the Federal Highway Act of 1921) the lower operating costs of rail transit. Consequently, the shift to bus systems in many cities began.[28] A full one-third of those firms that had abandoned streetcar lines replaced them partially with bus operations (Hilton and Due, 1960; Dewees, 1970; Saltzman, 1977).

Early highway legislation was directed toward improving intercity truck, agricultural, and industrial traffic. It was not until the New Deal that highway policy became an important part of personal transportation and urban planning policy. Roosevelt extended aid to urban highways in 1934 and 1936. Nevertheless, the New Deal was severely constrained by the fiscal crisis of the thirties. In this period, the policy of state intervention through fiscal support, technical assistance, and urban planning began. The National Resources Planning Board (NRPB), the Reconstruction Finance Corporation (RFC), the Public Works Administration (PWA) and the Bureau of Public Roads (BPR) all acted to construct the constraints and biases of planning that would promote automobile use after World War II.[29] Local and regional planning authorities were encouraged to draft proposals that would increase federal support of highway projects (PWA Administrator Harold Ickes, November 13, 1933, NA, RG 45, File 840, Box 56). State planning commissions were set up with federal assistance. Of particular concern to them was transportation.[30]

However, would planning be democratic at state and regional levels, or would it become controlled by businessmen and technocrats (e.g., planners and highway engineers)? The records of the NRPB show that chambers of commerce, manufacturers' associations, and other business organizations encouraged states and local communities to build roads through recommendations to state planning commissions. State legislation increased tax supports for municipal road building, and planners and engineers argued that these roads should be built parallel to railroad rights of way (NRPB, NA, RG 48, File 840, Box 56). Under the direction of the NRPB, development commissions within state planning commissions promoted urban development and, therefore, transportation planning. The corporate car coalition was overrepresented on all transportation planning bodies encouraging federal financing for road building (W. W. DeCherrie to NRPB, March 2, 1943, NA, RG 48, NRPB, Box 56, File 840).

Local officials acted to reduce the expense and inconvenience of auto ownership. Traffic regulation was interpreted to mean increasing traffic flows. Parking regulations, one-way streets, traffic signals, and other regulations were adapted to the needs of auto usage (*Motor Age*, December, 1923:28; Barrett, 1976:400–1; Flink, 1975:162–3). Such regulation was promoted by GM through automobile clubs (*Detroit News*, July 7, 1929). Unlimited automobile accommodation through new taxes, improved roads, expanded parking facilities, extensive surveys, and new regulations became the goal of local planning policy. In the process, the neglect of public transportation became institutionalized.

The impetus for such regulations came from the emerging profession of urban and traffic planning, automobile interests and motor clubs, and business interests that were worried about how regulations might harm central city shopping. Planning was a response to situations and problems, not a method for anticipating them. This notion of problem solving, so dominant in the urban planning tradition, was exemplified by local transportation policy. Moreover, it left urban development particularly vulnerable to corporate opposition to mass transportation.

Everything was done by state policy to promote the automobile, nothing to constrain it. Germany's transportation policy during the thirties had demonstrated to planners that successful road-building programs could not only stimulate the economy but also promote state policies (Committee for Economic Development, 1965:30).

The automobile complex gave birth to the Highway Lobby, which informally developed national transportation policy.[31] As the Automobile Manufacturers Association (AMA) (Memo to AMA Committee on Highway Economics, November 1, 1959, GM Files R-89) pointed out:

From the beginnings of the automobile industry in the United States, vehicle manufacturers have recognized their direct stake in highway development and financing policies. Both through industry-wide programs and through leadership by industry executives, continuous activities have been carried out through the years.

As early as 1913, the National Automobile Chamber of Commerce had joined with tire, parts, and cement companies to map and promote the first transcontinental highway. These corporations contributed money to build "seedling miles" of the highway to demonstrate its utility. They also contributed to the highway promotion work of the American Automobile Association (AAA). Federal aid to roads began "after an industry delegation met with President Woodrow Wilson and won his support for proposed federal highway legislation" (Memo to AMA Committee on Highway Economics, November 2, 1959, GM Files R-89). In 1932, GM President Alfred P. Sloan, Jr., established the National Highway Users Conference (NHUC) as the main highway lobbying organization, with the support of truck and bus operating associations and rubber, petroleum, and automotive industries.[32]

The membership of the National Advisory Commission for a National Highway Policy that designed the Federal Highway Act of 1956, [33] the lobbying activities of the NHUC sponsored by the AMA, the close connections among transportation associations, and the activities of individuals such as Francis V. DuPont, commissioner of the Bureau of Public Roads, and GM's Alfred P. Sloan, Jr., all contributed to the formation of a policy for financing highway construction.[34]

On the federal level, regulatory and enforcement procedures helped to accommodate automobile ascendancy. The Holding Company Act of 1933 made it impossible for concentration of ownership to occur between the transit and other public utilities industries. Saltzman (1977) has argued that this policy deprived the mass transit industry of needed capital for modernization. However, given the deleterious effects of utility-controlled transit firms after 1918, this argument seems questionable. The Holding Company Act had the intended consequence of depriving utility monopolies of transit properties. Unintentionally, it helped the automobile complex to replace the electrical industry/public utility faction in its control over transit and, thereby, to carry out its long-term motorization strategy. By removing the competition, automobile-dominated interests, working through trade associations, government bodies, and lobbies, were able to frustrate government regulatory policies. This strategy was critical in thwarting the investigation of the NCL and GM bus cases by the Antitrust Division of the Department of Justice and the FBI. Both agencies faced repeated obstruction from the Bureau of Public Roads, the ATA, and individual transit operators.[35]

On the state level, the NHUC, with 2,800 lobbying groups, decisively affected the creation of model state highway trust funds, which were free from competition with other state budgetary items. Through lobbying, campaign contributions, control of various lobbying organizations, and the influence of corporate representatives on decision-making bodies, highway building was insulated fiscally and politically from opposition.

A series of conferences sponsored by the auto industry through the Automotive Safety Foundation (founded by the AMA) and the National Committee on Urban Transportation (and later the Joint Committee on Highways) throughout the fifties and sixties specified the issues to be considered by state and local officials, traffic engineers, and city planners in transportation planning. Technically, transportation planning reinforced and expanded the patterns of auto domination established by the mid-fifties (Holmes, 1973:381–3). Through federal financing and private planning conferences, state highway agencies were freed from fiscal, legislative, administrative, and planning constraints in building freeways, primary and secondary routes, and feeder routes. This plethora of "technical solutions" gave state highway engineers enormous power to contour any coalition of local municipalities or civic groups committed to policy alternatives.

Highway planning reorganized transportation policy at

higher levels of government and, in successive stages, removed it from the sphere of public decision making. Because the 1962 and 1965 highway acts called for "comprehensive, cooperative, and continuous planning," the BPR was able, through various directives and instructional memoranda, to ensure that planning would be concentrated in and controlled by that bureau and state highway offices. Participatory planning was reinterpreted to emphasize the technical factors rather than the social effects of highway construction. Public hearings were not intended as popular referenda, but as trial balloons for testing local opposition, developing highway support, and creating a political strategy for any proposed highway route (Morehouse, 1965).[36] Moreover, as transportation planning through a metropolitan planning organization became institutionalized, control slipped from city hands. At the state level these procedures allowed complete agency control over transportation planning. A study by the U.S. Department of Transportation shows that in twenty-four out of thirty communities examined, the initiative for route selection, project staffing, and planning was taken by state rather than local agencies working through metropolitan planning bodies (Department of Transportation, 1976).

Increased opposition to highway construction in the sixties resulted in several court decisions that reinforced centralized planning. These decisions focused upon procedural rather than substantive issues. The courts determined that construction could be halted if the highway planners had made some mistake in the procedures. However, the powers of the community in public hearings, the social and economic impact of highways, and other issues were left untouched by the courts.[37]

Aside from the planning biases of federal legislation, economic biases abound. The apportionment formulas allowing heavy federal subsidization of highway construction almost eliminate other transportation modes. Less obvious is the anti-urban bias. Until the mid-seventies, states could not receive more than 12.5 percent of apportionment funds for other transportation modes. Thus, New York and Wyoming received similar mass transit allocations (Mantel, 1971:128–9). In the federal government's computation of costs and benefits of auto transportation, the improper valuations of land, pollution, residential dislocation, induced traffic, congestion, energy waste, and other social costs were excluded.

## Conclusion

The most important factor in national transportation policy was the strategies of the auto–oil–rubber industrial complex, which were designed to broaden the mass market and to provide the physical infrastructure necessary to sell their goods. Transportation policy also involved local and regional efforts to obtain capital to increase the development of land, fostering industrial construction and new housing starts so as to establish new bases to increase profits. Thus, capital at the national level involved in the most monopolized sectors, and capital at local and regional levels involved in more speculative, less directly productive areas, are unified politically and economically in motorized transportation.

Transportation policy reflects the profit-making and spatial-planning interests of particular large corporate interests. Historically, the profit-making function of transportation has dominated national developments. Such policy has been developed within corporate circles, expanded through "public" policy bodies supported by corporations, and transformed into state policy. Because rail transit hindered expanded production in new industries and profit making in urban land and housing, corporations worked to supplant rail with motorization policies. Although electrical transit was the climax of industrial growth associated with older industries (coal, steel, electrical machinery, etc.), it became an obstacle to the emerging of an ascendant faction of capital herein termed the *corporate car complex*. This new group worked to limit state transportation policy by its own investment and its influence upon the emerging mass market economy, and by struggling against older corporate interests associated with rail transit. Having established its influence, corporate control over transportation policy was secured as corporate leaders and their allies took an active role in policymaking at the federal and state levels. In short, the policy leading to transit's decline was one that minimized public control over transportation programs and maximized corporate benefits.

# 5

# Transportation politics: the case of Frankfurt am Main

## Transit change in Frankfurt

Local transit development illustrates how local urbanization, national industrial change, and concentration and political institutionalization influence the city. Transit ridership and motor vehicle registration illustrate Germany's differential rate of transit decline and increased motorization. In Frankfurt, ridership grew, with brief exceptions, until the thirties. Although there was some recovery during the late thirties, transit stagnated around the level attained during the Weimar period until decline set in at the end of the fifties (Figure 5.1 and 5.2). This pattern of stagnation and decline corresponds to increased motorization. As we shall see in Chapter 6, this pattern of decline differed sharply from that of Chicago. How can we account for shared yet strikingly different rates of transit ridership change? At the local level, the links between local planning and national economic, political, and corporate changes can be illustrated.

## General background

The late, uneven, and rapid industrialization and commercial expansion in Germany during the late nineteenth and early twentieth centuries is reflected in changes in Frankfurt's class structure. These changes, along with the physical structure established in an earlier era, created a unique set of transportation problems: to accommodate population growth and diversity associated with industrialization and to preserve the city's historical role as a financial and commercial center.

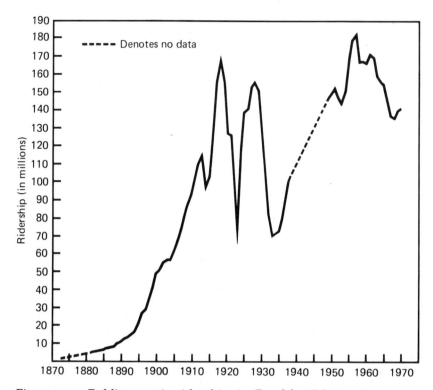

Figure 5.1. Public transit ridership in Frankfurt/Main, 1872–1970. (Sources: *Statistisches Jahrbuch Frankfurt/Main*, 1973:63; *60 Jahre Städtische Electrische Strassenbahnen in Frankfurt/Main*, 1958:45, 63; *Statistisches Handbuch der Stadt Frankfurt/Main*, 1907:249; 1928:395.)

Frankfurt lies in a valley between major stretches of forests and mountains in central Germany (the Taunus to the north and the Odenwald to the south). Its availability to easy water transportation, the rich farming soils of its valley, and its pivotal location close to other European countries are classic geographical elements that foster metropolitan growth. However, the pattern of urban growth and Frankfurt's role in the German system of cities changed over the centuries (Kurt, 1956:160–3; Isbarg, 1967). Its commercial past and the importance of finance capital in expanding consumer demand en-

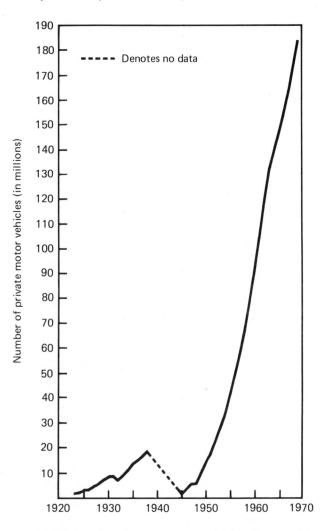

Figure 5.2. Number of private motor vehicles in Frankfurt/Main, 1923–69. (Sources: *Tatsachen und Zahlen aus der Kraftverkehrindustrie,* 1931:40; 1932:44; 1933:45; 1937:37; 1938:27; 1939:61; and *Statistisches Jahrbuch Frankfurt/Main,* 1962:Table 103; 1970:Table 86.)

abled Frankfurt to become uniquely important and central in the German urban system (Iblher, 1970; Klemmer, 1971).[1]

Major German cities have grown at widely varying rates. This variation is explained by political differences that enabled the cities to perform new economic functions or to preserve older ones (Mauersberg, 1960:73–5). Prior to 1866 and Frankfurt's annexation to Prussia, it enjoyed the status of a *Freistadt*, with more economic and political independence than other urban centers and nurturance of its commercial and craft interests.[2] This circumstance limited city growth and economic diversification until the late nineteenth century.

Frankfurt's slow industrialization inhibited its urbanization relative to other German cities. Its undisputed hegemony over the continental money and capital markets reinforced the political power of Frankfurt's financiers and businessmen and their wish to prevent manufacturers from competing for urban space and political control of the city.

Unlike banking centers in the Rheinland, Berlin, and Hamburg, Frankfurt's surplus banking capital was not used to promote industrialization; instead, investments were made in railroads, shipping, trade, government bonds, and business firms. Frankfurt was the major trading center for such stocks. Its business leaders preserved the city's commercial character rather than industrializing by joining the *Zollverein*.

Although Frankfurt's finance capitalists did not encourage industrial expansion until the 1880s, its role in expanding German capitalism was critical. With close ties to financiers and bankers in France, Austro-Hungary, and the Benelux countries, Frankfurt became a major distribution center, mobilizing consumer demand throughout Germany and other European counties (Riesser, 1911; Achterberg, 1956; Heyn, 1972:89–93). As a trading center, it spurred industrialization in other parts of Germany through its policy of extending credit and establishing large market areas.

Frankfurt's class structure and local politics reflected these unique circumstances. Late industrialization meant increased divisions among the established commercial and financial groups and the emerging working class. Frankfurt developed a rigid class structure in which the remnants of the old merchant class combined with the emerging finance capital group controlled the city.

The late fifties and early sixties . . . saw political and social divisions deepen and class lines became more rigidly defined. The haute finance merged into the social elite of the old established patricians and wealthy merchants; the rest of the more affluent citizenry formed themselves into moderately liberal upper, and somewhat more radical lower middle classes, and there arose the luminous spectre of a rapidly increasing fourth estate, the workers. Despite the hopes of the democrats that they might be able to contain and manage the rising labor movement, there was communist agitation in neighbouring Bornheim . . . The labor movement had come into its own and the liberal circles of the bourgeoisie gradually lost touch with what was becoming known as the proletariat. (Heyn, 1972:80)

The changing class structure of Frankfurt reflected the rate of population growth and the geographic distribution of population throughout the expanding city. Adjoining towns became urbanized and absorbed by the city through annexation. Demands arose for the physical and social services necessary to ensure economic diversification. In this context, transit was seen as a means of maintaining the spatial polarization of Frankfurt's class structure.

## Spatial decentralization and the concentration of political power

Bothe's (1906) examination of tax records shows that agriculture, retail trade, and handicrafts were the base of capital accumulation, in addition to country estates. Other sources of investment capital noted by Heyn (1972:4) included surpluses of wholesale merchants and trading companies, gains from currency or exchange and bullion speculation, profits of pawnbrokers, monopoly rents of landlords during trade fairs, capital imported by immigrants, and sharply regressive tax laws created by the Frankfurt Senate.

Manufacturing played a small role due to the power of the guilds, which regulated Frankfurt's trade and manufacturing. As capital accumulation became dominated by major banking families, dependency between the banks and the local merchants and guild artisans grew. Their shared interest in limiting Frankfurt's activities to credit and market expansion (Gley,

1936:75–6; Bohme, 1968 ) was mobilized to resist the legal reforms that promoted industrialization in other parts of Germany. For example, the ruling coalition of bankers, merchants, and artisans opposed *Gewerbefreiheit*, the right to manufacture or trade, until 1864. Financial loans for industrialists, citizenship and commerical rights, and participation in trading areas were all restricted until the nineteenth century. The absence of legal and financial reforms prolonged the dominance of trading and commercial groups in the city.

These characteristics of local political and economic power led to decentralized manufacturing. Manufacturing developed in Bockenheim and Offenbach to the west and east of Frankfurt, respectively, just beyond the borders of the city (Biel, 1922; Ludwig, 1940; Schneider, 1962). By 1880, Frankfurt was surrounded by smaller industrial suburbs.

Frankfurt's population and economy changed rapidly during the second half of the nineteenth century. Between 1850 and 1900 the population quadrupled, from 61,869 to 288,989. Only Leipzig and Charlottenburg grew faster, largely due to migration. The proportion of migrants remained about 60 percent of the total population, higher than that of other German cities (Emrich, 1974:139).

Following German unification and the end of restrictive migration and business licensing, the city experienced an economic boom (*Gründerzeit*) in manufacturing. During the closing years of the nineteenth century, employment in manufacturing grew twice as fast as total employment (*Statistisches Handbuch der Stadt Frankfurt/Main*, 1907:41–2). By the eighties, with the growth of the chemical industry, Frankfurt became known as the center of growth industries; this shaped its planning policies for decades to come.

Delayed industrialization, the rising demand for labor, and the changing class structure of the city led the older ruling coalition of merchants and bankers to demand governmental accommodation of urban growth and to prevent what was called *overproletarianization*. As population and manufacturing increased, the *Innenstadt* and areas adjacent to it no longer retained their residential character (Gley, 1936:81). Moreover, the wealthy, whose offices and homes had long dominated city

Table 5.1. *Annexation of neighbor-*
*ing townships, 1877–1928*

| Town | Year of annexation |
| --- | --- |
| Bornheim | 1877 |
| Bockenheim | 1895 |
| Niederrad | 1900 |
| Seckbach | 1900 |
| Oberrad | 1900 |
| Ginnheim | 1910 |
| Praunheim | 1910 |
| Huasen | 1910 |
| Eckenheim | 1910 |
| Heddernheim | 1910 |
| Niederursel | 1910 |
| Rödelheim | 1910 |
| Berkersheim | 1910 |
| Bonames | 1910 |
| Preungesheim | 1910 |
| Eschersheim | 1910 |
| Schwanheim | 1928 |
| Griesheim | 1928 |
| Nied | 1928 |
| Fechenheim | 1928 |
| Sossenheim | 1928 |
| Höchst | 1928 |

*Source:* Frankfurt Stadtarchiv, Eingemein-
dungen Verzeichnis

space, felt the pressure of increased population and business activities. As Gurlitz (1920:289) expressed this fear: "[the city] must through administrative-technical measures or through widening its boundaries prevent the intrusion of lowered building standards in its general region. Otherwise, the suburbs will grow with the city, increasing disease and proletarian overpopulation which usually works from the outside to the inside . . . a growth that is generally to be fought." The spectre of overpopulation and political challenge by the growing number of industrial workers spurred the Frankfurt Senate, city managers, and local elite to actively plan growth.

Sweeping annexation statutes gave the city the means of physical expansion (Lauck, 1926). The number of annexations increased swiftly between 1877 and 1928. The local govern-

ment and the ruling business coalition that for years had resisted manufacturing and the extension of the city's physical
boundaries, and that had restricted the right to participate in
municipal affairs, was now incorporating broad working-class
areas into the city's boundaries through annexation. What accounted for this shift in local policy?

In spite of changing strategies, the goal of the locally dominant class was the same – to maintain residential segregation
by class and control the use of urban space. With fundamental
changes in the population and local economy, new ways of
controlling the spatial segregation of classes were necessary.
Scholars of Frankfurt have demonstrated distinctive patterns
of residential segregation by class that developed over the
years (Gley, 1936; Emrich, 1974). The wealthy and middle
classes were concentrated in the Innenstadt, and by the close
of the century were moving into the western and northeastern
parts of the Anlage. The working class was concentrated in
the outskirts to the northeast and in towns on the city's periphery. Maintenance of the historic residential segregation of
classes guided mayoral politics from 1880 to World War I
(Miquel, 1886:10–20; Varrantrop, 1915; Emrich, 1974:295).

Prior to the 1880s, Frankfurt had faced persistent housing
shortages. As early as the 1860s, the public health department
had built public housing on the city's western periphery.
Quickly, the impetus for new construction shifted from social
reform to private profit making. Housing and real estate
speculation emerged as large businesses during the 1870s
boom period, dominated by firms such as the Süddeutsche
Immobiliengesellschaft and the Gütergesellschaft für Bau-
zwecke. Construction firms and land speculators increased
the density of housing throughout the city, particularly in
working-class areas, where the height and depth of buildings
were increased. This prompted local government to intervene
in housing and transportation practices (Hartog, 1965:41–50).

Before World War I, the mayor of Frankfurt was appointed
by the city's ruling class; voting rights were restricted to German property owners, and representation on the city council
was weighted heavily towards the old patrician and wealthy
merchant classes (Menne, 1964; Göb, 1966). The first mayor

84

during the growth period, Johannes von Miquel (1890–1), sought to regulate land and housing speculation. With the support of the city's old wealth, Miquel confronted the urban problems posed by the city's economic diversification and its effects upon settlement patterns.

Like other Frankfurt mayors, Miquel played an important role in the Verein für Gesundheitspflege (Association for the Preservation of Public Health). This organization was central to the German urban planning movement. Under Miquel, the goals of city government were defined by "professionals" and "experts." Soon after taking office, Miquel gained control over speculative investment and housing construction in the city; the municipal building code of 1884 restricted the building type and density in various sections of the city. However, uncontrolled building continued on the city's periphery. Regulation without annexation proved to be of little value in directing the city's growth.

Miquel foresaw the use of housing and transportation in urban planning and the further rationalization of urban growth. Close to the financial community of Frankfurt, he promoted the business potential of transportation as well. On June 12, 1882, he supported the initiative of a local merchant, J. Weintraut, and bankers W. Weiman and S. Merzbach, in establishing Frankfurt's first electrical tram to Offenbach. The Frankfurt–Offenbach Trambahngesellschaft (FOTG) connected the city center with the outlying manufacturing areas along the Main River to the east (Wiedenbauer and Hoyer, 1968:85–7). At the behest of the Rhein/Main Chamber of Commerce and Industry, Miquel supported a concession to Dr. Julius Kollman for an electrical railway to Eschersheim (Frankfurter Lokalbahn Aktiengesellschaft–FLAG).[3] The established Frankfurter Trambahngesellschaft (FTG) had concentrated its service in the wealthier neighborhoods of the city. Under increased pressure of competition from the FOTG and FLAG and a large number of petitions by residents of working-class areas such as Bornheim (where 1,500 signatures were gathered for such extensions), the FTG also extended service.

Miquel provided financing and regulation to expand mass transit. As Emrich (1974:339) notes:

He believed that new working class residential neighbourhoods would be encouraged by improving communication both within Frankfurt and between the city and its nearby suburbs. Here Miquel was thinking primarily of cheaper fares for workers to make it possible for them to commute to their places of work in the city from outlying areas where the cost of housing was lower.

Through Miquel's efforts, the city's profitable new contract with the FTG in 1888 forced line extensions, previously considered unprofitable, in an attempt to eliminate overcrowding and pressures upon wealthier neighborhoods in the city's center. The twenty-five-year contract also gave the city the right to renegotiate the contract within ten years and to purchase the FTG within twelve years if it so desired.

In the tradition of the Freistadt period, Miquel used local government to regulate housing construction and transit operators. Local regulation restricted profit making in these areas in order to preserve the existing neighborhoods within the city while expanding economic activities on the periphery. In a pattern that was strikingly different from that of U.S. cities, transportation was subordinated to economic expansion and rationalized urban development, deemphasizing the profit-making interests of land and transit speculators.

## Annexation and transportation planning: the Adickes period

Under Franz Adickes's mayoralty (1891–1913), transportation and city planning became even more extensive. Adickes's activities in Frankfurt brought him and the city worldwide recognition of its success in local planning.[4] As Frankfurt's traditional commercial and financial functions were supplanted by those of other major German cities, massive investments in the Frankfurt trade fair and water and rail transportation promoted the city's industrial growth and enhanced its traditional position as a national center of trade and transportation. Regulation of construction, the establishment of the first industrial park within the city, annexation, the expansion of public health and service facilities, the growth of the streetcar

Figure 5.3. Franz Adickes, Chief Mayor of Frankfurt/Main, 1891–1913. Under Adickes's direction, major infrastructural development, including that of transit, occurred through municipalization of services and active local government intervention in and regulation of the process of urban growth.

networks, bridges, and street construction, and the establishment of the university all came during these years (Menne, 1964:37).

## Physical planning measures

With the Aussenstadt invaded by multistoried housing for white-collar and skilled workers, and the growth of factories and shops, the city council and Adickes promptly blamed the existing building code. A breakdown of residential segregation would mean the realignment of urban politics in Frankfurt – something Adickes and the city's wealthy classes greatly feared. Clearly, stronger measures were necessary to preserve the residential staus quo while facilitating economic expansion; Adickes proposed protective land use regulations.[5]

The Zoning Act of 1891, his first major act as mayor, was designed "to preserve the established community character" (Müllen, 1976–77). Areas of the city radiating outward from the center were limited in building density and height. Class segregation was maintained, and the more visible problems of a growth economy were reduced. The zoning law represented the first application of the Prussian *Fluchtliniengesetz* (1975), which allowed for city master plans.

Adickes lobbied heavily for national legislation to expand local powers, promoting the *Lex Adickes* (1902) in the Prussian Landestag. In this critical law, which was later used throughout Germany, Adickes drew heavily from the Verein für Wohnungsreform (Association for Housing Reform), allowing Frankfurt to expropriate land as dictated by the needs of the master plan. Expropriation rights were central to rational urban planning. Under the act, up to 40 percent of the city's land area could be expropriated without compensation for use as parks and streets (Adler, 1904). This law allowed later city land purchases on the urban periphery for housing development and thereby discouraged speculation. It prohibited poorly constructed buildings, required improvement of existing structures, and enlarged the market for building lots, again avoiding harmful speculation (Müllen, 1976–7:10).

Finally, the Increment Tax (1903) taxed profits on housing and land speculation. Housing speculation had continually plagued Frankfurt and made construction of inexpensive working-class housing prohibitive (Adickes, 1900). This measure, along with other legislation, forced speculators out of the housing market.

In all these efforts, Adickes was supported by the strong local financial, commercial, and industrial interests that had recruited him as mayor. This wealthy and politically established group felt no obligation to smaller entrepreneurs involved in land and housing construction. Their overriding interest was in orderly and controlled urban expansion.

Straightening streets, clearing traffic bottlenecks, and subordinating housing lots to street development required an orderly land market. Once these physical barriers were removed, traffic could expand. Existing housing lots were subordinated to the need for transportation in opening new areas for future housing.

## Transportation politics under Adickes

Adickes saw housing, land annexation, transportation, economic development, and successful planning as issues requiring a unified approach to planning in local government:

> The use of commuter rail service for workers' housing is a problem since smaller outlying communities resist the associated social welfare costs . . . Through annexation we can create a master building plan which from the beginning makes commuter rail linkages a critical part of that plan. Commuter rail lines, streets, and stations become the spine of the master plan. (Quoted in Schneider, 1925:78)

Adickes's transportation scheme followed closely a plan developed by Miquel's Stadtbaumeister William Lindley; streetcar and street building would proceed in a radial pattern around the city center, joining the interstices of areas adjacent to the city. This ring development widened the streetcar network significantly (Magistrat, 1925:14–15).

The FTG denounced the Lindley program as too costly; Adickes retaliated by demanding renegotiation of the FTG's franchise. Simultaneously, the FTG's tranist fare hike became a popular issue. From January 30 to March 1891, a special committee of the city council heard testimony against the FTG's fare hike and Adickes's proposals for a new contract (FSA/R1770/II Bericht). Witnesses from the business community and working-class commuters demanded more transit services; calls for public ownership were heard for the first time.

In March 1891, the committee's final report proposed a compromise that would maintain private transit ownership. However, the city council forced major concessions from the FTG:

(1) it gave the city the right to review the issue of public ownership of transit every eight years; (2) it increased the amount of FTG profits going to the city as taxes; (3) it prohibited further selling of FTG stock; and (4) it forced the FTG to extend transit lines one kilometer for every 10,000 increase in population (FSA/r1770/II Bericht des Sonderausschusses zum Vortrag des Magistrats; Schneider, 1925:99).

A minority opinion in the city council offered by Martin Mor expressed the belief that the city had not gone far enough. The city had established all the "pre-conditions for city ownership" but, instead of proceeding, created a financial source of "loss for the city and the taxpayer" from concessions made to the private company (FSA/R1770/11).

Dissatisfaction with the contract increased. Three major objections were raised by the press and the city council over the FTG's compliance with contract provisions: (1) fares were rising, thus failing to encourage commuter traffic and suburban living by workers; (2) the FTG was accused of "foot dragging" in pursuing transit line extensions; and (3) the FTG refused to electrify transit lines which would allow more extended residential settlement (FSA/R1770/II).

In 1897, the city council voted for public ownership of transit. In spite of the cost, municipalization was promoted to catalyze urban expansion. One council member recalled: "Above all, there was the conviction that all enterprises with a monopoly character that used city streets and influenced the well-being of the urban population should be placed under city administration to be maximally efficient." (Quoted in Wiedenbauer and Hoyer, 1968:107).

Moreover, through public ownership of transportation and the market stimulation that ensued, Frankfurt would achieve Adickes's goal of "municipal industrialization" (Stadtisches Elektrizitätsamt, 1902; Guenther, 1913; Gottlieb, 1976:15). Local officials and businessmen mobilized local financial markets to fund public infrastructure for economic expansion.

Electrification, rationalization, and service extension became the agenda of the municipalized transit operation (FSA 1743/II, Strassenbahnen Generalia, November 20, 1907; February 22, 1909). As early as 1896, Adickes had argued that electrification would lower operating costs by one-third (Wieden-bauer and Hoyer, 1968:197). Soon after the council voted for public ownership, a contract was made with Siemens, Halse, Braun, and Boveries to electrify existing lines and construct extensions. The city took over the transit properties on January 1, 1898; electrification was completed by March 31 the following year. By 1897, the first regional transportation planning authority was created, the Preussisch-Hessischen Eisen-bahngemeinschaft. In 1904, the Waldbahn, Eschersheimer Bahn, and Frankfurt–Offenbacher Bahn were all integrated into the municipally owned transit system. Between 1900 and 1913, the length of track increased from 37 to 92 kilometers.

In a council policy paper, Councilman Wilhelm Riese presented the planning agenda:

It would be wise to municipalize those smaller rail systems which connect outlying areas with the larger city. The management of these lines, their placement, and fare structure have enormous significance for the future benefit of the city. In all major cities, a central tendency can be noted: the inner part of the city becomes dominated by business traffic while surburbs and exurbs become healthy and relatively low cost areas of housing. (Stadt-rat Riese, quote in Schneider, 1925:92)

Smaller cities were annexed to Frankfurt in exchange for transportation, sanitation, and electricity service extensions. By 1910, the remaining eleven communities surrounding Frankfurt had been annexed. The city also started community construction companies to build public housing in these outlying areas; they were later turned over to private housing companies (Menne, 1964:37–40).

Street building and transit fares were also part of Adickes's strategy of urban expansion. The mayor's office and the Stadt-baumeister used new land use and expropriation laws to remove all barriers to traffic through the Altstadt. Similarly, the radial *Landstrassen* stretching to the periphery of the city were widened and improved, and a new Ringstrasse was constructed around the outskirts of the city.

Transit subsidies and decentralization of working-class residences were promoted, thereby preserving central locations for upper-class residents and businesses. The Fare Ordinance (April 1, 1904) limited fares for long-distance travel (over 6

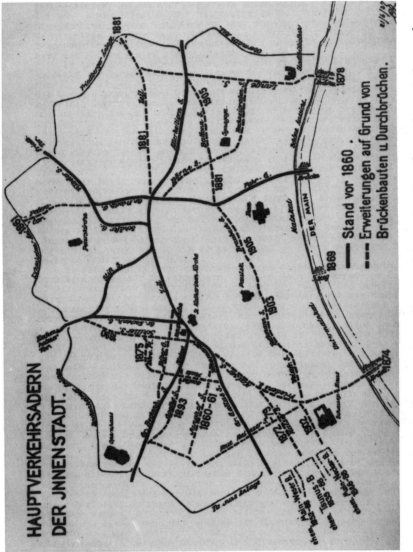

Main transportation arteries of inner-city Frankfurt, showing the major arteries and their dates of construction. (Source: Settlement Office, Frankfurt am Main, 1927.)

kilometers) to 20 pfennigs. Additionally, Adickes proposed weekly rates for work-related travel that, on the basis of a sliding scale, declined with the distance traveled.[6] These measures, along with Reich tax legislation allowing for income tax deductions for work-related travel on public transportation, spurred ridership.

Line extensions continued during this period before World War I. The goal of city planning was to promise both commuter traffic with the *Vororte* (suburbs) and to increase travel within the city.[7] Construction could barely keep pace with demands for service (*Frankfurter Zeitung*, "Notstand im Vorortsverkehr," 29 December, 1908). City council records indicate numerous demands for service, especially from factory owners and workers concerning work-related travel.[8] Requests were processed through SEBA (Staedtisches Elektrizitaets and Bahm Amt–Municipal Electrical and Rail Office). Consider, for example, this request from January 20, 1913:

The overburdened streetcar lines carrying vital work-related traffic between Bockenheim and the Industrial area near the Galluswarte has forced travellers to experience overcrowded conditions and inconvenient disembarkation at the corner of the Mainzerlandstrasse and Hohenzollernplatz . . . It seems, therefore, necessary . . . [to construct] a direct link to Bockenheim. (FSA, 1797/IV Frankfurter Trambahnbau, SEBA, 20 January 1913)

Positive responses to extend or increase service for work-related travel were received; recreational travel on the Waldbahn received less direct and immediate attention.

By 1918, ridership reached its highest point – 168,540,689 passengers per year. The timing of municipalization while transit business was flourishing enabled the city to use financial reserves from the company revenues to expand service, rather than waiting to take over an inefficient and debt-ridden operation.

Transportation, land use regulation, and annexation ordered Frankfurt's classes spatially in a way that was economically beneficial to urban expansion and yet suitable to the residential preferences of the city's upper classes. The working class was pushed to adjacent areas of the city and beyond, to suburbs that would be the location of future industrial growth. The inner and western parts of the city were preserved for the elite.

### Revolution, reform, and fiscal crisis: transportation politics during Weimar

World War I concluded in Frankfurt with a revolution. The Workers' and Soldiers' Council dominated local politics from November 1918 to November 1919. During that year the council, supported by the SPD and the USPD, demanded local services that previously had been neglected by municipal government, the labor parties, and their unions.

The Workers' and Soldiers' Council set up various *kontrollkommissionen* (commissions) to deal with local services and their administration. Immediately, unemployment compensation was increased.[9] After the food riots in March 1919, a Food Distribution Commission was also established. Similarly, and most important for the present discussion, the end of the war saw an enormous increase in the shortage of housing. The influx of refugees from other parts of Germany settling in Frankfurt, the increased number of marriages, and the shortage of housing construction left many homeless and others in overcrowded living quarters. The council distributed vacant apartments through its housing office to those needing shelter.

The council encouraged pubic transit through lower fares. Travel increased during this period and peaked in the summer months. Since the electrical utility and transit lines were run from the same city office and organization (SEBA), workers in those units supported the demands of the Workers' and Soldiers' Council and the use of the streetcar system for food distribution, housing planning, and the like. A city report later attributed low fares to "political reasons why it was impossible to entertain the idea of a fare increase in spite of growing economic necessities to have one" (Magistrat, 1925:19).

Immediately after the defeat of the Workers' and Soldiers' Council, the official city administration organized an independent transportation office directed by members of the city council (Magistrats-Beschluss Nr. 3052, 24 December 1919). By centralizing transportation organization, there was "coordination of all means of transportation" and the delivery of transportation service was depoliticized (FSA/R34 No. 4d, Magistrats Akten, 1919–30). This was part of a series of measures enacted by the city to eliminate the decentralization of service delivery (in housing, food, social services, and transportation) under the Workers' and Soldiers' Council (Protokoll Auszug der Stadverordneten Versammlung, Magistrats Beschluss Nr. 3235, January 6, 1920, Magistrats Akten, FSA/R34 No. 4d, 1919–30). The Frankfurter SPD followed the Reich SPD in denouncing the "council model" as a path of "extending democracy into the economy sphere" (Historisches Museum, Frankfurt, 1976:50.09–50.10).

The brief revolutionary period spanned transportation politics throughout the Weimar period. By institutionalizing demands through municipal reform, the local SPD leaders sought compromise with both the more radical working-class elements and organized capital. Social democratic power on the municipal level mirrored the compromises made nationally. Economic recovery and expansion required a more fully legitimated political order than the prewar system of local autocracy. Local government was organized to integrate, through centralization and planning, the continuing pressures by citizens groups and trade union locals for housing, transportation, and social service, as well as urban expansion for industry and commerce.

The city council under SPD Mayor Ludwig Landmann (1924–33) maintained political support by extending services (Gley, 1936:89; Rebentisch, 1975: passim). These measures placed enormous strain on the fiscal system because of fare subsidies. On January 6, 1923, a report from the newly formed Municipal Transportation Office demanded an immediate fare hike because "wage demands by transit workers and the rise of material prices have created a catastrophical economic condition for the streetcar system" (P34 No. 4d R1711, Magistrats Akten, 1919–30).

Furthermore, the report called for including business representatives in the Transportation Office since they were "required for administering [the transit system] due to this situation [of economic crisis]" (FSA/R1711, R34 No. 4d, Protokoll Stadverordenten Versammlung 6 February 1923).

The fare policy during the period of inflation decimated

Figure 5.4. Ludwig Landmann, Chief Mayor of Frankfurt/Main, 1924–33. Landmann maintained political support by extending urban services, which contributed to the city's fiscal crisis. Professional planning replaced citizen participation in transportation planning during his administration.

Figure 5.5. Ernst May.

ridership, which sank to its 1906 level (Magistrat, 1925:20; Schneider, 1925:188). As transportation use and system revenues declined, the settlement of peripheral urban areas decreased too, and the traditional overcrowding and shortage of working-class housing reappeared. In the face of this dilemma, SPD Mayor Landmann (Hoffman, 1974) and the head city planner and councilman, Ernst May, developed housing and transportation planing, not only for Frankfurt but for a whole generation of German planners.[10]

Shortly after coming to office, Landmann stated the major ideas of physical growth guiding his administration: "In order for Frankfurt to burst through its belt of current settlement and to promote natural and unhindered growth through annexation, we must facilitate economic expansion through housing, industrial, and settlement, as well as transportation

Ernst May's settlement plan, 1926–8. May's plan for "decentralized" residential settlements called for the first use of streetcar extensions for the settlement of areas that were not contiguous to the existing city settlements. (Source: Das Neue Frankfurt, 1928:125.)

policy" (quoted in Schneider, 1925:197). Landmann and May's goal was to close off the central city through physical planning, thereby preserving it as the focal point for financial, commercial, and administrative activities. In order to accomplish this division and the specialization of land use within the city, residential patterns shifted to the city's outskirts (Beusster, 1916:12–21; Weitzel, 1924:102). In 1925, Landmann introduced the first general construction plan for the city (*Generalbebauungsplan*), which replaced concentric expansion (i.e., the annexation of adjacent areas) with what May called "decentralization," the creation of satellite suburbs beyond the periphery of the city (May, 1928:112–15; May, 1930:28–30). The plan separated the city into distinct industrial, residential, and recreational areas. Industry was offered local subsidization for locations near the Main and along rail routes. For completion, the plan required another massive wave of annexation in 1928, when remaining adjacent areas were incorporated into the city. Heavily industrialized areas to the east (Fechenheim) and to the west (Hoechst) were brought within the city. Also, socialization of housing finance through worker supported building funds created 10,000 more units in the first five years and began urban renewal in older sections of the city (Menne, 1964:31–5).

Further transit plans focused upon linking the central city with neighboring areas that were to be annexed by 1928 (e.g., rail links from Bergesheim to Vilbel, from Riederhöfe to Fechenheim, and from Griescheim to Hoechst) (Schneider, 1925:199).[11] Reduced fares encouraged travel along these routes. Plans for increasing circulation between neighborhoods were ignored as the priority shifted to the transportation goals of May's settlement plan.[12]

Transportation became a means of decentralizing residential settlement.[13] Decreasing travel time to work and creating sufficient residential housing for the growing industrial workforce were considered crucial (Schultze, 1929).

On October 17, 1925, coordination between plans of the Settlement Office and the Transportation Office became part of city policy (Frankfurt Trambahnbau, FSA, R1797/IV, Memo, October 17, 1925). In city council meetings, local policy papers, and the press, the importance of transportation in physically organizing the city was continually discussed. For example, a policy paper by the Frankfurt Transportation Office stated:

Precisely the problem (of the multiplicity of economic requirements by different work situations) lies in a huge city with its complicated multilayered economic relationships where the daily time spent for the journey to and from work, education, and recreational locations becomes increasingly large and at the cost of labor time. We travel always more and work less. (Magistrat, 1927:78)

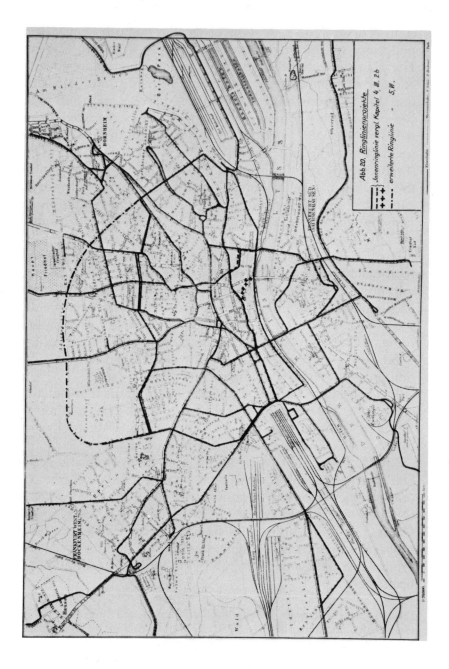

Abb. 20. Ringlinienprojekte.

Innenringlinie vergl. Kapitel 4. II. 2b
erweiterte Ringlinie    "    5. II.

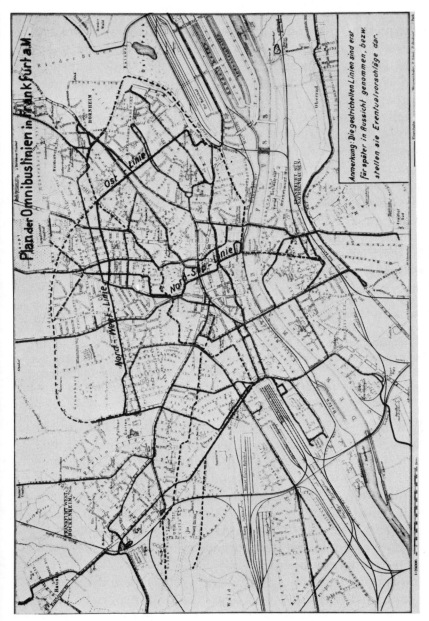

Frankfurt's streetcar and bus systems (1925). Both rail and bus were used in a coordinated manner to increase settlement of outlying areas contiguous to the city, as well as to increase circulation between those areas. (Source: Frankfurter Magistrat, Frankfurter Verkehrsprobleme und Beiträge zur ihre Lösung, 1925.)

Consequently, the Transportation Office argued, work-related travel should be restricted to commuter lines in order to reduce inner city congestion. As a result of this study, transportation construction concentrated upon commuter links with suburban areas.

Finally, during the Weimar period, the nascent conflict between cars and railways in urban transportation began to emerge. Of particular concern was the congestion caused by industrial and commercial trucking traffic throughout the city (Magistrat, 1925:51–3). More regulation was required to segregate various types of travel (industrial, work-related, recreational, etc.). The Transportation Office recommended construction of commuter rail lines that would remove traffic from existing streets, rather than construct new ones. Police President Zimmerman wrote the Transportation Office on November 11, 1927:

In Frankfurt/Main, the highly unfavorable street system makes traffic regulation difficult. Therefore, there is a need to correct this problem . . . Transportation and safety reasons make it immediately necessary to do so. In order to accommodate increased traffic, it is important that rail traffic be unhindered [by cars]. If this is accomplished in the near future, unforeseen disadvantages for the general economic area of the city of Frankfurt will be averted. (Magistrat, 1927:3–4)

That same year, Zimmerman strictly enforced auto traffic measures that would enable a free flow of commuter rail traffic. On July 1, 1929, the Municipal Transportation Office suggested that "it would seem a good idea, particularly, that the administration of the municipal automobile department be integrated into the motor bus section of the Street Rail operations" (FSA, R1711, Magistrats Akten, 1919–33, R34 No. 4d). Automotive regulation was administered through street rail operations and dominated by it.[14]

Transportation politics during the Weimar period reflected the contradiction between the demands for transportation and other urban services by a mobilized working class and the need for economic recovery and capital expansion by the business community. In short, public transportation became an object of class conflict. Themes of Adickes's city expansion movement and the 1918–19 revolution were institutionalized during this period. In order to accommodate these conflicting goals, the SPD government under Landmann and May forged a program replacing socialism with social policy, and public participation with professional planning. Eventually, the attempt to reconcile social and economic functions of public transportation contributed to the urban fiscal crisis of the late twenties.

Technocratic planning goals required more centralized organization and coordination with regional government. The control commissions were replaced by separate planning offices within the municipality. Neighborhood transportation needs were ignored, and suburbanization was promoted as a solution to both industrial locational problems and working-class housing shortages. The insulation of the central city from residential development was pursued by line extension, fare reductions and, most importantly, municipal construction and annexation programs.[15]

Many Weimar social policies, particularly in housing and transportation, were inherited by the Nazis together with a generation of planners and established local government organizations that defined social reform as technical planning.

## German fascism and transportation politics in Frankfurt

Changes in urban transportation during this period reflected the increased importance of the auto–oil–rubber industries in the national and regional economies, and centralized political power eliminated the possibility of local opposition to motorization. By 1933, the Rhein/Main area had become a national center of oil and chemical (I. G. Farben), rubber (I. G. Farben and Dunlop), and automobile (Adam Opel and Adlerwerke) manufacturing. Germany's highway lobby, the HAFRABA, was founded and headquartered in Frankfurt.[16] These industrial intersts forged national motorization policies and affected local politics as well. The economic interest of these industries converged with the planning interests of other regional businesses in expanding the urban market through decentralization – the dispersion of industry and housing to the peri-

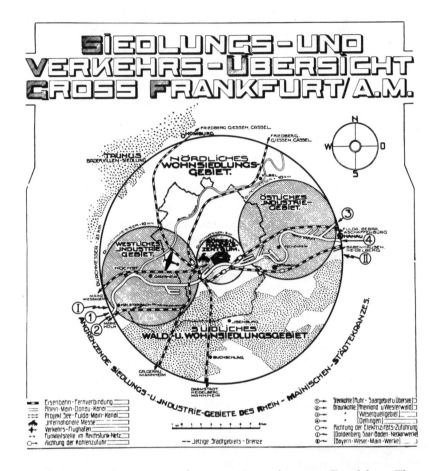

Settlement and transportation overview of greater Frankfurt. There was a general attempt by city planners in the twenties to divide Frankfurt into eastern and western industrial areas and northern and southern industrial areas, and to preserve the city center for commercial activities. (Source: A. Weitzel, 1924:103.)

phery. Local officials and planners argued that rationalized urban growth could be accomplished only with more centralized political power – something German fascism was more than ready to provide.

Agitation for motorization policies in Frankfurt preceded the emergence of fascism. As early as 1931, Willy Hof of the

HAFRABA lobbied the Municipal Council to support Reichstag proposals for financing a model stretch of the autobahn (Memo to Dr. Heun, Magistratsrat, 23 March 1931, FSA, 3416/1; Frankfurt/Main Wirtschaftsamt, 13 April 1931). In 1932, Landmann agreed to permit Hof to represent the city at meetings of the International Autobahnkongress and to host that Congress (Hof, HAFRABA to Landmann, 13.4.32, FSA 3461/2). Nevertheless, the lack of national financing for local road building kept such plans in abeyance.

Because of Frankfurt's geographical position and the importance of motorization lobbying groups in its local economy and government, the city became a center of national motorization policies. On August 18, 1933, Fritz Todt, the general director of German highways, converted HAFRABA into the official Gesellschaft zur Vorbereitung der Reichsautobahn (GEZUVOR). On September 23, 1933, Hitler appeared at the opening ceremony for the construction of the first autobahn stretch from Frankfurt to Darmstadt, praising the city that was realizing his vision of a motorized Germany (*Die Strasse*, May 1, 1935; *Frankfurter Volksblatt*, May 19, 1935). The planned Frankfurt Junction was the central exchange of traffic for the whole autobahn system. National planning meetings of the GEZUVOR were held in Frankfurt. At the May 19, 1935, meeting, Chief Mayor Friedrich Krebs told the gathering: "Frankfurt/Main, 'the city of streets' is proud to have become, through the iron will of our Führer Adolf Hitler, the birthplace of the Reichsautobahn" (FSA, 3416, 1933–40, Reichsautobahnen).

Local business interests were intimately involved in the shift to motorization. The local GEZUVOR planning group in Frankfurt included representatives of the automobile clubs, various local chambers of commerce, business and financial interests, and the automobile industry (Tätigkeitsbericht, GEZUVOR, SEK. 8, 28.11.33; Memos 24.10.33.11.33, FSA, 3416/1).[17]

Opel, GM's German subsidiary, applauded the Nazis, stating that "under the protection of the national socialist regime" Opel's plant became the largest auto manufacturing factory in Germany (*Die Opelwerke, Die Strasse*, May 1935:63–5). I. G. Farben recognized the direct relationship between transportation planning and the profit motive:

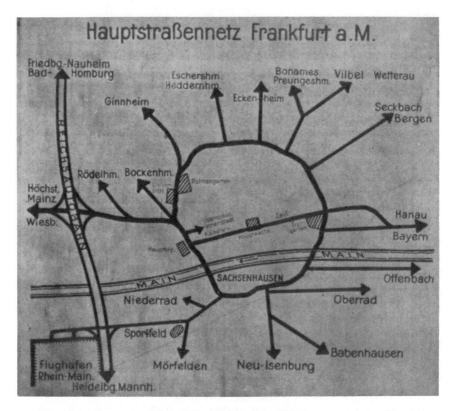

Major street network of Frankfurt (1936). Street construction was used during the Third Reich to enclose the city center and expand traffic to outlying suburban areas. The first Reichautobahn was also constructed during this period, making Frankfurt a center for inter-urban travel. (Source: Städtisches Anzeigeblatt Frankfurt am Main, 1936.)

The consequences of extensive street planning is [sic] apparent in various areas. Not only immediately upon transportation, but upon industry in general which will be stimulated by new highway construction. For I. G. Farbenindustrie, which in this area has various factories, this has particular importance. (Reichautobahnen und I. G. Farben, *Die Strasse*, May 1935:53)

Nationally centralized planning was promoted by the new highway lobby. Fritz Todt personally sent instructions to

Mayor Krebs concerning the physical planning of the city, local economic policy, and the need to shift labor to various residential settlement and transportation work projects (Todt to Krebs, 17 May 1934, Krebs to Landesarbeitsamt, 20 June 1935, FSA, 3416/1).

Local business interests under Nazism reorganized transportation planning (Stadtisches Anzeigeblatt, October 2, 1936:-594–6). As Menne (1964:34) notes:

During the national socialist period, the direction of the Reich's administration, politically coordinated through Berlin, brought everything together under a fortified centralism . . . [that centalization of political power] influenced change in the economic sector of Frankfurt. Economic incentives to the construction sector, the automobile industry, and the favorable location of Frankfurt on the intersection of . . . the autobahn network influenced the transportation sector.

Motorization and centralized planning were extended to the Frankfurt Rhein/Main region. In 1931 *Stadtbaurat* Rheinhold Niemayer, who succeeded Ernest May as the principal city planner in Frankfurt, complained that he lacked the centralized political authority necessary to accomplish the spatial decentralization goals of the city's master plan. He believed that all physical planning required centralized political power to ensure that housing construction considered all related costs, specifically the journey to work (*Frankfurter General Anzeiger*, 10 April 1931).

Through his position as *Stadtbaurat*, Neimayer argued that the Rhein/Main Regional Planning District was "torn by political frontiers . . . [whose] arbitrary nature . . . aggravated organic regional planning and the uniform development of communications" (Niemayer, 1931:195). In presenting HAFRABA's plan for a system of international autobahns connected through Frankfurt, he argued that a plan for secondary traffic routes in the core of the Rhein/Main area would open new areas for decentralized settlements and isolate the city center (Niemayer, 1931:198).

Niemayer's proposals were incorporated into Frankfurt's transportation policy. This was a logical development, he argued, because urban decentralization could be accomplished

# Das Automobil schafft Arbeit

Anzahl der Beschäftigten in Deutschlands größter Automobilfabrik

Der 30. Januar 1933 wurde zum Wendepunkt in der Geschichte des deutschen Automobils. Bereits am 11. Februar wurde die Regierungsmaßnahme angekündigt, die das Automobil von seinen Fesseln befreite; die langersehnte Steuerbefreiung brachte den beabsichtigten Erfolg: eine bedeutende Belebung der deutschen Wirtschaft und eine sehr erhebliche Entlastung des Arbeitsmarktes.

Die Zahl der Arbeiter und Angestellten in Deutschlands größter Automobilfabrik stieg von diesem Zeitpunkt an bis zum Juni dauernd und beträgt seitdem rund 10 000. Diese Zahlen drücken jedoch noch nicht restlos die Steigerung der Beschäftigung aus, da in der gleichen Zeit, in der die Zahl der Beschäftigten um durchschnittlich 40 Prozent gestiegen ist, die Mehrleistung an Lohnstunden 104 Prozent beträgt. Es sind also nicht nur mehr Arbeiter eingestellt worden, sondern der einzelne Arbeiter hat auch weit mehr Lohnstunden leisten und dementsprechend mehr verdienen können als im Jahre 1932. Die Steuer- und Konsumkraft des einzelnen Arbeiters erfuhr dadurch die so erstrebenswerte Steigerung.

Aehnliche Erhöhungen der Beschäftigungsziffer zeigen die etwa 900 deutschen Lieferwerke der Adam Opel A.G. — Mit der Herstellung deutscher Kraftfahrzeuge sind schätzungsweise 45 000 Menschen beschäftigt. Außerdem finden in den Lieferstätten dieser Industrie, im Verkauf, bei der Pflege und Bedienung des Kraftfahrzeuges, der Herstellung von deutschen Kraftstoffen weitere 550 000 Menschen Arbeit und Brot. Rechnet man die Familienangehörigen hinzu, so ergibt sich, daß heute in Deutschland rund zwei Millionen Menschen vom Kraftfahrzeug leben.

Opel

Für Deutschlands Fortschritt, für Deutschlands Verkehrsentwicklung

Figure 5.6. Adam Opel AG and transportation politics. This advertisement, proclaiming that "The Automobile Creates Labor," typifies the propaganda surrounding the Nazi motorization program. The advertisement is from a Nazi publication. Opel executives, with help from their GM counterparts, helped to formulate national transportation policy and local decisions in Frankfurt, in addition to their independent efforts and activities through the automobile trade association, Der Reichsverband der Automobilindustrie (RDA). (Source: *Nationalsozialismus in Staat, Gemeinde, und Wirtschaft*, 1935.)

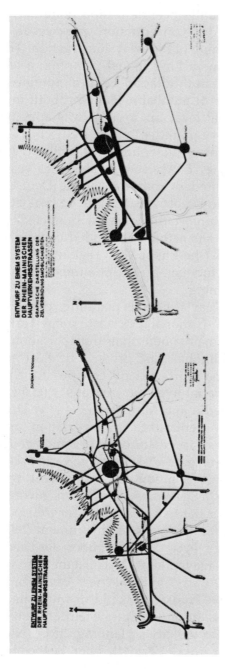

City planner Rheinhold Niemayer's highway design. Niemayer succeeded May as principal city planner and ascended to national prominence under the Nazis. His promotion of highway building and centralized planning authority facilitated motorization policies. The map indicates proposed highway links to further suburbanization and "sanitization" (the term used by the Nazis for urban renewal) of the inner city. [Source: *Das Neue Frankfurt*, 5 (Nov./Dec.) 1931, p. 197.]

only through further political centralization of authority. Fascism provided the needed concentration of power to accomplish the regional planning of highway construction. That was Niemayer's basic argument for regional planning, a technical argument that required authoritarian political administration.

Niemayer was active in autobahn planning both in Frankfurt and at the national level. In 1934 he was appointed by Todt to head an "expert committee" of the Deutscher Gemeindetag to oversee and plan autobahn construction (Ferenz to Krebs, 13 January 1934, FSA/3416/1). Later that year, Niemayer was also appointed as chairman of the Deutsche Gemeindetag (Niemayer to Krebs, 29.5.34, FSA 1233-14-26/BD. 1) and thus became an important figure in municipal politics throughout the Reich. His activities included coordination of Section 8 of GEZUVOR (the Rhein/Main region), participation in the Deutscher Gemeindetag, and appointment to the Reich Academy for City Planning.

Under the Nazis, May's liberal planning policies were transformed into the National Socialist framework. Niemayer, for example, maintained that transportation policy was a key to the additional vast urban renewal ("sanitization") necessary in Frankfurt and other cities for "population, political, and racial-hygienic reasons" (Confidential Summary of Trip to Berlin and Munster, 14, 15, 17 December 1934, FSA). Politically centralized transportation and city planning were necessary to create one "organic" geographical area that would overcome dissension at various levels of government. Niemayer's solution was consistent with the *Führerprinzip,* whereby a *Reichstatthalter* (Reich governor) for Rhein would administer the technical plans for transportation and urban renewal at higher levels of government (Niemayer to Krebs, 28 November 1934, Vermerk über die Dienstreise nach Bonn, FSA). Niemayer kept in constant contact with various governmental, party, and business organizations in order to make sure that Frankfurt would maintain its central position as the hub of the autobahn system and keep road building at the center of the city's planning effort (Niemayer to Krebs, 3 September 1934, Vermerk über Besprechung in Berlin, Confidential, FSA 1233-144-16/BD.1).

Another active personality in transportation planning was Stadtrat Dr. Robert Lingnau, who was involved with the Commission for Local Transportation of the Deutscher Gemeindetag.[18] That commission set basic public transportation policies, subordinating rail transit to the goals of motorization. The commission concluded that several basic policies should be pursued in running the existing rail transportation systems: (1) expenditures should be limited as mandated under the Community Fiscal Statutes passed according to guidelines approved by the central government; (2) fares should be raised in accordance with the cost of service, eliminating special discounts for particular groups – the elderly, workers, the unemployed, students;[19] (3) labor costs should be lowered over a period of time;[20] and (4) bus routes should replace streetcar service and be integrated into public transportation through the motorization and settlement policies mandated by the central government (Lingnau to Krebs, Reports on Berlin Commission Meetings, 20 November 1935 and 22 January 1935, FSA).

The liberal-technocratic planning theories and practices that had developed in Frankfurt over the previous decades degenerated under Fascist transportation policies. The focus shifted from planning rational and aesthetically pleasing spaces, housing, and transportation (as under Ernst May) to reducing the state's cost of public goods through private housing and transportation policies. This required the destruction of local autonomy through centralized regional planning that unified housing and transportation policies.

The National Socialist regime saw numerous political and ideological advantages to motorization and decentralized housing. Under fascism massive urban renewal began, along with large-scale suburban residential construction.[21] Spatial decentralization was not simply a goal for reordering the city physically; it was a political act. Decentralization would allow industrial labor to be complemented by agricultural tasks, thus lowering food costs; working-class communities would be politically defused; and housing construction costs would decline through the participation of residents. The settlements would provide a stable source of labor (*Stammarbeiterschaft*) for economic recovery and the remilitarization of industry and the economy. Most importantly, it was argued, creating accessible individual housing units would replace class solidarity with the ideology of individual achievement among workers by establishing "racially pure people's communities." Reich Labor Minister L. Seldte described the process:

> The *Kleinsiedlung* [single-family unit settlement] is the residential-ideal for all those workers out of the broad mases of the working classes which want to achieve private property. Those workers which are objectively, ideologically, and racially suited will receive *kleinsiedlungen* which eventually, after a three year probationary period, will become their private property. It will be seen to that rents for apartments are tolerable. For those party members which do not receive *kleinsiedlungen,* publicly owned apartments with gardens will be available. (F. Seldte, 1938, quoted in Historisches Kommission Frankfurt, 1976:53.05)

Frankfurt became a showcase of Nazi urban policy. The decentralization of population and industry was accomplished by centralizing planning authority in the Reich's policy and governmental organizations. Hitler noted that urban decentralization required a cheaper means of transportation. Motorization and decentralization were linked together in regional and urban planning during the Third Reich. Frankfurt Stadtbaurat G. Schroeder noted:

> The demands of the automobile industry through the promotion of the idea of the Autobahn are well known . . . of particular importance is the enclosing of unpopulated areas by the autobahn, and, as well, the closing off of the large city, thereby enabling the accomplishment of the settlement of the German people. (Schroeder to Krebs, 19 June 1934, FSA 3416/1)

The Nazis promoted highway building as the sole solution to the transportation needs of a coalition of old and new capital in Frankfurt. Under the Nazis, motorization aided the older commercial and financial groups that had long sought to insulate the city from pressures of urban growth and maintain it as an administrative center. Highway building would close off the central city and spur decentralization of industry and residences, thereby displacing the working-class communities whose militant traditions had long challenged local authorities and big-business interests. More importantly, motorization served the interests of new capital (auto–oil–rubber) industries that required state intervention to support their growing market through infrastructural investment, consumption subsidies, and the like. Along with Frankfurt's geographic centrality in the evolving national transportation network, the shift toward new industries in the local economy and the desire of the local elite to control downtown development created an overwhelming bias toward motorization.

These goals would have never been met without fascism. The consolidation of motorization interests required a centralized political authority. To successfully promote new auto-related industries, the local government had to overcome the traditional commitment to rail transportation and its subsidization of working-class riders. The tradition of local planning autonomy and rail transportation was destroyed by the Nazis. Centralized planning coordinated from Berlin through nationally linked local corporations and regional planning organizations allowed motorization to go unchallenged. Planning technicians such as Lingnau and Niemayer worked closely with business leaders such as Luer (Opel and Rhein Chamber of Commerce), von Schnitzler (I. G. Farben), Hagemeier (Adlerwerke and Reichsverband der Automobilindustrie), and others to motorize Frankfurt.

Fascism in the thirties brought economic stagnation, reduced ridership, and fare hikes. Ridership declined drastically from 156 million in 1928 to 70 million in 1933. In 1932 and 1936, rate increases further reduced ridership, which continued a long period of stagnation and decline. By 1938, public transportation had decreased by nearly 30 percent of the Weimar level.

At the Reich level, motorization was promoted and revival of mass transit was impeded. The Prussian Law over Budget Administration for Communes (1933), passed shortly after Hitler came to power, forced cuts in local spending; transportation expansion, maintenance, and ridership then declined. Meanwhile, street building associated with the autobahn program was given priority by the city council controlled by Fascists (Magistrats Beschluss #1491, 4117/1 Bd. 1). Similarly, centralized planning was required by the Reich Law Controlling Communities (1936), which eliminated all vestiges of local autonomy. Stronger annexation facilitated autobahn construction and furthered Nazi settlement and urban renewal policies (Niemayer, 12 June 1935, FSA 1233/14-26; Bd. 1; Mazerath, 1970). By the end of the thirties, Frankfurt had become the most motorized city in Germany (*Statistische Monatsberichte Frankfurt/Main*, 1959:153).

## Reconstruction, urban growth, and the rise of the corporate city: transportation and planning politics in postwar Frankfurt

In divided postwar Germany, Frankfurt's industrial, commercial, and administrative importance was enhanced (Iblher, 1970:14–17), and demands on the city's transportation infrastructure grew proportionately. The war had destroyed approximately half of the city's buildings. Nevertheless, the location of U.S. Occupation forces in Frankfurt, the loss of other urban centers in the east, and the existence of a politically agressive ruling coalition of business and labor leaders contributed to Frankfurt's newfound importance as a national urban center.[22] The increase in the number of commuters, in which Frankfurt ranked first in Germany, and public transport users, whose number skyrocketed at the end of the war, increasing until 1957, was stimulated by the massive expansion of the workforce (*Statistisches Jahrbuch Frankfurt/Main*, 1951: Table 1929; *Frankfurt Statistiche Berichte*, 1975:74–5). The government granted rent subsidies to encourage labor migration to Frankfurt.[23]

Prior to World War II, workers commuting from beyond the city limits were served by railroads and streetcar extensions. After the war, the territory from which workers were drawn expanded. The resulting increases in heavy traffic required extensive street and highway construction, which weakened public transit. By 1970, ridership had decreased by about 20 percent of its 1959 level (*Statistisches Handbuch der Stadt Frankfurt/Main*, 1952–72). As traffic congestion increased, the municipality initially extended bus service to avoid the cost of large-scale rail line extensions.

In this context, the motorization that had begun during the thirties continued at a rapid pace. The number of registered automobiles in Frankfurt had increased by nearly 100 percent during the Nazi period (Asemann, 1959:101–3). From 1951 to 1961, it rose from 17,647 to 104,484. By 1971, that number had again doubled (*Statistisches Jahrbuch Frankfurt/Main*, 1952, 1962, 1972).

Highway construction and motorization of this scope required reconstitution of the pro-automotive measures that had been established on a national level under fascism and articulated through local government. Nevertheless, in spite of its decline, Frankfurt's mass transit system survived a pattern of motorization similar to that experienced in the United States. The resilience of public transit can be attributed to the survival of institutionalized political support for public transportation, which occurred during the pre–World War I and Weimar periods and which are not to be found in the United States.

On November 11, 1945, Chief Mayor Kurt Blaum gathered 100 local business leaders to discuss the economic future of the city. He argued that reconstruction and economic expansion depended upon a close working relationship between the business community and the city government: "These are questions [of urban reconstruction] that relate directly with the activities of the Frankfurt local administration and that can be solved only through the closest cooperation with relevant economic branches [of industry] and the Chamber of Industry and Commerce" (Blaum, 1946:21).

In the discussions that followed, there was general agreement that local government should rebuild and expand physical services and infrastructure to ensure that the advantages Frankfurt had gained by Germany's division would not be lost. There was also a general recognition that urban expansion could best be administered by increasing regional governmental powers through the State of Hesse and regional governmental units (e.g., transit and utility authorities) (Blaum, 1946:26). During the immediate postwar period, much of the city's expansion and many of the changes in land use practices were accomplished under the broad legal powers for annexation and expropriation given to local and regional governments by an SPD-sponsored Reconstruction Law passed in the Hessian parliament in 1948 (Böhm, 1953:3).[24]

Physical reconstruction and transportation planning were to play a critical role in transforming Frankfurt's rubble in the immediate postwar era into a "world metropolis."

The first requirement (for expansion) is to complete the autobahn so as to provide good access to existing streets and to further construction of the (whole) autobahn system. Land for access roads is to be kept clear of construction and later purchased. It will be especially important to make the east side of the city accessible through an efficient north-south axis between the autobahn around Frankfurt's east side. Also, the streetcar system in Frankfurt needs only a few alterations. It should confine itself to the needs of the urban population . . . opening up neighboring communities near the Taunus. (Blaum, 1946:25)

Frankfurt's reconstruction policies were identical to the plans that had been interrupted by the war (*Städtisches Anzeigeblatt Frankfurt,* October 2, 1936).

The continuity of control over Frankfurt's transportation politics that spanned the pre- and postwar eras is observed in both policy formation and administration. In spite of changes from CDU to SPD local administrations, the policies and personnel in important planning positions remained under the control of planners from the thirties. Denazification affected only the most visible local politicians; administrators of transportation policy remained in place. Like transportation policy at the national level, local politics continued to be dominated by urban corporate powers.

Even though the Allies controlled appointments to local government, they acted primarily upon the recommendations of established business leaders. For example, the persons chosen to administer gas and transportation improvements in the city were A. Weikel of the Firma Deugsa (an oil firm) and Peter Herman, the local Mercedes Benz dealer (April 6, 1945, FSA 4127/1–1942–52). A few months later, the temporary organization of the Transportation Coordination Office was centralized under the economic office of city government. This action, taken by the military, placed all major transportation decisions under the control of Stadtbaurat Robert Lingnau, who had been active throughout the years of Fascist rule. Lingnau regrouped the city's motorization and pro-growth interests in the Street Traffic Office and the Municipality's

Transportation Office, which were reestablished in January 1947. The former was controlled by a committee consisting of members of the Chamber of Commerce and Industry, artisans, trade unions, and the Automobile Users Association (ADAC). Its membership was weighted toward motorization interests. However, the committee's broader than usual makeup, required by the U.S. occupational forces, was later condemned as "inefficient" by city officials, who dissolved it in July 1948. The committee was replaced by an appointed staff from the Municipality's Transportation Office that would oversee the postwar expansion (FSA, 4127/1, Fahrbereitschaft, Allgemeines, Geschäftsführung). Most transit extensions were confined to the completion of earlier plans. New rail extensions were questioned because of their cost. The streetcar/bus debate arose repeatedly in the city council. The city then purchased more buses and improved bus transportation and ridership rose accordingly. The streetcar/bus issue was resolved by instituting bus service in outlying areas while maintaining streetcar traffic for the nearer suburbs (Wiedenbauer and Hoyer, 1968).

A key figure in the reconstitution of highway interests during the postwar period was Dr. Walter Leiske, former head of the Frankfurt Chamber of Industry and Commerce. As mayor, Leiske set up the Department of Economic Initiative, the major municipal office coordinating Frankfurt's reconstruction and economic growth. As part of this task, Leiske regrouped those individuals and organizations that had been involved in HAFRABA and GEZUVOR during the twenties and thirties (Kolb to Harder, September 26, 1951, FSA 4127/25).

Later, under Mayor Walter Kolb, Leiske continued his work as chairman of a special committee for "Further Construction of the Autobahns." Kolb and Leiske organized a meeting on March 11, 1952; in attendance were Willy Hof (Director of the German Automobile Club), H. Linsenhoff (German Construction Industry Organization), Dr. A. Fricke (Organization of German Construction Materials Industry), Dr. von Brunn (Association of the Automobile Industry, VDA), and K. Friedrich (German Asphalt Industry). The meeting's goal was "to begin plans to bring HAFRABA back to life [and] with the help of auto users [through taxation] to complete as soon as possible the autobahn network" (Niederschrift, March 5, 1952, FSA, 4127/25:3). In founding a new lobbying organization for motorization, von Brunn, representing the automobile industry, suggested that motorization would accomplish the economic renewal of Germany – assisting foreign trade, domestic commerce, and market expansion. The meeting concluded that its lobbying efforts should be centered on and coordinated from Frankfurt.

By May 14, the group had met with their parliamentary allies in both the SPD and the CDU. With the advisors of Chancellor Konrad Adenauer, they coordinated a legislative program for federal aid for highway construction. This lobbying group became known as the "Frankfurter Circle for Autobahn Questions." As an informal coalition of municipal, business, and industrial leaders, they formulated new highway policies for Frankfurt and the rest of the Federal Republic (Reisebericht, Leiske, May 17, 1952, FSA 4127/25).

The 1953 Land Use Plan developed by the city was based largely upon the 1926 General Construction Master Plan developed by Ernst May. The separation of recreational, industrial, commercial, and residential areas was the basis of postwar city policies. The major difference between the 1926 and 1953 plans was in transportation. The 1953 plan based all industrial and residential decentralization upon motor transportation. A transportation supplement to the 1953 plan (presented in 1958) required more road construction and accessibility for auto commuters and commercial trucks (Schmidt, 1958). The Master Plan focused upon consolidating existing suburban communities and new housing construction in semi-autonomous satellite cities (e.g., the Nordwestadt) (Böhm, 1953).

Most importantly, the 1955 plan focused upon converting various areas of the central city and immediately adjacent residential areas to office and service use. The higher demands for office space nearer the central city reflected a vision by Frankfurt's corporate leaders that the city would become a world-metropolis. As city and Chamber of Industry and Commerce literature suggested, Frankfurt's traditional role as a commercial and financial center was to be broadened to coordinate and administer tertiary economic functions.

Such planning increased the concentration of land ownership in the Innenstadt and Westend during this period. The need for expanded investment in real estate and construction was on the rise. By increasing land use, higher returns on capital could be assured. In his study of land ownership concentration, Vorlaufer (1975:15) notes:

a change in the structure of the ownership of properties as well as a change in the potential for expanded construction in the downtown residential area demanded large investments of capital. Therefore, the intensification of the process of restructuring the city center could only be realized through groups of proprietors – themselves being agents of structural change – which could get a high amount of credit from banking capital. Only on a basis of a strong alliance between groups with new interests in the use of land, on one hand, and the credit institutions, on the other, could a structural change of the downtown occur.

Although middle-class residents (merchants, professionals, craftsmen, and civil servants) were the major landowners in 1947 (53.3 percent), their share dropped to 24.5 percent by 1972. Meanwhile, corporate use of the land increased from 9.2 to 57.9 percent between 1947 and 1972. Real estate offices, insurance firms, corporations, and banks became the principal landowners in the area after World War II.

By the time the 1961 Master Plan was drafted to restate the goals of earlier plans, the pressure for office expansion was immense. After considerable efforts by residents, the city allowed residential use to continue in some areas of the city. However, "exceptions" were granted on a case-by-case basis to landowners who wished to convert their properties to commercial or higher-density residential uses. The structural transformation of the city continued with the creation in 1961 of "city expansion areas," where priority was given to trade, transportation, banks, insurance, service, or governmental offices. A final blow to the city was the "Finger Plan" of the early sixties, which allowed the main transportation arteries of the city – the "fingers" – to be used for offices and parking spaces.

Both private and state-directed banks concentrated investment capital in city real estate development. This influx of capital, combined with urban policies, encouraged urban specialization in the tertiary sector. Urban activities and places – residences and workplaces, industrial and commercial activities, recreation and education locations – were segregated and increasingly separated from each other. In a period of rising motorization nationally, transportation planning became even more crucial to build highways and accommodate cities to automobile traffic.

## The organization of planning

To comprehend this outcome, it is important to understand the role of the predominantly SPD municipal government that forged a "pro-growth coalition" (Mollenkopf, 1975) between private construction, financial and industrial groups, and labor unions, which were the SPD's traditional base of support. In this period of postwar reconstruction, the local SPD was permitted relatively uncontested control over the city. The function of local government was to guarantee a stable and productive labor force by increasing city services while facilitating the city's physical expansion. High wages and low unemployment characterized the economic situation of the city. The function of local government was to accommodate the business expansion prescribed by the corporations.

The local SPD's interest in political control over its constituency and that of local business in economic control over market expansion through city growth were coordinated in a plan to further centralize and rationalize housing and transportation planning through governmental reorganization. Centralization permitted private interests to take part in housing and transportation decision making, as documented by various community struggles.[25] Autonomous community interests were largely excluded from planning. The postwar SPD local government was no longer the defender of local autonomy, but instead the central administrator of national policies. This redefinition of the role of local government had begun with the destruction of local autonomy by the Nazis and the subsequent institutionalization of central state intervention in local

120

affairs. This trend increased during the restoration of German capital after World War II and became part of federal–state–local relations in the Federal Republic.

Planning power, especially in transportation, was concentrated in municipal bodies. Municipal Department IV for Planning and Construction was controlled by strong bureaucratic figures whose decisions often affected transportation. Dr. Hans Kampffmeyer, long-time head of that unit, prided himself on making planning decisions without popular consent. Until 1972, he used his powerful position to promote Frankfurt's growth and its changing economic, social, and physical structure. In describing his success and personal responsibility in making Frankfurt the major postwar financial center of the Federal Republic, Kampffmeyer reveals his arrogance:

> In a particularly decisive question, I fully and in an authoritarian way . . . – without asking anyone – kept the Deutsche Bundesbank from transferring [its headquarters] to Cologne . . . I have preserved the banking tradition and did everything conceivable to make Frankfurt number one in banking. And this was all done in spite of the provincial attitude of the population that has an amorphous consciousness structure. And thus, as I've said, I personally accepted the goal to make out of this destroyed and beaten down body [of a city] the preconditions for creating a world metropolis. (Quoted in Roth, 1975:16)

Hans Adrian, who succeeded Kampffmeyer, was also active in forging alliances with business interests to maintain the local growth strategy. Other important appointed administrative bodies influencing transportation planning were the Construction Committee of the Municipal Councilmen, headed by Erich Nitzling and Otto Thomazewski; the Municipal Architectural Commission, made up of architects who were often designers of major office and housing complexes; the Construction Committee of the City Administrators, headed by Dr. Dieter Hoffman; and the general service and business directorate of the Municipality (Allgemeine Dienst–und Geschäftsanweisung für die Stadtverwaltung), headed by Rudolph Lortz. The Hessian state minister of Economies and Regional Planning Units (e.g., the Regionale Planungsgemeinschaft Untermain and the Frankfurter Verkehrsbund) were also important in local transportation planning. Bureaucrats in these offices circumvented the requirement, mandated under the federal government's urban renewal and planning laws, to receive suggestions and criticism from the public (Roth, 1975:99–139).

SPD Chief Mayors Walter Möller and Rudi Arndt, as well as Mayor Rudi Sölch, acted against the decisions of various SPD neighborhood and city organizations in pursuing pro-growth strategies (*Frankfurter Rundschau*, May 5, 1975). This rejection of grass-roots opinions and actions was the outcome of growth coalition politics. The SPD leadership sacrificed the support of some neighborhood groups for the guarantees of increased employment that would bring broader electoral support. More directly, the SPD and municipally owned corporations received financing and contracts from the housing and transportation construction that came from restructuring the city. State- and party-owned banks (e.g., Hessische Landesbank and Bank für Gemeinwirtschaft), housing construction companies (Neue Heimat, Hellerhof, and Aktienbaugesellschaft für kleine Wohnungen), and transportation construction firms (Frankfurter Aufbau AG) had shared interests (often culminating in cooperative projects) with private capital in the large-scale construction projects that dominated the city's changing skyline.

Finally, the role of private associations such as the Chamber of Industry and Commerce and the Frankfurter Society for Trade, Industry, and Economics, a club of the city's industrial and financial leaders, in planning Frankfurt's future was often noted in the local press. Later, the club admitted a few municipal officials in order to communicate more informally their proposals for urban and transportation planning (Roth, 1975: 145–46; *Deutsche Messe Zeitung*, May 5, 1956:3–5).

### Transportation conflicts: streetcars and autobahns

Frankfurt's transportation system faced problems created by regional economic and demographic changes. Iblher (1970) and Klemmer (1971) have shown that by 1970, Frankfurt had become the dominant German city, leading all others in commerce, finance, education, science, and transportation. As a result, Frankfurt had the highest proportion of white-collar and civil service employment in the Federal Republic (55 percent in 1974) and the second highest proportion of tertiary sector employment (62 percent in 1974) of all German cities (*Frankfurt Statistische Berichte*, 1975:11–19).[26]

The rapid rate of population growth (20 percent between 1939 and 1970) and the significant changes in the city's employment structure from the industrial to the service sector strained the transportation system (Müller-Raemisch, 1967; Stöber, 1964). The growth of service employment and the concentration of 25 percent of the workforce in 1.5 percent of the city's area forced the decentralization of housing and pushed families to the city's periphery and the broader Rhein/Main region. The national policy supporting highway transportation increasingly pressed for the motorization of Frankfurt.

Because of the conflict between residential decentralization and greater demands for labor within the city, commuter traffic has increased significantly since World War II. Between 1950 and 1970, the percentage of suburban commuters to urban workplaces grew from 25 to 38 percent. As a result of higher local costs for public transit extensions, plus increasing subsidization of street and highway building by the federal government, transportation planning increased motorization during the fifties.

Consequently, Frankfurt became steadily more dependent upon the automobile for the journey to work. By 1960, Frankfurt had become the most motorized city in Germany (330 auto registrations per 1000 people). Automobile transportation for work-related travel became increasingly popular, jumping from 24.6 to 52.1 percent of all commuter traffic in a single decade (1960–70), while public transit constantly declined.[27] Competing work, trade, and recreational traffic flows increased street traffic and limited parking space; Frankfurt became the most congested city in Germany (887 people and 221 autos per kilometer of streets) (*Statistisches Jahrbuch deutscher Gemeinden*, 1973).

Although street construction rose heavily, new roads promoted further auto use, worsening the congestion. In 1961, an effort was made to resolve conflicts between commuter, business, and recreational traffic. The proposal was to redirect commuter traffic onto an improved public transit service while reserving the streets for trucking and business auto traffic (*Frankfurter Allgemeine Zeitung* [*FAZ*], February 3, 1963). This was to be accomplished through constructing a U-Bahn (subway) and extending the S-Bahn into a commuter rail line. The strategy, as Chief Mayor Möller (1968) presented it to the city council, was to overcome the spatial constraints of parking and urban architecture, along with traffic congestion, by coaxing commuter traffic off the streets, thus freeing arterial street traffic for other transportation purposes.

This first major General Transportation Plan was to be used to improve all modes of travel – the street system and public transportation – while coordinating transportation planning with urban renewal efforts to expand the central business district by converting residential property into business property. The new transit system did not keep up with the increased displacement of urban housing, leaving commuters often with no alternative to the automobile. The result of the plan was a "broader individualization of transportation coming into the Inner City and a city plan directed at the structural transformation of the Inner City area" (Schächterle and Holdschür, 1965:54).

From the beginning of the sixties, numerous plans, revisions, and conflicts surrounded the General Transportation Plan (*Gesamtverkehrsplanung*, 1961, 1973). The Social Democratic city government was committed to both a growth economy and the extension of transportation as a public service. The General Transportation Plan was intended to meet both commitments. Thus, it supported both increased public transit and increased highway and road construction. Unwittingly, in this way, the plan promoted competition and disharmony rather than much needed cooperation between public and private transportation.

As part of its growth coalition strategy with capital, the local Social Democratic government effectively promoted private transportation. Local policy accommodated the privately made corporate decisions to expand both city and highway construction. In this constant accommodation, dominant class interests were routinely considered by local planners and administrators.

Planners and administrators of the General Transportation Plans demonstrated how institutionalized pro-automobile biases had become during the postwar period. The plan based construction schedules upon extrapolations of increased auto use and declining rail ridership. It failed to consider how a shift away from the policy of making Frankfurt an "auto accessible city" could change these trends. This faulty reasoning reflected the deep biases that permeated the methods and theories of the planning profession. Wünschmann (1972:4) points out the extent of this bias in Frankfurt:

> The fathers of the General Transportation Plan . . . strongly identify with their product. After achieving a goal to which they so long aspired, they are understandably not ready to let . . . their product be questioned . . . these experts responsible during the time of planning were captured by one-sided perspectives: at the universities, transportation planning was equated with the planning of individualized [automotive] transportation. In the offices of the city planners, there prevailed, to put it simply, the very same opinions as that at the automobile clubs. Hardly anyone was consious at the time that transportation planning is subject to social and economic forces.

The General Transportation Plan failed to examine the impact of rail extensions, park-and-ride possibilities for commuters, or the land use influence of public transit expansion. Although the rail expansion program was approved in 1968, the 1965 revision provided no disincentive for auto travel into the inner city. Only when the 1974 "middle range transportation program" was adopted were attempts made to exclude automotive traffic from various areas of the city and create "transportation cells" within the city that were accessible solely by pedestrian or public transportation (*FAZ*, December 12, 1974; Magistrat, 1973).

Rail building (U-Bahn) was an enormously expensive endeavor (estimated at $2.2 billion). The city formed the Frankfurter Verkher-und Tarifsverband (FVV), a special transportation authority incorporating, for taxation purposes, numerous outlying areas that the U-Bahn system was designed to serve. These areas resisted heavy taxation, requiring the city to raise needed funds in the private credit market (*FAZ*, July 27, 1974). By 1966, city funds for the project were depleted and Frankfurt was suffering further indebtedness to private banks.

Some relief came in 1967, when the federal government allowed the gasoline tax to be used for public transportation. Nevertheless, Frankfurt became the most debt-ridden city in the Federal Republic (2,595 deutsche marks per capita in 1974), in part as a result of infrastructural construction. (Wiedenbauer and Hoyer, 1968:215).

A series of unpopular fare hikes occurred between 1973 and 1974, opposed by the central trade union organization (Deutscher Gewerkschaftsbund [DGB]), SPD organizations, various organizations of the left, and an independent citizen action group (Null Tarifbewegung). In May 1974, violent confrontations between anti–fare-hike demonstrators and the police occurred. Clashes broke out every day during the evening rush hour for nearly a week (May 12–16) (*Kampf gegen die Fahrprieserhöhung*, 1974).

The Planning Department divided the city into areas of varying land uses, increasing the competition between public and private transportation. The lag in public transportation construction and the simultaneous expansion of highways gave private transportation a continuing edge in commuting to the city. The continued focus upon ring construction of highways also placed public transit at a disadvantage in allowing personal access to the city (Wünschmann, 1972:10–12).

Finally, the construction of commuter rail systems fell prey to pork barrel politics. Cost overruns and delays resulted from the SPD local government's use of public works projects to promote its coalition with private capital. The three firms involved in U-Bahn construction – Hoch-Tief, Holzman, and Ways and Freytag – were heavy contributors to the local SPD's campaign funds. An investigation by the Federal Accounting Office in 1971 exposed and sharply criticized the procurement policies of the local government:

The city government was reprimanded by the federal accounting office report for the way the municipality distributes contracts for city projects. [The Federal Accounting Office] . . . shows an inexcusable favoritism towards the firms Holzman AG, Ways and Freytag, as well as Hoch-Tief, which as a consortium planned the U-Bahn and then received a lion's share of the construction projects for the U-Bahn as well. (*Frankfurter Rundschau* [FR], July 7, 1971)

126

A later investigation in 1975 revealed ownership connections between these firms and the four largest financial establishments involved in urban renewal and construction projects throughout the city during this period (Commerzbank, Merck-Finck Bank, Deutsche Bank, and the Aktiengesellschaft für Industrie). These institutions were closely involved in concentrating land ownership throughout the inner city and the Westend, as well as supporting the local SPD and its semipublic housing and construction organizations (Roth, 1975:125–38; Vorlaufer, 1975:512).

Although public transportation was supported, its role was weakened by private transportation planning and the physical restructuring of the city. The case of the Autobahn A 80 around the northeastern parts of the city illustrates this process. As auto traffic on city streets increased, especially on the ring streets encircling the city, Frankfurt agreed to Hessian Minister of Economics and Development Heinz Herbert Karry's proposal to build an autobahn (with federal funds) through the city, thereby circumventing the ring streets and reducing traffic on them.

Highway construction was planned for the Northend and Bornheim areas of the city, both mainly working-class neighborhoods. More than 700 apartment buildings would be condemned for road construction. Community groups and SPD local organizations opposed transportation plans that conflicted with local housing needs (*FR*, May 5, 1975). On August 31, 1972, the SPD Commission on Transportation Planning wrote, "In the past years, the consciousness of our citizens has grown against environmental compromise . . . From that, it must result, that housing needs have priority over through traffic in city planning" (quoted in Wünschmann, 1975:7).

Over the next several years, neighborhood opposition to the highway in Bornheim and the Nordend increased. "Citizens initiatives" against the highway opposed both the process and the substance of the transportation program that would construct a freeway through their community. One community group, calling itself "Inhuman Autobahn," wrote:

At a time when [citizen] participation in city development is understood and "officially" emphasized in Frankfurt this action [on A 80] can only be

127

seen as an affront [to the people] if our attempts for participation on such an important matter are strangulated (by the city administration) through hasty measures.

Other activists opposing the autobahn noted the effect it could have upon their neighborhood. They believed that the freeway would destroy the communication and organization of social life that had long thrived in the area. A citizen group called the "Action Group of Wetteraustrasse and Günterburgspark," wrote:

There should be black flags not only here, but in the windows of Nordend and Bornheim too. As a result of the planned A 80, it will be impossible for people who cannot or do not want to drive a car or don't have one to reach the Güntersburg park, Friedhof, Huthpark or the surrounding quiet and safe parks. Gardens and fields will disappear. Hundreds of young mothers with infants and toddlers, fathers and grandmothers, adolescent children wanting to bicycle, handicapped persons who can walk only a short distance, the socially weak, the pensioners, widows, etc–for all of them, indispensible paths will be destroyed. (Quoted in Roth, 1975:159).

In spite of such community organization, Mayor Arndt and the municipality came under increased pressure to ignore popular sentiment and approve the autobahn plan. Minister Karry wrote: "When the city rejects the State's proposal for A 80, then I see no further possibility any longer for a decisive contribution to the solution of Frankfurt's transportation problem to be made [by Hesse]."

The threat of losing state and federal support for other parts of Frankfurt's transportation program led Arndt to lead a successful battle *against* community groups and his own party opposing highway construction. Arndt repeated the traditional job creation litany of motorization: Highway construction meant more jobs, especially for Frankfurt Aufbau AG (the municipally owned construction company), which faced an unemployment crisis in 1973–4 (Roth, 1975:158–62).

Transportation politics in Frankfurt is characteristic of the postwar denouement of local Social Democratic politics. The SPD government remained in power only so long as it successfully pursued a pro-growth policy that united the interest of the party's working-class base in more jobs and corporate capital's interest in business expansion. As the local government sedulously pursued fiscally stimulative policies that would keep corporate capital supportive of its social measures, the SPD's traditional social base was physically displaced by urban renewal, transportation, and housing policies within the party and in neighborhoods threatened by city planning and real estate speculation (e.g., housing occupations, tenant strikes, antihighway and fare hike movements, etc.). Corporate capital became suspicious of the SPD's ability to maintain a legitimate political order for business expansion. The growth coalition that had brought the SPD into power began to unravel. In 1976, the first CDU government in more than two decades took power.

For Mayor Rudi Arndt and the local SPD leadership, transportation was not really a public service, but rather part of the pro-growth strategy that had kept them in power for so long in spite of threats from the right (the old Frankfurt aristocracy) and the left (students, neighborhood organizations, and young SPD dissidents). Through transportation planning, inner city land use would be restructured from residential to commercial use, commuter traffic would be removed from city streets to allow the expansion of commercial traffic, and more jobs would be created.

These goals had contradictory and unanticipated outcomes for the local SPD; in their pursuit, the social and spatial structures of communities that had long supported social democracy were destroyed. The SPD's voting base declined, along with the "success" of its planning and renewal policies in creating a world metropolis.[28] As neighborhoods such as Bornheim, Nordend, Bockenheim, and Westend fell to the bulldozer, working-class communities were scattered and progressive voters involved in citizen's initiatives on local issues became alienated.

The pursuit of the corporate city destroyed the social fiber of Frankfurt's neighborhoods. The social interaction, humor, and community that had long injected an element of vibrance into Frankfurt politics were replaced by the rise of a corporate technocracy whose centralized organization, planning procedures, and language were more amenable to private than public interests. Frankfurt's politically active neighborhoods became increasingly demoralized as one defeat followed another in struggles over housing and transportation. One resident of working-class Bornheim described the situation in these graphic terms: "Frankfurt is going to become a Ghetto, that will slowly be walled up, dismembered, and gassed" (quoted in Roth, 1975:163).

# 6

# Transportation politics: the case of Chicago

## Transit change in Chicago

The national collapse of mass transit is reflected in Chicago's history. Although Chicago's transit system survived, its atrophied service routes continue to be a source of fiscal and administrative conflict in state and local politics. Chicago's great and rapid rate of transit growth dissipated around World War I, stagnated during the twenties, and began to decline in the thirties, a decline that accelerated during the post–World War II period (Figures 6.1 and 6.2). In Chapter 3, we noted that transit history in the United States was characterized by the continuous subordination of planing to short term profit, first by local transit operators and later by transportation equipment producers and related industries. This case study illustrates the mechanisms of local transportation politics over a century of planning.

## General background

In the second half of the nineteenth century, Chicago was the fastest-growing city in the United States–a manufacturing center, a commercial metropolis, and the hub of transportation activities in the westward expansion (Hoyt, 1933:294; Mayer and Wade, 1969:140–54). Virtually every analysis of Chicago's urban geography views its patterns of transportation change as a central independent variable (Burgess, 1926; Barton, 1948; Duncen and Lieberson, 1970; Weber, 1971; Berry, 1976).[1] These studies, however, place less emphasis on the equally important role played by transit companies and

131

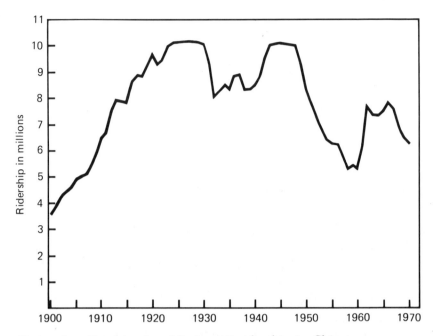

Figure 6.1. Combined public transit ridership in Chicago, 1900–70. Chicago surface lines' ridership, 1900–46, based on fiscal years ending January 31 the following year. All other ridership 1900–63 based on calendar years. Ridership 1964–70 based on 52-week fiscal year except for 1966, which is based on 53-week fiscal year. (Source: Chicago Transit Authority, General Operations Division, Operations Planning Dept., "Riding Habits," 1979.)

land speculators, on the one hand, and financial, manufacturing, and commercial interests on the other.

The corporate decision making of Chicago transit executives at the turn of the century attempted to maximize the profits from real estate and commercial investments in the central business district while promoting the housing and land development efforts of real estate and transit speculators on the urban periphery. Although these interests were not always dissimilar, conflicts erupted regularly (Maltbie, 1901:7–8).[2] The contradiction that divided business interests was overlaid by periodic mobilization of small landowners, small business-

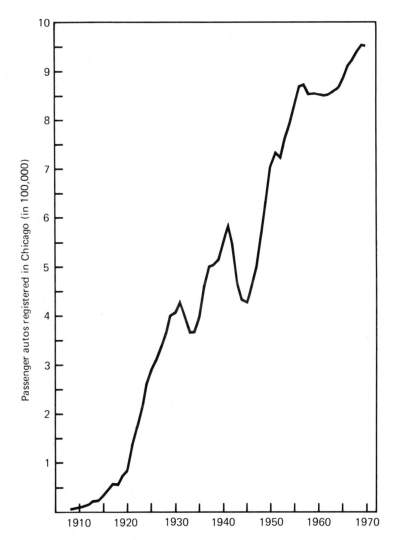

Figure 6.2. Number of private motor vehicles in Chicago, 1908–70. (Trucks and other vehicles included through 1909.) 1908–19, figures for May–April; 1920, figures for May–December; 1921–70, figures for January–December. (Source: Chicago Transit Authority, General Operations Division, Operations Planning Dept., "Riding Habits," 1979).

men, working-class communities, and transit workers, who challenged, sometimes successfully, a variety of policies that businessmen promulgated (see Weber's discussion of the "Southport Wars," 1971:200–5).[3] Chicago's physical structure was therefore continuously influenced by class actors reacting to the changes caused by the city's development as a metropolitan center.

The first step in this process was developed by Potter Palmer, the "first merchant prince of Chicago." Having amassed a fortune in dry goods and bond holdings during the Civil War, Palmer diversified his assets, building wealth in real estate and construction. In 1867, he bought two-thirds of State Street and proceeded to convince the city council and other landowners to widen it. This move changed the direction of the whole spatial development of the city. The central business district shifted from what had been an east–west axis along Lake Street to a north–south axis along State Street, vastly increasing the value of Palmer's landholdings (Mayer and Wade, 1969:140–2).

With the advent of horse-drawn trolleys, the first wave of wealthy residents dispersed to a suburban perimeter that was expanded repeatedly with electrification. Since the immigrant working class was largely engaged in low-paying, unskilled labor, their residential areas were located close to the manufacturing districts on the north and west sides of the city. Over time, these areas became more and more densely populated. By changing the direction of growth of the central business district, Palmer relieved the pressure from lower-class residential areas that constrained commercial development (Ward, 1971:81–121, 128–41).

The Chicago fire of 1871 consolidated the central business district and speeded up residential displacement from the urban core. The cable cars of the eighties and the electrification of transit in the nineties afforded greater mobility to immigrants who had appeared on the Chicago scene a generation earlier. Areas to the south and west of the city were left to eastern and southern European immigrants in the first of numerous "waves of succession" described by the early Chicago School sociologists (Park and Burgess, 1925:51; Cressey, 1939:

59–69). The extension of transit lines to the southwest allowed the central and northern European immigrants who had come to Chicago in the fifties to escape the urban center (Lind, 1975; Warner, 1976:46–66).

## Transportation conflicts before World War I

Despite the assumptions of ecological theory, the pressures of population succession alone do not explain early rail extensions. Archival evidence indicates that transportation planning was designed to funnel traffic flows toward the Loop in order to accommodate centralized commercial, retail, and administrative activities.

As early as 1863, transit companies began dividing the city in an effort to minimize competition. The Chicago West Division Railway Company operating west of the North and South branches of the Chicago River, the Chicago City Railway south of the river and east of the South Branch, and the North Chicago City Railway north of the river and east of the North Branch all agreed to prohibit transfer privileges. By this action, the downtown district was made a terminal for crosstown traffic. This artificial division of the city was maintained by streetcar entrepreneurs as a means of maximizing fare revenues (Maltbie, 1901:7–8).

When the Chicago and Blue Island Elevated Railway sought permission for construction, businessmen persuaded the governor to pressure the city council to comply (C. W. Dean to Gov. S. Brown, July 8, 1979, Dean Papers, CHS). As elevated railway construction continued into the nineties, property owners and commercial tenants in the central part of the city pressured city councilmen for ordinances securing service. In arguing for a station in the Lake Street area, one property owner wrote: "In this way, the great shopping and business crowd coming downtown will be first brought to our own doors . . . bring the people to our doors and we will do the rest" (J. D. Wallace to H. C. Durand, March 21, 1894, Durand Papers, CHS). In the same letter, this person stresses the importance of electrifying transportation as soon as possible to increase the flow of people into the downtown area for commercial purposes: "Electricity should be used as the motive power as soon as practicable. I feel confident that such numbers placed on our street will greatly increase the rental value of the property" (J. D. Wallace to H. C. Durand, March 21, 1894, Durand Papers, CHS).

Transportation had no coherent effect upon settlement patterns because it was motivated by a concern for expansion of land available for speculation (Hoyt, 1933:280). As traction moguls such as Charles T. Yerkes concentrated transit holdings, they expanded service (from 131 to 344 miles of track) in order to maximize the value of suburban property while simultaneously feeding people into the cental business district and raising commercial property values there.[4] This was a typical form of electrical transit system expansion that was not in the interests of rational transportation development but made large profits for transit operators, land speculators, and bankers. Consider the following testimony by Ralph S. Bauer before the Federal Electrical Railway Commission (1920:1622):

I further found that the ground hogs in different communities – land speculators – had brought certain influences to bear on the local governments which compelled the street railway to build extensions into property for the sake of adding rental and sales values to pasture land, and the politicians in charge of the localities in those times brought sufficient influence to bear on the railway to compel them to build that kind of extensions which were never profit producing lines.

Such line extensions imposed heavy traffic upon existing neighborhoods; local merchants and property owners in the affected middle-class and working-class neighborhoods resisted the axial building of streetcar lines that disrupted neighborhood life (Deuther, 1926:14; Weber, 1971:202).

The local transit monopoly, led by Yerkes, maintained its power through state and local political corruption that was often investigated by journalists. The expense of often unnecessary extensions drove fares up. In this situation, Chicago neighborhood organizations and streetcar workers united in their opposition to what was popularly called "the transit trust." Their shared recognition of common interests led to united action: The first important streetcar workers' strike in

1885 was followed by public campaigns against the streetcar companies by consumers upset over the lack of transfers, the length of travel time, fare hikes, poor crosstown service, and business–government corruption (Flynn and Wilkie, 1887; Harrison, 1935).

Ultimately, when Yerkes requested new state and city legislation to extend his transit charter,[5] popular resistance coalesced into the Independent Anti-Boodle League (IABL), which protested the whole array of utilities that had "monopolized the streets above and below ground" (1899:1). Numerous mass meeting, ethnic, and neighborhood groups were involved in this struggle (e.g., the South Water Street Merchants Association, Southside Rapid Transit Employees, Great Swedish Mass Meeting, Ninth Ward Polish American Organization, Colored Democratic League of Cook County, Cook County Socialist party, and others).[6]

Employees of the various transit companies opposed the extended monopolization of transit as well, in support of the communities that had aided them in earlier strikes. The Employees of the Southside Rapid Transit Company wrote: "Whereas said corporations have destroyed organizations of their employees, thereby denying them the right to organize . . . we oppose extended franchises and are against any monopoly of the street railways" (quoted in IABL, 1899:2).

This popular resistance to Yerkes's monopoly inspired demonstrations in the city council chamber when franchise ordinances were considered. Deuther (1926:15) recalled:

Popular indignation was at its height and . . . so great was the demonstration against these several ordinances that the galleries of council chambers were filled to overflowing, some enthusiasts even bringing with them ropes formed in nooses, which were dangled over the gallery balconies. None of these ordinances passed and . . . Yerkes met defeat.

After his defeat, Yerkes sold his properties to the U.S. Construction Company, a syndicate that was controlled by William Elkins and George Widener, East Coast Transit moguls (Maltbie, 1901:33).

Yerkes's business practices came to be considered indiscreet, unsound, and a threat to the general stability of local business operations and city expansion (Lloyd, 1903; Prentiss,

FRANK LESLIE'S ILLUSTRATED NEWSPAPER

No. 1,555.—Vol. LX.] NEW YORK—FOR THE WEEK ENDING JULY 11, 1885. [Price, 10 Cents.

Illinois.–The strike of the conductors and drivers of the west division street railway, Chicago. Strikers overturning a car.

Figures 6.3 and 6.4. Transit strikes and traction politics. Chicago public transportation workers struck in 1885 (facing page) and 1903 (above). In both strikes, community support for the striking workers was often directed against the police, who tried to keep the street-cars running. Transportation workers and consumers were united in their struggle against streetcar magnates such as C. T. Yerkes until 1907. The continued militance of transportation workers and their success in raising their wages eventually led corporate leaders to consider other transportation modes not given to such politicization. (Source: The Chicago Historical Society. 6.3–IChi = 04895; 6.4–DN = 3540.)

1903; Andrews, 1946:176–85). Corporate reform groups such as the Municipal Voters League, the Chicago Civic Federation, and the Chicago Association of Commerce favored an end to long franchises.[7] Many corporate reformers were also involved in rival transportation schemes (e.g., elevated construction) and wished to see city franchises shortened for their own benefit.

The Citizens Association Committee on Street Railways and Bridges annually reported several operating defects in the street railway system, but its suggestion for relief was to encourage the construction of elevated railways which would provide competition and force the surface lines to improve their service. Some of the competitive schemes for surface and elevated roads enjoyed an endorsement from reform elements. In addition, many reformers personally invested in potential rival corporations. In 1865, many of the anti–99 year law activists subsequently backed the Wabash Railway company . . . Two of its investors who were also members of the Common Council, played an important part in creating public awareness of the 99 year bill . . . In the late 1890s, when the Civic Federation established a special committee to deal with street railways, two of the most prominent members had both been involved in separate railway projects. (Weber, 1971:104–5)

As Arnold (1905:3–7) points out, the multiple fare system and territorial competition between divisions perpetuated travel in its particular area, thereby eliminating the possibility for rational expansion of the city and coordination of physical growth. These reform elements were therefore concerned with efficient operations and lower transportation costs in order to foster residential expansion. As Weber (1971:223–4) explains:

The only consistent definition Chicago had of the function of transportation related to real estate. Speculators and developers of outlying land viewed transportation basically as an adjunct to the stimulation of their sales. Although most of the reformers did not participate in real estate development, the idea that transportation should serve the interests of speculators enjoyed substantial support in Chicago. The reformers themselves still conceived of transportation in terms of land.

Corporate reformers justified urban expansion as part of the assimilation process of foreign immigrants and "buckwheat" rural migrants. The "moral influence of transportation" was to provide a "safety valve to relieve congested districts" (Warner, 1961:26);[8] this ethic was used to legitimize the process of disorganizing working-class communities spatially and, therefore, politically as well. Such a position was frequently articulated by members of reform organizations, the business groups supporting them (e.g., the Chicago Association of Commerce), and designers of surface and elevated transit extensions.[9]

Reform business organizations and working-class communities were temporarily united in their opposition to Yerkes's domination of city transit. Yet, in that struggle the opposing transportation interests of labor and capital emerged. In the popular drive to end transit corruption, consumers and transit workers came to define their goal more broadly – to provide cheap and publicly responsible transit service. This goal contradicted the desire of the local business community to subordinate transportation service to the needs of urban spatial expansion. This conflict became the axis for the next wave of "traction questions." Interests in transportation were not defined solely by the class position of workers, consumers, or businessmen; instead, they were created by conflicts over transportation during these years.

## The struggle for public ownership

By 1900, the struggle against corruption, poor service, and high fares had been transformed into a fight for public ownership of transit, which was solidly opposed by the business community. Despite three referenda (1902, 1904, 1907) in which Chicago residents voted for municipal ownership, the transit companies remained in private hands.[10]

In the aftermath of Yerkes's defeat, actions at the state and local levels dealt with the transportation problem. In 1899, Illinois Governor John P. Altgeld argued that the city should lease operations to a private company. Chicago Mayor Carter Harrison appointed a Street Railway Commission (1899), and the city council later created a Local Transportation Committee of aldermen (1901) to oversee transportation decisions. The Street Railway Commission, headed by Colonel Milton J. Foremen, was appointed by the mayor and represented both

THE STREETS
OF CHICAGO BELONG
TO THE PEOPLE

PERSONAL LIBERTY
EQUAL RIGHTS TO ALL.
SPECIAL PRIVILEGES
TO NONE

CARTER H. HARRISON
FOR OUR NEXT MAYOR.

NO BLUE LAWS
FOR CHICAGO

Figures 6.5, 6.6, 6.7. The fight against streetcar boodleism. Carter H. Harrison made his debut in Chicago politics on the wave of public indignation directed toward the streetcar companies and their attempts to control the city streets. After continued popular support for public ownership, Harrison switched to the corporate plan of city and later state regulation, which ended urban population involvement in transportation policymaking. Transportation and other issues of collective consumption (public utilities) were an important part of the urban political agenda during the first decade of the twentieth century. (Source: The Chicago Historical Society. 6.5–IChi-17302; 6.6–lChi-17301; 6.7–lChi-17303.)

# CARTER H. HARRISON

AGAINST THE

# BOODLERS!

Every citizen of Chicago should
come down to the CITY HALL

# To-Night

## MONDAY, DEC. 12TH,

and EVERY MONDAY NIGHT THEREAFTER while the Street Car Franchises are under consideration and see that the interests of the City are protected against

# BOODLEISM!

## CITIZENS, AROUSE AND DEFEAT THE BOODLERS!

KIRCHNER, MECKEL & CO. 94 PRINTERS, 85 FIFTH AVE.

Figure 6.6

# MONDAY EVENING.

## A Great Mass-Meeting of Citizens.

### Shall the People or the Street-Car Companies Rule?

A mass-meeting of citizens interested in the cause of street-car reform in Chicago will be held at Greenebaum's Hall, 76 and 78 5th avenue, on Monday evening, June 28.

This meeting will be preliminary to other and larger mass-meetings to be held throughout the city. The object is to outline the policy to be adopted by the street-car patrons of Chicago on and after July 1.

Representative business men will address the meeting. Good speeches will be made. The earnest workers of the N. S. N. F. movement will be present. It is time to act. Now or never.

### By THE COMMITTEE.

## Put a Stop to Street-Car Bossism.
## Put an End to Street-Car Bribery.
## Put a Period to Street-Car Outrages.

# TURN OUT MONDAY EVENING

Figure 6.7

business and working-class communities that had successfully opposed Yerkes. Their compromise recommendation reflected the contradictions between the two groups: "The Commission is of the opinion that it would be wise for the City at the earliest practicable time, to acquire ownership of the trackage and of whatever may form a part of the public street, without going to the extent of ownership and operation of rolling stock" (Tideman, 1939:2).

Many found this recommendation of partial public ownership unsatisfactory and petitioned the city repeatedly as agitation for broader public ownership increased. At the behest of the Civic Federation of Chicago, Yerkes opened the books of his transit operation to public inspection. The result was a scathing report by Milo Maltbie (1901) exposing the overcapitalization of the street railway system and the dishonest accounting practices. With the release of the Maltbie Report and the agitation it inspired for public ownership, the Local Transportation Committee made its first report on December 11, 1901, requesting a referendum on municipal ownership of the transit line. The advisory referendum passed overwhelmingly on April 1, 1902 (142,825 for and 27,998 against) (Deuther, 1926:16).

After this first referendum, local corporate leaders sought technical solutions from a traffic engineer, Bion J. Arnold, and legal alternatives to public ownership from Walter L. Fisher,[11] city traction counsel. These efforts in the public sector mirrored private industry's move toward scientific management. The goal of the mayor's office and the business organizations was rationalized public regulation of privately controlled transit companies.

Arnold sought to promote unified public transportation with the slogan "One City–One Fare." While maintaining existing routes through downtown terminals, he attempted to unify the operations and better manage them (Arnold, 1905). Fisher prepared enabling legislation for municipal ownership by issuing "street railway certificates" redeemable through the income of transit properties. This allowed the city to mortgage the street railway properties and gave the financial institutions control over any municipally run system.

This hybrid was opposed by the popular movement for public ownership. A key organizer of the public ownership struggle was Margaret Haley, president of the Chicago Teachers' Federation. She had led a campaign by teachers to get the streetcar companies to pay taxes that would provide revenues for wage raises for teachers. When that campaign was unsuccessful, she became directly involved in the public ownership issue. Along with others in the labor unions, ward committees, and ethnic organizations, Haley organized the Municipal Ownership Delegate Convention. The convention consisted of elected representatives from labor unions, craft organizations, community improvement associations, and sports clubs who held weekly meetings and elected delegates to a citywide body to promote measures for public ownership and publicly responsive transit planning (Tidemann, 1939:3).

By April 5, 1904, another referendum was held on municipal ownership. Two proposals were on the ballot: The proposal supported by the convention, labor union, and other populist organizations called for the immediate and direct expropriation of the transit lines; the Mueller Law proposed a state-regulated transit authority that would slowly buy transit properties through public financing. The latter proposal passed by a smaller margin (121,957 to 50,807).

Public support for municipalization was undermined by a judgment by U.S. Circuit Court Judge Peter S. Grosscup, who, on May 28, 1904, sustained the constitutionality of the nineteenth-century ninety-nine-year franchises held by the companies. This court decision seemingly left the traction properties in private hands for the foreseeable future. Grosscup later left the bench due to his suspicious personal involvement in transit companies (Deuther, 1926:16).

The city government sought a compromise between the popular demand for public ownership and Grosscup's decision. The Local Transportation Committee proposed a tentative ordinance with the Chicago City Railway Company, seeking a franchise that would continue private ownership with more city regulation. This ordinance was defeated by a wide margin (59,013 for and 152,135 against), indicating that the voters were clearly opposed to any form of continued private ownership.

That same year, 1904, Edward F. Dunne was elected mayor on a platform advocating "immediate public ownership."

On April 3, 1906, yet another referendum was submitted for municipal ownership under the Mueller Law. This referendum passed, although by a narrower margin (121,916 to 110,323). Walter Fisher then opened negotiations with the traction companies to improve transit service and increase the public accountability of the transit companies while avoiding public ownership (*Chicago Daily News*, April 3, 1906). Over the next year negotiations produced the compromise "traction settlement ordinances," which granted a twenty-year franchise to existing companies. The goal of these ordinances was the eventual purchase of transit lines through Mueller Certificates and a Traction Fund established by 55 percent of the traction companies' private revenues.

Mayor Dunne disavowed Fisher's efforts as a "sellout" to the transit companies and vetoed the ordinances. However, on February 11, 1907, the Republican-controlled council overrode the mayor's veto and set a referendum for the April 2 election. Over the next two months, a major campaign was mounted by the traction companies and corporate reformers to secure passage of the settlement ordinances. These complicated ordinances provided maximum city regulation while maintaining the option to exercise future municipal ownership. Aside from the Traction Fund and Mueller Law financing set up for that purpose, the ordinances guaranteed transit extensions upon request by the city council, through routing of passengers and transfers, a five-cent fare, and adequate service. However, other provisions would prevent these goals from being realized.

Nevertheless, the settlement ordinances were advertised as the solution to the traction problem. Two major organizations led the campaign for passage, the Citizens' Non-Partisan Traction Settlement Association (CNPTSA) and the Straphangers' League (Deuther, 1926:15–19).

The CNPTSA was the larger group, reporting a membership of more than 100,000. However, its support was drawn largely from the business community and the middle-class neighborhoods in the Chicago Lawn, Gage Park, and West End areas.

The major corporate support came from the Chicago Real Estate Board,[12] the Chicago Commercial Association, and the Builders and Traders' Exchange.

Frederick M. Bode, president of both the CNPTSA and the Chicago Commercial Association, argued that "the people want the traction muddle disposed of at once . . . they are thoroughly wearied of the old conditions and are looking for something better" (*Chicago Tribune*, March 31, 1907). For the first time, the argument that planning problems were best left to experts was raised. At the final meeting of the association prior to the election, Bode stated:

The ordinances we are asking the voters to support are not snap ordinances in any sense of the word. They are the product of the best legal and professional advice the city of Chicago has been able to secure. They were not prepared by representatives of the traction companies, nor have they been prepared by the officials of the city of Chicago. They are the result of joint conferences between representatives of the city running over eight months. They concede to each interest all that is due such interest in law and they clarify a situation which if the courts were resorted to would require years of litigation to settle. (*Chicago Tribune*, March 31, 1907)

On the critical question of municipal ownership the CNPTSA remained neutral, advertising the ordinances as the only possible way to achieve such ownership "should the city choose." Bode noted, "the members of this body as an organization have not been opposed to municipal ownership, nor have they advocated such a policy" (*Chicago Daily News*, March 31, 1907).

Whereas the Non-Partisan Association claimed independence, Republican mayoral candidate Fred Busse supported the ordinances and the association. In one interview he stated that "the people are heartily tired of having the traction question dragged into every political campaign. There is the desire on the part of every citizen who has the interests of the city at heart to reap the results of property that will come with the settlement of the traction question" (*Chicago Tribune*, March 30, 1907).

The campaign to pass the ordinances cost close to $3 million. The Non-Partisan Association sent more than 1,200,000 mail solicitations for support of the ordinances. Traction work-

ers were assured by their companies of a two-cent hourly raise if the ordinances were passed (*Chicago Examiner*, April 6, 1907).

The other, smaller organization supporting the ordinances was the Straphangers' League, which claimed to be made up of transit riders. The identity of its directors and officers, however, reveals that it was mostly supported by major figures associated with reform politics and corporate planning (e.g., Frederick A. Delano, H. L. Ickes, and Charles H. Merriam).

Opposition to the ordinances came from Mayor Dunne, who was accused by business leaders and the *Chicago Examiner* of "obstructionism." Alderman William Dever, the streetcar employees, and the Chicago Federation of Labor also rejected the ordinances. Immediately prior to the election, organized labor demonstrated against them, stressing their opposition to private management and support for municipal ownership ("Chicago Ownership Looks Good to Us," *Chicago Tribune*, March 21, 1907).

Throughout March, a debate over the settlement ordinances between Democratic Alderman William Dever and Republican Alderman Charles Werno was serially printed in the *Chicago Daily News*. Dever demonstrated why the ordinances, although leaving the door open to municipal ownership, would not accomplish it. First, there was no provision for a referendum on municipal ownership; it was left to the city administration. Second, the ordinances locked the city into a five-cent fare precisely at a time when other cities were lowering fares. Third, the city would have to pay cash for the properties, although the financing provisions allowed only $75 million in Mueller Certificates to be issued. The ordinances agreed upon a capitalization of the properties that would push the purchase price far beyond that amount.

Dever's indictment of the ordinances proved correct. Although the settlement ordinances had eliminated $59 million of overcapitalization on the traction properties' books, overcapitalization was accepted as part of accounting procedures (Fisher, 1907:9). Barrett (1975:487) explains:

In order to induce the companies to undertake a far-reaching modernization program, the city agreed that unexpired franchises, contractors' fees, and bank charges, and brokerage fees on bonds would be enshrined as part of the companies' capital value. That valuation was fixed in the law as the price the city must pay should it ever attempt municipal ownership, no provision was made for amortization, and every subsequent track extension or renewal was added to the total. In order to obtain what it hoped would be good service under private ownership, the city accepted terms that encouraged the companies to keep and extend obsolete facilities, held back the merger of competing companies, and prevented municipal ownership for forty years.

On April 2, 1907, the settlement ordinances passed (167,366 to 134,281), most voters believing that they would be a step toward municipal ownership. On April 15, the Supreme Court of Illinois declared that the Mueller Certificates, which would finance future municipal ownership under the ordinances, were illegal since they would surpass the city's debt limit. This eliminated any possibility of municipal ownership.[13]

The transit companies, utilities, and financial and commercial groups not only won the battle over the ordinances but defeated the urban populist movement for public ownership by proposing regulation instead. Even during the fight with Yerkes, "state regulation of Chicago transportation was proposed by streetcar executives as a method of escape from city control" (Barrett, 1975:491). The corporate reformers of the Chicago Commercial Association, the Chicago Commercial Club, the City Club, and the Chicago Civic Federation sought a similar escape through city-level regulation established in the 1907 ordinances. The Board of Supervising Engineers was organized on May 7, 1907, with members appointed by the city and the transit companies (Board of Supervising Engineers, 1927).

For the first time, transportation was no longer a local issue to be decided through direct democratic referenda, but instead by an appointed city bureaucracy. The Cook County Socialist party concluded its analysis of the "traction question" as follows:

For twenty-five years, the people of Chicago have been jostled and jammed, plucked, plundered and bounced by the street-car companies . . . Three times the people of Chicago have voted substantially in favor of municipal ownership. Yet every time the politicians and companies have found some way to circumvent the will of the people. (Stedman, 1914:1)

By the 1880s the first wave of annexation had started, involving residents and developers in adjacent areas of Chicago anxious for the expansion of urban services, particularly transportation. Aside from the expansion of surface lines under Yerkes, the Chicago Southside Rapid Transit Company was extending transit south under the sponsorship of the city's major downtown commercial and financial interests (e.g., Marshall Field, C. W. Wacker, E. L. Lobdell, and W. R. Walker). The first elevated line was completed in time for the 1893 Columbian Exposition, which began the "city beautiful" movement in urban planning. That movement sought the rationalized and aesthetic development of cities. The exposition was sponsored by major Chicago capitalists who had reservations about what the free market had done to the city, although they were satisfied with their own success in it (Gilbert and Bryson, 1929; Leech and Carroll, 1938; Fogelsong, 1976:10).

Elevated construction expanded rapidly after 1893, following rectangular routes along section streets and main arteries. Downtown financial and commercial groups controlled the elevated lines which became the key to expanding settlement north and south while centralizing the flow of traffic towards the Loop area (Davis, 1965; Weber, 1971).

With the 1893 exposition's success, steps were initiated by Daniel P. Burnham to develop his classic plan for Chicago. Burnham's work, started in 1902, was encouraged and supervised by members of the Merchants Club (particularly Charles H. Wacker, a wealthy merchant; Charles D. Norton, an insurance executive; and Frederick A. Delano, president of the Wabash Railroad).[14] In 1907 the Merchants Club became the Commercial Club of Chicago, and its first act was to sponsor the continuation of Burnham's work for presentation to the city government. Aside from harbors, parks, and commercial districts, central to the Burnham Plan was a complete street system of boulevard circuits, radial arteries, and a main east–west axis. The wide streets and diagonal thoroughfares were reminiscent of Haussmann's plan of Paris.

In November 1909, Mayor Fred Busse presented the Burnham Plan to the city council, requesting that an "independent

Centralization of Transportation Facilities With Loop Terminals Determine Chicago's Policy of Development.

*Figures 6.8 (above) and 6.9 (facing page.)* Big business domination of route planning. Over the years, increasing antagonism arose in outlying neighborhoods because of the lack of crosstown routes connecting them, rather than feeding traffic into the Loop area. Instead, all routes radiated from the Loop area, requiring passengers to transfer at Loop terminals to get to other parts of the city. This centralization of transportation facilities resulted in continued extension of urban settlement rather than settlement of contiguous areas in the city. This eventual land use pattern was the result of political decisions made by the corporate interests that dominated transportation politics at the time. As early as 1909, a subway was suggested that would further congest the Loop area. Samuel Insull, who also owned the city's public utilities, formed a coalition with State Street interests to promote subway construction. (Source: The Northwest Side Commercial Association, Chicago Historical Society. 6.8–IChi = 17481; 6.9–IChi = 17479.)

# "Come on now — Everybody — Through the Loop!"

Why should we jump at the crack o' the whip?

commission" be set up to implement it. His introduction explained the plan's inspiration.

> This plan is not to be considered as the embodiment of an artist's dream or the project of theoretical city beautifiers who have lost sight of everyday affairs and who have forgotten the needs and interests of the mass of people. On the contrary, the men who produced the Chicago Plan are all hard-boiled business men. (Quoted in Bach, 1973:134)

Busse then appointed C. H. Wacker, who had been head of the Merchants Club's original planning committee, to chair the "independent" Chicago Plan Commission.

The goal of the Burnham Plan was to emphasize Chicago as a "center of industry and traffic" in order to maintain and benefit the centrality of the downtown area. Thus, it was designed for "removing the obstacles which prevent or obstruct circulation" (Mayer and Wade, 1969:276). The Burnham Plan was influenced by earlier Commercial Club efforts to promote road building in the Chicago area (Interurban Roadways Committee of the Commercial Club of Chicago, 1908). Numerous elements of the Burnham Plan were oriented toward expanding transportation, which would eliminate working-class residential areas and remove traffic from the central business district. Railroad facilities and terminals were consolidated. There were provisions for expanding surface and subway loops around an enlarged central business district. Finally, there was commitment to building more streets and roads in order to benefit the entire community, but especially business interests. Two hundred miles of street widenings, extensions, and improvements were planned (Burnham and Bennett, 1909:34–5, 41–2, 88–90; Hooker, 1914; Merriam, 1929:8; Burnham and Kingery, 1956; Crane, 1971; Condit, 1973).

The city institutionalized corporate plans through the Chicago Plan Commission, which implemented the Burnham Plan over the next thirty years. This plan had some thoroughly negative effects, contributing to massive residential displacement, increasing congestion in the central business district, and the decline of public transportation. Scott (1969:108) captures the major limitations of the Burnham Plan:

In many respects the Chicago of the Burnham Plan is a city of the past that America never knew notwithstanding the facilities for transportation and transit, the network of roadways for automobiles, and the generous provisions of recreation areas for the people. It is an essentially aristocratic city, pleasing to the merchant princes who participated in its conception but not meeting some of the basic economic and human needs. In this metropolis for businessmen there are, with the exception of the central business district, no carefully designed areas for commercial enterprises, well distributed throughout the city. Nor are there any model tenements for workers, much less model neighborhoods.

Until the Depression, the street-widening efforts often met with opposition. A classic case was the widening of Michigan Avenue at a cost of $16 million, half derived from assessments made on property owners and half financed through a bond issue passed in 1914. The special‑assessment drove many lower-income property owners to sell. The residents opposed the street widening as a concession to "rich automobile owners" and argued that it would promote the "swells," a

Figure 6.10. The fight against the Traction and Subway Commission proposal. Mayor "Big Bill" Thompson, closely associated with Samuel Insull, first offered the voters a chance to approve subway construction in 1915. The referendum proposed using the Traction Fund, created by the 1907 Traction Ordinance for the eventual municipalization of public transportation, to finance subway construction, thus eliminating the possibility of public ownership and serving increased suburbanization and downtown traffic at the same time. The voters rejected the subway proposal overwhelmingly. By 1930, with high unemployment and economic stagnation, corporate interests were able to mobilize support for the same proposal, which was then accepted by the voters. (Source: The Northwest Side Commercial Association, Chicago Historical Society. IChi = 17480.)

contemporary expression for urban sprawl. After the bond issue passed, the property changed hands. However, by 1935 property values along with the thoroughfare had increased to twelve times the amount of the special assessment (Adams, 1935:203; Mayer and Wade, 1969:300).

In 1909, Mayor Busse also ordered a study to consider the construction of a subway to the central business district. The plans were influenced by earlier designs provided by other engineers working for the Chicago Association of Commerce (Roewade to Alderman Francis D. Conery, January 9, 1902, Roewade Papers, CHS). On January 31, 1911, Bion J. Arnold, chief of the Board of Supervising Engineers, reported to the Local Transportation Committee that subways would be useful in removing congestion and facilitating traffic flow to the Loop area.

In April 1911, Mayor Carter Harrison appointed a City Harbor and Subway Commission to draw up plans for a comprehensive subway system. This commission, representing downtown commercial and financial interests, proposed a $100 million bond issue, which, along with $14 million from the Traction Fund, would finance subway construction. This referendum for subway construction was soundly defeated in the 1914 election. The public was strongly mobilized against the commission's proposals. As one pamphlet explained:

Within the district bounded by the river, Lake and Twelfth streets the real estate is about equal in valuation to about all other real estate in the city of Chicago, and 75% of the city's business is done in this district. Those who control the traction system intend to operate it for the purpose of increasing the population downtown, and intensifying activities within the loop, so that valuations will increase. Their pretense is that a subway will relieve the present crowding . . . Big business, big grafters, big political sandbaggers, big department stores, demand franchises that will dump you where you will increase their business and profits. (Stedman, 1914:1)

Opposition on the subway scheme came mainly from working-class residents and small businessmen on the Northwest side who wanted more diversified transportation service. Tomaz Deuther, a community leader from that area, presented an alternative plan that would link outlying areas of the city.[15] In presenting his plan before the Local Transportation Committee, Deuther said:

The Harbor and Subway Commission is beginning at the wrong end of the problem . . . The first duty of the authorities is to secure improvement of service from existing agencies – not merely improvement of service to and from the downtown loop district, but also early development of certain greatly needed crosstown lines, particularly lines running north and south in the western division of the city. (*Chicago Daily News*, October 2, 1913)

## The consolidation of private power over public transportation: 1913–30

On November 13, 1913, the city council passed an ordinance allowing the unification of the two major systems, along with thirty-seven other transit properties, under the management of the Chicago Surface Lines (CSL). It was argued before the council that unification was necessary to extend service to various growing industrial areas of the city (e.g., Cicero and Calumet) (Deuther, 1926:23; Cramer, 1952). In exchange for a unified fare and transfer systems achieved through consolidation, the city accepted the accounting practice adopted by the Board of Supervising Engineers–a method that used overcapitalization and kept municipal ownership a more elusive goal than ever.

The elevated lines experienced similar unification through the Chicago Elevated Collateral Trust (1911), established by J. B. Hogarth and the National City Bank. The financiers of the city believed that this unification would provide a more rational expansion maximizing real estate investments and benefiting city expansion. As the elevated continued to go into debt over unpaid bills to Commonwealth Edison, it fell under the control of that company and its owner, Samuel Insull.

Insull, who had obtained control of public utilities throughout Chicago and the Midwest (Andrews, 1946:266–82), used his new control over the elevated to expand its network to the north, south, and west of the city.[16] His financial power was used to create public policy concerning transportation and public utilities, and the Illinois Committee on Public Utility Information (ICPUI), established by him, vigorously fought any suggestion of public ownership. The results of Insull's efforts was the State Public Utility Commission Law of 1913, which successfully shifted regulation from the city to the state level (McDonald, 1958:248–53).

With the establishment of a gubernatorially appointed state Public Utilities Commission, even the city council's limited power over transportation in the settlement ordinances was removed. All rate, service extension, and routing decisions were then elevated to the state level, and transportation decisions were further insulated from public control.

Both elevated and streetcar operators sought state regulation, which facilitated extensions to outlying areas. These extensions, although unprofitable for the lines, were highly profitable for real estate speculators and downtown business interests. For example, Insull's extensions usually benefited his own real estate investments, first in Wilson, Irving, and Rogers Park and later in more outlying areas such as Niles Center and Westchester (Insull, 1929:11; Andrews, 1946:266–82).[17]

State regulators also approved the creation of competing surface routes served by the Chicago Motor Coach Company, a bus company that operated parallel routes in the areas of highest population and ridership (Chicago Transit Authority, 1952:458). This company was founded in 1922 by James A. Ritchie and John Hertz; Ritchie, it will be recalled, was later a director of GM's Bus and Coach Division and the Omnibus Corporation, GM's first experiment in sponsoring bus conversions.[18] He was aided by Charles Mallough, a Chicago banker, William Wrigley, Jr., the chewing gum magnate, and members of the Armour and Swift families in financing the bus operation, which became a successful competitor of Chicago's rail systems (*Bus Transportation*, 1922:221–4; GM pamphlet file, G250; *New York Evening Telegram*, October 10, 1922).

However, although this bus competition hurt rail transit, it did not dominate it at this time. The financial institutions of the city holding transit stock and bonds, as well as the Insull empire, were still interested in maintaining rail transit.

Mayor Bill Thompson appointed Insull's lawyer, Samuel Ettleson, as corporation counsel of Chicago. Through Ettelson, Insull was able to ensure that transit decisions would be in his interests.[19] Thompson was often referred to as "Big Bill the Builder." Under his first administration, which lasted until 1923, transit extensions were encouraged and a Traction and Subway Commission was appointed. The commission urged further unification of surface and elevated roads, along with revitalization of the previously defeated plan to build a subway financed through the Traction Fund (Mohler, 1912:42–3; *Chicago Tribune*, September 11, 1915; Chicago Traction and Subway Commission, 1916; City Club of Chicago, 1936:9).[20]

Seeking new financing for transit extensions, Insull used his position as chairman of the State Council for Defense Planning during World War I to secure funds from the federal government through the U.S. Housing Corporation (USHC). With the assistance of Burnham and the Chicago Plan Commission, Insull was successful in getting the USHC to finance increased transportation services to Chicago's southeastern industrial district (USHC, December 21, 1918; NA, USHC, RG3, Boxes 406, 407).

Insull was also active in seeking state legislation in 1917 and 1919 to extend his consolidation of the elevated lines, as well as to broaden Surface Lines's operations and extend its franchises. In July 1919, a strike by streetcar workers for higher wages brought the CSL and the Chicago Elevated to seek higher fares (*The Union Leader*, March 29, 1952). This fare hike was fought by streetcar workers, unions, and consumers. The Public Utilities Commission reinstated the five-cent fare guaranteed by the 1907 ordinance. However, by 1920, the companies had managed to obtain a State Supreme Court decision ruling this fare as "confiscatory," since it was far below the costs of service. The court forced the state commission to raise the fare to eight cents (Mohler, 1919:481–93; People's Streetcar Ownership League, 1928). The court decision eliminating the five-cent fare resulted in a 458 percent increase in streetcar receipts, whereas the cost of the service increased only 88 percent (Mohler, 1923:7).

The Chicago banks played a significant role during this period in directing the operations of the CSL (Lyman Lobdell Papers, CHS; Leach, 1925; James, 1938:555–62).[21] Holding first-mortgage bonds of the transit properties as securities for other loans, they refused to extend financing for further service extensions that were required by the 1907 ordinances. The banks, which held traction bonds, achieved another victory over the 1907 settlement franchise when they received a favorable judicial decision. The Lobdell decision stated that 8 percent of transit receipts, earmarked for renewal and modernization of transit equipment, were to be paid to bondholders instead. By January 31, 1927, CSL was bankrupt; it was 250 miles behind on required service extensions.[22]

Similarly, the banks refused financing to Insull for new

equipment and extensions for the elevated lines. In 1930, Insull's transit properties went into receivership as well. Earlier, he had appointed a Banker's Committee to draft a transit ordinance that would consolidate all transportation properties under his leadership.[23]

With the end of public franchises and the beginning of bankruptcy receivership, a concerted effort was made by financial, transit, and public utility interests in the city to consolidate and secure their control over public transportation for the indefinite future. This coalition, led by Insull, succeeded in passing a series of state laws in 1929 that made such control possible with city approval.

This legislation had three goals: (1) to extend the twenty-year limit on franchises granted to private transportation companies to forty years; (2) to unify surface and elevated lines; and (3) to permit the construction of a subway. The legislation also provided that transportation franchises would be granted through a "terminable permit," which promised to allow the city to terminate the franchise at any time and either buy the property or transfer it to another transit firm. In reality, the law ensured that the franchise would be permanent, since it set a purchase price at the overcapitalized level of $260 million while dissipating the $55 million Traction Fund in subway construction, allowing only 3 percent of transit revenues to go to the city for possible eventual purchase.[24]

Similarly, the law promised to return authority to Chicago through a "Home Rule" Act, allowing control over transit matters to be shifted from the Illinois State Commerce Comission to a Transit Commission appointed by the mayor. The actual ordinance, passed through Insull's control over the city council, ensured that Transit Commission decisions would be subject to review by the state, granting effective veto power over all city decisions.

After passage of the legislation, Mayor Bill Thompson (again Mayor until 1931) appointed the Citizens' Traction Settlement Committee to meet with representatives of bondholders, public utilities, transit owners, and city representatives in order to draft appropriate ordinances for a public referendum. Walter L. Fisher, drafter of the 1907 ordinance, and

Sidney S. Gorham, a corporate lawyer and officer of the Chicago Motor Club, were appointed counsel for the committee. This so-called citizens committee addressed the various interests involved, but as one attorney for the CSL noted, its main responsibility was to draft an ordinance enabling corporate interests "to sell it to the people" (Proceedings of the Citizens' Traction Settlement Committee, 1929:41).

The Non-Partisan Citizens' Traction Ordinance Committee was organized by various transit interests – the Chicago Association of Commerce, the City Club of Chicago, the Chicago Real Estate Board, and other corporate groups – to mobilize support for the ordinance.[25] The selling of the consolidation ordinance concentrated upon the promise of home rule, city control through the terminable permit, and a "fair and equitable settlement . . . whereby the various properties can be united under one control and ownership and necessary extensions can be made" (Chicago Association of Commerce, 1930:2). Moreover, in the midst of rising unemployment, the ordinance promised economic recovery through the construction of subway and transit extensions. In a classic statement of the business viewpoint on transportation, Insull wrote:

Improve the traction facilities, and property values will be increased and business stimulated through the area of the existing transportation system. And wherever a new line is run, wherever an extension reaches, there will be so tremendous an increase in business and values that the people of such neighborhoods will themselves be amazed. This is the history of every extension, every addition. (Insull, 1929:6)

Ordinance advertisements promised more jobs, more transportation, universal transfers, and prosperity. Most remarkably, Insull suggested that the ordinance would provide "community ownership":

Set up the right kind of financial plan, founded on true economic principle, and the money necessary will pour in from Securities . . . and we will have a transportation system truly owned by the community – owned by our own citizens as small investors, just as most of the other Chicago local utilities are owned today. (Insull before the Chicago Association of Commerce, December 18, 1929, Lobdell Papers, CHS)

The consolidation ordinance was opposed by a broad coalition of liberal reform elements (the Liberal Club of Chicago) some unions (e.g., the Structural Iron Workers and Street Railway Employees), consumer groups (the Better Transportation League), neighborhood organizations (the West Side Alliance), and the Chicago Traction Committee of the Public Ownership League.[26] These groups, having formed a coalition called the Citizens' Committee Against the Traction Ordinance, argued that "exploitation of public services for profit should end." They stated:

This franchise, if passed, will fasten upon the city of Chicago and its people for all time to come a gigantic merger-monopoly. The same interest that now controls electric light and power, the gas and telephone utilities will control also the transportation facilities of the city. Moreover, by the control of transportation in Chicago and the suburban territory, these interests will also have a land and real estate monopoly. They will be able to buy up land in the surrounding territory, run their transportation lines into that section, improve and develop it and sell this land at greatly increased prices. (Thompson, 1930:3)

## Transit decline and highway building, 1930–45

The 1930 ordinance passed, but the collapse of Samuel Insull's empire made its implementation infeasible. On September 29, 1933, the federal court supervising the receiverships of both the surface and elevated properties appointed Walter L. Fisher to bring the city, financial institutions, and transit companies together to devise a financial reorganization agreement.

Transit began its long period of stagnation and decline for the following reasons: (1) the failure of the financial reorganization of transit properties; (2) the disinvestment in public transportation by banks and subsequent deterioration of service; (3) the growing power of the local highway lobby in city planning and government; and (4) the growing centralization of highway-oriented transportation planning at regional, state, and federal levels.

Controversy surrounded Fisher's efforts at financial reorganization of public transportation. Stories of scandals relating to the drafting and approval of the 1930 ordinance began to unfold at the city council. Councilmen and state legislators who had been crucial in passing the ordinance were said to have been on Insull's payroll, and charges of bribery and col-

# VOTE FOR

## Jobs for the Unemployed;
## Doubled Transportation and a Subway;
## Universal Transfers at a Single Fare;
## Prosperity for All Chicago.

---

### *Help Chicago Win Its 30-Year Fight For Progress*

---

A BALLOT MARKED "YES" MEANS:

A VOTE FOR—

Work for tens of thousands of men and women now unemployed.

A revival of prosperity in all lines of business.

Universal transfers—free from "L" to surface lines or subways.

No increase in fares and elimination of present double fares.

Expenditure of $65,000,000 in three years for extensions and improvements; a minimum of $200,000,000 (and probably double that amount) in ten years.

In addition, a $100,000,000 subway which will not cost taxpayers a cent. (A grand total of $165,000,000 of new transportation WITHIN THREE YEARS).

A general revival in the building industry, meaning the spending of tens of millions more dollars, bringing prosperity to all business and workers.

Relief to automobile congestion.

Increased values for homes and real estate.

Millions of dollars saved to the people in time yearly through increased rapid transportation.

Home rule for Chicago.

The city will get more transportation facilities within 10 years than it has had in the last 75 years.

Chicago is the only city of its class in the world which does not have a subway. New York, Philadelphia, Boston, Paris, London and Berlin have subways.

If Chicago loses this fight on July 1, THERE IS NO RELIEF IN SIGHT; NO EXTENSIONS WILL BE BUILT; THE CITY'S PEOPLE MUST CONTINUE TO STRUGGLE AGAINST THE UNBEARABLE TRANSPORTATION CONDITIONS FOR YEARS TO COME.

## Mark Your Ballot [YES] [X] on Tuesday, July 1
### POLLS OPEN 6:00 A. M. TO 4:00 P. M.

Figure 6.11. The 1930 Traction Ordinance. This advertisement supporting the 1930 Traction Ordinance shows the effort made by the Chicago business community to use unemployment, promises of economic development, and a universal transfer system (promised in earlier referenda) to secure support for the unification of all public transportation into one private company after the bankruptcies of the surface and elevated lines. (Source: The Chicago Historical Society. IChi = 17304.)

lusion filled the local newspapers. Under the leadership of Paul Douglas, the city council refused to extend the ordinance, which would have allowed Fisher's proposed reorganization (Douglas, December 29, 1933, speech before city council, Douglas Aldermanic papers, CHS; Amended Reorganization Plan and Amended Reorganization Agreement of Chicago Local Transportation Company, 1934; Schwartz, 1935:45)[27]

Financial reorganization failed because of the conflict between banks and city officials over whether bondholders or improved transit service should have first claim on fare revenues. Furthermore, the banks wanted public subsidization of transit debt through continued overcapitalization as the base for figuring fare increases.[28] These conflicts were not resolved until the establishment of the Chicago Transit Authority in 1947. In the words of one observer, "capital simply could not be induced to rescue the two companies (CSL and Chicago Elevated Railway) from receivership and bankruptcy" (*The Union Leader*, March 29, 1952), and in general, "new capital ceased to flow into the two properties" (Budd, 1952:3). Service cuts resulted, and transit routing failed to keep pace with new residential settlement patterns, leaving the automobile as the only alternative for many commuters.[29]

Corporate and state leaders judged that Chicago's regional expansion would be better served by highway transportation. This highway–automobile orientation was rooted in the Burnham Plan proposed decades earlier. Pro-highway initiatives climaxed in 1937–9 in a series of reports that provided the plans for massive highway expansion in Chicago. Barrett (1975:480–4) suggests that three major groups influenced the automobilization of Chicago during the pre–World War II period: (1) transportation planners and engineers working for the city; (2) automobile dealers and auto owners' associations; and (3) downtown commercial and financial interests. My research supports this analysis; however, futher examination uncovers the linkages between these groups that spurred automobile use.

The Burnham Plan advocated wider streets for unrestricted motor car movement. By the mid-twenties, most of these boulevards were constructed along a grid pattern providing continuous routes and auto right-of-way at simple X-type intersections (Barton, 1948:19). Wider intersecting and cross-streets within the city, however, did not solve the problem of connecting intraurban traffic with traffic originating in the broader Chicago region; highways might.

For more than twenty years, highway interests had been active at both the local and state levels. In 1912, Edward F. Dunne, dubbed by the Chicago Motor club the "first Good Roads Governor of Illinois," successfully legislated state support for highway building. Like most of the early efforts, the first plans to support highway development were oriented toward road building on the urban periphery and in rural areas of the state. The Chicago Regional Planning Association urged improved major roads leading to and from Chicago. Further, as one early study established, this construction led to increased demand for streets intersecting with such roads that would serve "traffic . . . originating in suburban communities around Chicago and having its destination in or near Chicago's central business area" (Taylor, 1929:372). In short, the boulevards specified in the Burnham Plan had to be connected with the major highways leading to the city.

In 1924, Cook County and the U.S. Bureau of Public Roads suggested that a concerted effort be made to overcome the resulting congestion by building more highways connecting state and urban roads (Chicago Regional Planning Association, 1925:3).[30] The next year, the Chicago Motor Club (the local auto lobby representative) established a coalition with various city, county, and state planning agencies and downtown commercial interests to promote highways.

In September 1925, the Chicago Motor Club joined with the Chicago Regional Planning Commission to propose traffic regulations facilitating automobile travel and promoting highway building. In the process, it successfully halted rail expansion that would compete with highway building (*Motor News*, June 1926:3). These efforts culminated in September 1926, when Cook County Board President Anton Cermak appointed a highway advisory committee co-chaired by the Chicago Plan Commission's D. H. Burnham and his business associate, Rufus Abbott (*Chicago Tribune*, August 19, 1926). This committee was hailed by the Chicago Motor Club and the automotive industry as critical in coordinating highway planning efforts. In supporting the committee, an underlying justification for highways is revealed: the reorienting of urban transportation toward distribution and consumption, rather than industrial production:

It is easy to advance many reasons for road widening . . . Wider roads make possible increased speed in hauling in so far as transportation is concerned, reduction in time amounts to a decrease in the distance from market centers. *This is important in view of the fact that the economic problem of today is one of distribution rather than production.* Wider roads will tend to relieve the periodical congestion of markets while accruing benefits to producer and consumer alike. (*Motor News,* September 1926:3; my emphasis)

The committee's work resulted in the Chicago Plan Commission's Superhighway Plan. Superhighways were to run parallel to elevated tracks into the suburbs. These superhighways planned were in cooperation with the Chicago Regional Planning Association, the Chicago Association of Commerce, and the Highway Improvement Department of the Chicago Motor Club (*Motor News,* January 1930:4). Consequently $340 million was spent on street improvements before World War II, with funding coming from bonds, real estate taxes on adjacent property, or general revenues. Barrett (1975:484) observed that "Chicago drove itself into debt with street improvements quite early in the game."[31]

Job creation was another aim of highway building plans in the thirties. Moreover, former Chicagoans in the Roosevelt administration (Frederick Delano at the National Resources Planning Board and H. L. Ickes as Secretary of the Interior) helped leverage federal funding for Chicago's highway projects. As the National Resources Planning Board set up state planning agencies, Chicago's existing local and regional planning bodies took a major leadership role. Robert Kingery, one of Burnham's close associates, became head of the Illinois State Planning Board, and C. W. Elliot II, of the Chicago Regional Planning Association, became involved with state planning efforts that benefited Chicago (C. M. Moderwell to Robert Kingery, May 24, 1933, NRPB Records; H. L. Kellogg to C. W. Elliot II, January 23, 1929, NRPB Records, NA RG187, File

840, Box 56). These planning bodies were closely involved in state legislative efforts to supplement highway funds. They succeeded in arranging for the state of Illinois to pay one-third of municipal highway costs.

Two major documents outlined the future development of Chicago's urban transportation system: the Chicago Plan Commission's Master Plan of Residential Land Use in Chicago (1939) and the city's Comprehensive Local Transportation Plan for Chicago (1937). These planning statements, along with a series of other city reports, outlined a system of subways and superhighways radiating out from the downtown area to better handle the demands of suburban-oriented travel.[32] Financing for both subway and highway construction was made available through the Federal Aid Highway Program, the Defense Highway Act, and the Public Works Administration. Subway equipment was bought with aid from the Reconstruction Finance Corporation.

The shift from rails to highways was facilitated by increasingly centralized local government (Burton, 1939). In 1939, the Department of Subways and Traction was abolished and replaced by the Department of Subways and Superhighways, headed by Philip Harrington, chief researcher for the subway and highway studies conducted by the city.

The locus of transportation planning moved further away from city control. In 1942, the Cook County Highway Authority was created. City and regional planning commissions united local, state, and federal planners in a call for a statewide agency. By August 1943, the Cook County Highway Authority was dissolved and replaced by the Illinois State Superhighway Commission. Throughout the remainder of the decade, Mayor Edward Kelley and Governor Dwight Green worked closely together to finance and plan the superhighway system. A series of decisions by the various planning agencies ensured the subordination of rail to highway planning.[33]

Chicago's new orientation to transportation planning continued residential and manufacturing decentralization and allowed for subway construction that would preserve the commercial and administrative centrality of the central business district.[34] But subways and superhighways would not solve

Chicago's transportation crisis, particularly the needs of urban neighborhoods, which were aggravated by the continued deterioration of surface and elevated rail service. Instead, urban transportation planning was designed to solve the problems of those controlling the planning process – commercial and financial groups that owned Loop property and highway interests that sought a wider market for their products through residential and industrial decentralization. A citywide subway system was impossible due to the dispersal of single-family housing. Yet subways to the neighborhoods of higher-income employees and shoppers would serve downtown interests. Prior to 1937, downtown property owners had agreed to a special property assessment of up to 35 percent in order to cover subway construction costs. However, with the availability of federal loans and grants during the New Deal, property owners paid nothing. The Better Chicago League, a community action group, pointed out:

> the property which is adjacent to the [subway] exits is not being assessed any part of the cost, and the car riders will gain practically nothing from the subway routes as planned. They will not save time, nor will they be delivered where they want to go. The only beneficiaries of the expenditure of over $40,000,000 of pubic funds for six miles of subway will be the owners of the six blocks of State Street from Randolph to Van Buren. (Better Chicago League, May 16, 1939, Douglas Aldermanic Papers, CHS)

## Public ownership and private control: the Chicago Transit Authority and decline of public transportation

After World War II, there were three major changes in Chicago's transportation system: (1) the creation of the Chicago Transit Authority (CTA); (2) the conversion from rail to bus service on surface routes; and (3) a massive increase in highway construction. Control of transportation planning and administration shifted from local government to Chicago's major corporations. Consequently, local transportation plans were unresponsive to demands for better public transportation, thus hastening the advent of automobilization.

By the forties, transportation was no longer a key public

policy issue. After years of transportation decisions dominated by the federal courts, the Illinois Commerce Commission, and various regional and federal planning agencies,
only 15.4 percent of the electorate bothered to approve a
referendum reorganizing public transportation in 1942; this
was in sharp contrast to the pre–World War I era, when
voter turnout was over 40 percent (*Transportation Journal
News*, June 6, 1942:225). Unencumbered by a politicized electorate, the courts, planning agencies, business groups, and
the city drafted various reorganization schemes for Chicago's
transit properties.[35] However, many of these plans were
turned down by the Illinois State Commerce Commission in
1943 and 1944 (Department of Subway and Superhighways,
1947:48–54).

The commission's objections were based upon the overcapitalization of the transit properties. The Securities and Exchange Commission overcame that problem by slashing the
elevated's valuation from $91 million to $11 million, and ruled
that the CSL's valuation could be reduced considerably from
previous equity cases (Chicago Department of Subway and
Superhighways, 1947:56; Barrett, 1975:487–8). Chicago's major
banks, acting as trustees for the transit properties, then
agreed to a public ownership scheme that would pay them
more than $92 million for the transit properties they held as
court-appointed receivers (MacMurray, 1945:28; *Passenger
Transport*, October 1947).

State legislation created a regional transit authority, the Chicago Transit Authority (CTA)–"a contractual alternative to
public ownership" (Budd, 1952:8). Three constraints have affected the operation of the CTA: no taxing authority, right of
refusal by participating suburban municipalities in the Chicago region, and bank control over the operating budget (*Chicago Daily Tribune*, August 28, 1947).[36]

This arrangement limited the CTA's ability to develop effective mass transit. The CTA was forced to finance modernization of a dilapidated system through operating revenues. To
build ridership and rebuild transit service without massive
subsidization was an impossible task. The mismanagement of
transit modernization hastened rail transit's decline and the

eventual decline of total public ridership as well. The huge financial burden of modernization and demands for suburban extension saddled the CTA with deficits by the mid-1950s (Budd to *Chicago Tribune,* February 15, 1954; American Public Transport Association, 900.01 Chicago). Fares rose, service was reduced, and ridership declined (Overton, 1955:480; Banfield, 1961:91–106).

In 1956, the CTA proposed that $30 million of state fuel tax funds be used to finance transit extensions and improvements (*Mass Transportation,* July 1957). The Chicago Motor Club and the Illinois Highway Users' Conference (IHUC) reacted immediately to defeat the "gas tax raid" (*Motor News,* May 1957).

This defeat exemplifies the power of the highway lobby on a local level. The National Highway Users' Conference sent two full-time workers to coordinate the defeat of the measure by a public relations committee consisting of members of the IHUC and the Chicago Motor Club.[37] Concentrating upon outlying suburban communities in the Chicago region, they pressured state legislators to reject any attempt to "endanger the state highway program" (Banfield, 1961:109–11).[38]

Alternative proposals to finance transit through bond issues or suburban or city property taxes were also defeated. A coalition of downtown commercial interests and suburban dwellers avoiding property tax increases, auto-related corporate interests opposed to fuel tax diversions, and regional planning agencies seeking to keep planning authority away from the CTA joined in opposing transit subsidization.

The defeat of transit subsidies was the result of long-term efforts by corporate groups such as the Chicago Central Area Committee and the Chicago Association of Commerce and Industry. These groups represented broader class interests than the single-issue politics of associations such as the Chicago Motor Club. The Chicago Central Area Committee represented downtown commercial and industrial interests.[39] The Chicago Association of Commerce and Industry included many of these same interests and reflected the growing power of auto-related interests in the local capitalist class. Standard Oil, for example, was one of the association's main financial supporters (Banfield, 1961:115).

170

After the fuel tax diversion defeat, the Central Area Committee and the Association of Industry and Commerce financed a study by the Northwestern University Transportation Center of the CTA's expansion plans and subsidization measures. The study rejected residential service extensions as unnecessary and fiscally unsound; however, it suported extensions into industrial districts (such as the Clearing area). It strongly opposed subsidies and accused the CTA of overstepping its authority in planning expansion, claiming that planning authority should revert to the regional level – the Northeastern Illinois Regional Planning Commission and the Chicago Department of Planning (*Chicago Daily Sun Times,* August 12, 1958; *Chicago Daily News,* June 6, 1961).

From 1963 on, CTA deficits grew. However, it was not until 1973 that the state government began providing operating subsidies in the face of massive service curtailments (Berry et al., 1976:20).

The conversion from rail to bus on surface routes contributed to transit's further decline. During the first ten years of the CTA's existence, its modernization budget of $150 million relied almost exclusively on bus conversion (CTA Annual Report, 1952:72–4); only $46 million had been spent on new equipment in the previous four decades. Earlier streetcar equipment purchases were criticized by the city as manifesting "improper judgement." The City Council Committee on Local Transportation echoed the popular notion that "the modern trend in transportation is to get away from a fixed surface operation" (Annual Report, 1952:72–4).

The individual responsible for Chicago's bus substitution policy was CTA Chairman Ralph Budd. An understanding of why Budd preferred bus conversion exemplifies the general process that has led to the demise of mass transit.

Budd was no stranger to the transportation business, having been president of both the Great Northern and the Chicago, Burlington, and Quincy (CB&Q) railroads. Budd was also no stranger to GM. He worked closely with Charles F. Kettering, GM president, both of whom had served as members of the board of Great Northern. Both played important roles in planning the dieselization of the locomotive industry.

Budd had also worked with GM executive C. R. Osborne, assisting in the development of the Silver Streak and Pioneer Zephyr. Later, during World War II, as transportation commissioner on the National Defense Council, Budd collaborated with GM President William Knudsen, who served as the council's industrial production commissioner.

Budd's thinking about the dieselization of locomotives and the motorization of public transportation was greatly influenced by his contacts with GM. As president of Great Northern and the CB&Q, he converted the nation's principal coal carriers, the railroads, to diesel engines. As president of Great Northern, Budd was one of the first to substitute buses for short-haul branch passenger trains. Later, as a director of the CB&Q, he supported the incorporation of the Burlington Transportation Company to operate buses on highways (1929). In 1937, Burlington joined with other companies to form National Trailways Bus Company, which competed with railroads for interurban traffic (Overton, 1955:421, 462).[40]

Under Budd, the CTA rapidly converted to buses. In 1953, he declared in a speech before the Chicago Association of Commerce and Industry:

The substitution of modern motor buses for street cars has moved forward at a rapid pace. Of the 52 street car routes being operated when the CTA acquired the surface lines [1947] only 10 remain, and all but two or three are to be converted within the next year or two. The old red street car is vanishing. It's on the way to the scrap heap. In two years, perhaps three, it will be only a memory. (Budd, 1952:3)

In selling bus conversion, Budd sought to expedite the flow of traffic: Maneuverability in street traffic would improve one-way streets and relieve congestion, and street paving would be simplified. To hasten the conversion, Budd directed the CTA to contribute $300,000 a year for paving Chicago's streets. GM, of course, received most of the supply contracts for buses.[41]

The Chicago experience reinforces St. Clair's (1981) finding that for all U.S. transit operating systems, bus conversion was the least economical way to provide mass transit and furthered ridership decline. In Chicago, higher fares and service cuts were necessary to finance bus conversion; ridership and running time suffered as a result (*The Union Leader*, March 29, 1952:28; Budd, 1952:3; CTA Annual Report, 1962:11–12).

## Highway planning and the restructuring of Chicago

From 1947 to 1971, as a result of the CTA's bus conversion program and the dominance of highway planning, mass-transit ridership declined 65 percent. By 1956, all CTA surface routes had been converted to bus routes. Compared with the CTA's subway and elevated operations, surface bus routes declined most rapidly after that year. The CTA's elevated ridership did somewhat better due to rail median service on the Eisenhower (1958), Dan Ryan (1969), and Kennedy (1970) expressways.[42]

After World War II, Chicago, like many other cities, decentralized. Residences, employment, and industrial and retail activity moved toward the suburban periphery,[43] reversing travel patterns toward employment centers outside the city. Industries developed along the new highways as railroad corridors were abandoned (Berry et al., 1976:13–46).

While Chicago declined, "Chicagoland" (the Chicago region) grew massively. The Chicago Association of Commerce and Industry noted that the Chicago region had the highest rate of industrial and residential construction of all major cities in the country, mostly outside the city. The most rapid suburbanization of population and employment occurred between 1960 and 1970 (Berry et al., 1976:11–12).

Chicago was also a center for national corporate capital. From 1956 to 1972, branch office, administrative, and auxiliary employment of the Fortune 500 industrial corporations increased by 252 percent. Fifty-five of these corporations made the city their headquarters. More than half of these corporations based in Chicago were linked to the auto–oil–rubber coalition, which was involved in national and local highway lobbying.

Earlier, we noted how the Public Works Administration, the Illinois State Planning Commission, and the Chicago Plan Commission had planned highway development for the Chicago region during the thirties and forties. The Chicago

Master Plan of 1943 specified radial expressway routes con-
verging at the central business district and inner and outer
circumferential routes tying the radial routes together (Chicago Plan Commission, 1945). Land use along these routes
was prescribed by the planners for industrial park and residential uses, exacerbating the decline of housing and industry
within the city and heightening racial polarization (Berry et
al., 1976:52–71).

With the routes planned, administrators waited only for
federal financing to begin construction. With the 1956 Highway Act, highway construction took priority over every other
form of transportation planning. With highway construction,
the city government's role in planning declined. The Federal
Highway Administration reported that nearly all final route
decisions were made by state highway planners and the
Northeast Illinois Regional Planning officials.[44] Highways
were built so rapidly that route duplication occurred, as illustrated by the financial disaster of the Chicago Skyway (Berry,
1976:17).

With the increasing suburbanization of the Chicago electorate, local government supported highway planning and related efforts of suburbanites that opposed the interests and
goals of inner city wards, which had been the traditional basis
for Chicago politics (Kasperson, 1971:410). Thus, the shift of
population and employment caused by highway construction
led to a reorganization of city politics.[45]

The conflicts surrounding the construction of the Crosstown
Expressway, which occurred during the late sixties and early
seventies, typifies these political shifts.[46] The Crosstown was to
follow a circumferential route between the inner and outer
rings on the western periphery of the city limits. In 1964 Mayor
Richard Daley, in an attempt to satisfy suburban commuters
and local business interests, appointed a suburban- and busi-
ness-dominated Transportation Advisory Group to study the
Crosstown route and grant its "citizens' " approval (Transportation Advisory group, 1965). The associations representing
eastern European and black neighborhoods that would be dev-
astated by the highway construction were excluded.

By the early seventies, the Crosstown was embroiled in controversy. Faced by court rulings requring broader citizen review, the Crosstown's construction was repeatedly delayed by the Anti-Crosstown Coalition organized by the Citizens Action Program of Chicago.[47] The Anti-Crosstown Coalition was affected by the lengthy procedures of highway review and the growing polarization of Chicago neighborhoods, which made the building of interracial coalitions exceedingly difficult (Pavlos, 1972; *Chicago Tribune*, May 19, 1972).

In the summer of 1972, the Crosstown Executive Board, a corporate coalition of the Illinois Division of Highways, the Chicago Association of Commerce and Industry, and highway constructors decided that the best way to defeat the Crosstown's opposition was to propose a long series of route alternatives that would exacerbate conflicts between black and white neighborhoods along the route and prolong hearing procedures, sapping the organizational strength of community opposition (Minutes, Crosstown Executive Board Meeting, August 17, 1972, Highway Action Coalition Files). After more than a decade of controversy, in the late seventies, a slightly altered Crosstown route named the "Daley Expressway" was developed and received final approval.[48]

This case study of Chicago reveals how political fragmentation of local government powers and increasing power of federal and state governments removed the urban population from urban transportation planning. Along with the professionalization of transportation planning, organizational changes in policy and planning permitted easier penetration by local corporate interests nationally tied to auto, oil, and rubber corporations that were motorizing urban transportation. Few U.S. cities had greater potential than Chicago for developing a transportation system balanced between private and public modes and serving a diverse population. Few cities boasted the survival of rail and rubber, public and private transportation. Nevertheless, Chicago succumbed to the national process that automobilized America.

# 7

# Conclusion: Urban transportation for whom?

Steel rails and concrete molded urban growth in both the United States and Germany. Transportation policy and technological choices reshaped community life and reorganized local, state, and federal policies. Personally and politically, private and public decisions accommodated transportation changes. These changes in urban transportation captured and shaped the consciousness of city dwellers like no others had. This study has attempted to weave together diverse levels of analysis – cross-sectional analysis of German and U.S. cities, cross-national policy comparisons, and local case studies – in order to reassess the social origins of transit change.

In contrast to the orthodox position that technology or the use of urban space determines urban transportation, macro-comparative historical evidence presented here demonstrates the importance of changes in class power in shaping cities and their transportation systems. This evidence, it is hoped, has illuminated the conflicts surrounding transportation and the controls used to resolve them. At the national and local levels, it is possible to view the conflicting functions of urban transportation: industrial and personal travel versus short-term profits for transportation equipment and related industries. The conflicts between community and corporate interests in transit or motorization policies offer a unique opportunity to examine the interaction of private interests and public policy. Although there are many similarities in the decline of public transit in Germany and the United States, differences in the level of transit service are attributed to the changes in corporate power and variations in the timing and form of government intervention in urban transportation policy and planning.

## Conclusion

The study neither disregards nor dismisses the role of technology, urban space, and demographic factors in contributing to transportation change. These factors are embedded in the broader history and theory of modern capitalism and its effects upon urbanization. The comparison of Germany and the United States allows us to make historically specific generalizations about transportation change. Conclusions can be drawn about the influence of the changes in corporate power and the institutionalization of state policy upon urban transportation. In short, the research demonstrates the politico-economic conditions and policy mechanisms that produce a trade-off between public and private transportation.

## Ecological and politico-economic factors

This research confronts two different traditions in urban studies—human ecology and urban political economy—and generates testable hypotheses. Identifying variables from both and using them together clarify more about transit change than either alone. Neither can claim exclusive understanding of these fundamental changes in urban life. The utility of considering aspects of corporate power, local economic structure, and class relations suggested by urban political economy is demonstrated; so too are the spatial limits of transit growth. It is hoped that this research and its implicit challenge to earlier conceptions of how cities work suggest the importance of further theoretical synthesis between these areas.

### Germany

In Germany, corporate power and industrial production, which were more diversified than their U.S. counterparts, accompanied an early concentration of economic power. Highly concentrated and intertwined coal, steel, iron, chemical, and electrical manufacturing industries, which were tied to the large banks that financed German industrialization and economic concentration, viewed transportation from the perspective of corporate consumers. This promoted rail transportation and institutionalized it as part of national and local public policy. By the turn of the twentieth century, the national government had developed commuter rail service to major cities, and through its fiscal policy, promoted rail travel. Local governments expanded mass transit through public ownership and fare subsidization as part of a general program of municipal industrialization facilitating private industrial development. The Reich Transport Ministry and municipal transportation offices served the transportation needs of those industries that dominated the urban economy.

The interpenetration of U.S. and German capital after World War I and the global strategy of GM reduced the dominance of older monopolies and promoted the rise of automobile-related industries. The shift toward the interests of transportation producers converged with Nazi interests in motorization and militarization; the eclipse of public transit began. After World War II, automobile-related industries were important for economic recovery and growth. Consequently, motorization continued at the expense of mass transit. However, in order to explain the later and less precipitous decline of public transit in Germany compared to the United States, we must refer to specific differences in the timing and composition of economic concentration in German industry and the early institutionalization of state intervention into transportation policy, which preserved competing interests in transportation service and established a strong commitment to rail transit. These same factors could also explain potentially why, after the 1973 oil crisis, German cities experienced an unparalleled revival of mass transit and U.S. cities did not.

How did these elements of German economic and political history affect city growth and transportation changes? The analysis of cross-sectional data for German cities in 1900 and 1970 addresses this question.

In 1900, the linkage between the local economy and the core industries (heavy capital goods industry) increased the level of transit. The workers' need for rapid means of travel and political demand by labor and capital for transit services encouraged urban expansion. This process spurred rail transit construction. Similarly, growing tertiary employment increased transit ridership. The expansion of the transit system was necessary for the coordination and integration of a growing system of German cities.

In 1970, the historically derived ecological structure of the city supported higher levels of mass transit. Urbanization associated with older waves of industrialization created a built environment supporting a transit network. Similarly, public transportation was responsive to variations in labor force concentration in the older industrial sector.

But another conflicting process was also at work. Corporate power in 1970 reflected the radically changing nature of Germany's central growth industries. Growth rates in heavy industry were overshadowed by the massive expansion of the auto–oil–rubber sector. Significantly, increased corporate power resulted in decreased transit ridership. Corporate producers and suppliers of highway transportation equipment made travel demands; the answer was private, not public transportation. This negative impact of the auto–oil–rubber coalition is confirmed again when we consider the effect of these corporations alone upon the level of transit ridership. Again, we observe that because cities depended on the pro-automobile industries for employment, transit ridership decreased.

Although these static models of mass transit in German cities in 1900 and 1970 are informative, they do not account for the dynamic processes involved in transit decline. In a statistical analysis of transit decline from 1929 to 1970, corporate power was the only independent variable with a statistically significant impact. Consistent with earlier statistical results and historical evidence, concentrations of corporate power resulted in greater transit decline.

In the case of Frankfurt, additional evidence confirms propositions about differences between the U.S. and German transit systems, as well as the linkages between them and the impact of corporate power. Commercial, financial, and industrial interests long dominated Frankfurt and its transportation planning. Public transit was used to disperse the growing working-class population and reduce its competition with local dominant classes for limited central city space. Rail transit developed areas contiguous to the city and decreased travel time to decentralized industrial locations. In contrast, Chicago's system developed radial paths fragmenting land use. Based largely upon U.S. experience, human ecologists have argued that rail technology limited development to corridors radiating from the city center, unable to develop the interstices of land between them. This limitation allegedly stimulated the shift to more flexible buses and autos. In both Frankfurt and Chicago, demands by outlying residents and commercial groups for crosstown and ring routes were noted. In the former case, construction routes led to the settlement of underutilized space; in the latter, settlement occurred only through highway development. This demonstrates, I believe, that there was nothing inherent in rail technology limiting spatial development; the limits were largely political. Local politics, class interests, and the urban economy determined the use of space and the balance between transit modes.

At the turn of the century, strong mayors such as Miquel, Adickes, and Landmann linked the German tradition of local autonomy (albeit in the context of an autocratic central state) to planning policies, including mass transit, that rationalized state-mediated economic growth. After World War I and the granting of universal suffrage, municipal politics reflected not only the growth policies of local industry but also the increased social, economic, and political demands of the newly enfranchised working class. Political and class issues were imbricated in Frankfurt and are illustrated in the demands for transit service under Social Democratic planning during the twenties. By contrast, in Chicago by that time, such demands were no longer important public issues after the early defeat of municipalization.

As new growth industries concentrated in Frankfurt, the traditional importance of mass transit in organizing city space for administrative, commercial, and financial activities was supplanted by the highway construction needs of motorization industries. The growing centralization and coordination of transportation planning resulted in conflicts between highway and transit building. Transit construction was geared to providing service along specific travel corridors, as was the traditional U.S. use of transit technology. Service workers were ferried from suburbs to the city center, and the travel needs of more nearby populations were ignored.

However, the resilience of mass transit amid rapid motorization in Frankfurt can be attributed to the history of public investment in transit services and the tradition of municipal service dating from the first decades of this century. Traditionally, urban transportation was an issue not only for professional planners but for the public as well. Public support of and consumer demand for continued transit service mitigated the disastrous effects of motorization policies that occurred in the United States. Intraclass competition and interclass conflict over the development of urban transportation in Frankfurt illustrates the importance of political and economic factors in urbanization and their interaction in city growth.

## The United States

U.S. urban transportation was subordinated first to the interests of transit operating firms and later to the interests of equipment producers and their industrial allies. The electrification and expansion of rail transit by operators, utilities, and land developers represented overhead investment for profits in increased electrical consumption, housing speculation, and private development. Transit service was rarely the primary goal of the firm; corruption and inefficiency plagued these transit systems and led to their bankruptcy.

In contrast to Germany, economic concentration occurred later in the United States and coincided with the increasing importance of the auto manufacturing, oil, and rubber industries. The growth interests of this highway coalition dovetailed with the local interests of real estate speculators, developers, and local industrialists seeking the spatial expansion of cities for industrial plants, commerce, and housing. Thus, national corporate interests paralleled regional and local interests to develop locational advantages within regional systems and between competing cities.

The United States lacked an industrially diverse economic structure that might have contested the dominance of the narrow interests of auto-related firms in transportation planning and policy. Also, unlike Germany in the twenties and the post–World War II period, there was no pressure to channel class conflicts over urban service into institutional forms of mass transit support subject to governmental administration. Accordingly, public policy promoted the interests of motorization industries. In contrast to Germany, where state intervention in transportation preceded the rise of the motorization lobby, in the United States both occurred at the same time. Road building rather than rail expansion was the focus of governmental policy.

How were these processes articulated in the national urban system? To what extent did corporate power, urban centrality, the nature of local industry (i.e., diversity or specificity in a given place), and urbanization (size, density and age) affect changes in urban mass transit? How are these factors interrelated?

U.S. data for 1900 and 1970 reveal that intercity variation in mass transit depends upon the amount of corporate power, economic diversity, and timing of the rate and process of urbanization. Analysis indicates the weakness of earlier theories focusing solely on static measures of proximate, visible, and easily calculated dimensions of urban structure. The findings for 1900 indicate that a competitive and diversified corporate and industrial environment, and the central position of a city in the growing national urban system, benefit public transportation.

For 1970, the effects of centrality, corporate power, and local economic structure on the level of public transportation are largely mediated by urbanization. The built environment of cities filters and reflects historical conditions previously described through the spatial structure of cities that preserved an atrophied mass transit system. The rise of monopoly power in the auto–oil–rubber industries, their link to the local economy, and urban centrality in a petroleum-based economy are associated with transit decline either directly or through the form of urbanization they encourage. Additional evidence suggests that cities that resisted motorization and/or municipalized transit before its decline suffered less reduction in services and ridership. Although this statistical analysis is limited, it indicates the importance of historical factors affecting transit change.

Urban form can, therefore, be better understood as the outcome of earlier business, economic, and governmental institutions that are linked to various places within the national urban system. Evidence from Chicago's history confirms this analysis at the local level.

Organizations of the powerful classes – business and corporate civic associations – staffed and dominated the commissions, study groups, and offices of government transportation agencies. Corporations, whose dominance was threatened by public opposition during the Populist era before World War I, divided the interests of transportation consumers and workers and simultaneously removed the transportation issue from electoral politics. These organizational barriers to popular participation in transportation planning limited transit. This built-in unresponsiveness to transit demand limited the mobility of public transportation. As local corporate power and employment became linked to the auto–oil–rubber growth industries, planning shifted toward highway construction.

## Corporate strategy, state power, and urban transportation

Mass transit in both the United States and Germany faced continuous financial, operating, and service delivery problems during this century. In this study, a number of questions have been raised. What explains the different rates of decline between the two countries? How have corporate concentration, control, and combination in various industrial complexes blocked or promoted specific interests? How have labor processes and class relations in specific industries influenced the rise of corporate power? How has the relationship between corporate strategy, transportation policy, and travel needs changed over time and varied between Germany and the United States?

In both countries, corporate strategy impinged upon state transportation policy by creating an environment in which it could be controlled. The policies of corporations and their trade associations limited and skewed alternatives for transportation policymakers. Although the timing of motorization and the industrial conditions leading to it differed, the continuity of corporate control over urban transportation in both countries is evident.

Even without direct political representation, auto, rubber, and oil companies were able to mold public policy to their needs (e.g., market expansion and control over ground transportation). Nevertheless, to ensure that their interests would be protected, large corporations placed their representatives at all levels of government.

Variations in transit decline in Germany and the United States are closely related to differences in industrial composition. Urban transportation policy was largely the outcome of competition between various groups within corporations and the state. State transportation policy came to reflect and enhance the interests of the largest corporations. Such policies had the consequence, if not the intention, of eliminating transportation alternatives, thereby assuring that earlier policies would not be revived and challenges by other classes would be defeated.

A comparison of the German and U.S. experiences indicates that the variation in transit decline is rooted in the internal relations and historical background of old and new industrial coalitions. As we discussed in Chapters 3 and 4, the labor process in German and U.S. industry was transformed at vastly different rates. Craft traditions and labor organizations in Germany held back the introduction of the assembly line, which was so important in the early dominance of auto interests in the United States. Thus, the impact of class relations upon the labor process affected the differential rate of corporate growth in highway-related industries. This factor, along with Germany's early monopolization and concentration in older industries, retarded the emergence of the pro-automobile coalition. Moreover, this economic structure had a definite effect on the political structure necessary to achieve motorization. Although pressures for motorization and labor process rationalization were rising in Germany prior to 1933, the resistance by both labor and competing industries was eliminated with the rise of fascism.

The timing and strength of institutionalized state intervention contributed to different transit outcomes in the United States and Germany. The changing relationship and structure of local, state, and federal governments increased the ability of corporate power to penetrate state policies. The political fragmentation of governmental units that controlled transportation policy, government regulation, and the increased centralization of public investment and subsidy decisions all contributed to new directions in urban transportation.

## *Germany*

A strong tradition of local autonomy combined with a central government bureaucracy sympathetic to rail transit contributed to the extensive public transportation network in German cities during the first decades of this century. Bismarck nationalized the commuter lines of the Prussian railways in 1878 in order to transport labor from the hinterlands to Germany's rapidly industrializing cities. Simultaneously, the central government promoted rail expansion by providing tax benefits for workers and employers using rail transit and tax relief and subsidies for rail systems.

During this same period, the role of local government changed from caretaking to more active planning and intervention. The goal was to transform German urban areas from stagnant central European cities into modern industrial metropolises. Strong mayors such as Miquel and Adickes in Frankfurt increased local planning, including transportation. Public ownership facilitated the electrification and expansion of public transportation, provided the necessary infrastructure for economic growth, and expanded urban settlement. Annexation and increased regional authority of local government permitted broader planning schemes than in the United States. Local government designed, financed, located, and controlled public transport facilities in order to attract and retain population and economic activity in the Frankfurt region. Transit politics satisfied the interests of industrial and commercial consumers of transit before World War I in order to provide them with locational advantages. Priority was given to suburban and regional travel rather than intracity traffic.

This policy remained unchallenged because the urban working classes were disenfranchised until after World War I. With the challenges of the 1918–19 revolution and the Weimar period, local government had to satisfy the demands of different and competing classes for transit services. As a result, planning bureaucracies at the local and regional levels proliferated, moving planning decisions out of the public realm.

With its national shift toward motorization industries, fascism eliminated local power over transportation planning. Increased centralization through the fragmentation of governmental units came to dominate transportation planning. The administration of the streetcar systems was left to the municipality; however, directives from the Reich forced service cuts and fare hikes. Highways were planned by the local section of GEZUVOR, a Reich-appointed and controlled planning arm. These various levels of transportation planning were coordinated by the regional state (*Reichhaltsteller*) and party (*Gauleiter*) organizations.

With the centralization and proliferation of governmental bureaucracies, local autonomy was destroyed, permitting motorization interests to dominate national and local planning and promote highways. Financing and budgeting at the national level were transferred from public to private transportation modes.

After World War II, the reconstituted highway lobby helped to formulate national transportation policy. In spite of a recovery during the fifties, urban mass transit did not regain its prewar levels until the seventies. Nationally, transportation planning concentrated upon building highways and subsidizing auto owners. However, the rise of the SPD to national power in the late sixties and early seventies, and the enormous traffic congestion in German cities, revived earlier commmitments to transit planning.

As local transit operations fell deeply into debt, the federal government intervened increasingly by the mid-sixties. New transit authorities with special taxation and borrowing authority were created as agencies separate from local government. By 1965, with SPD cabinet participation and control of the Transportation Ministry, gasoline tax revenues were spent more on transit than on highways. By 1976, two-thirds of all transportation subsidies went to transit. Simultaneously, the federal government increased highway construction and vested the coordination of transportation planning in regional transportation authorities (*Nahverkehrsverbände*) and state governments (Länder).[1]

The outcomes of this process for transit were ambiguous. Since transit subsidies were tied to the gas tax, reduced fuel consumption reduced tax revenues (a similar dilemma confronted the U.S. Highway Trust Fund in the seventies). Meanwhile, with rising energy costs, the expenses of serving an increased ridership grew. To cut expenditures, the federal government reduced transit investment by more than 3 billion deutsche marks in the 1976 budget (Bundesminister für Verkehr, 1976:11); highway construction continued unabated.

The rehabilitation of the highway lobby after the war, its penetration of various governmental levels and agencies, and its impact upon transportation policy and planning have been documented in the case of Frankfurt. Federal policies, regional government, and special transportation authorities overcame opposition to highway building and transit fare hikes and transformed Frankfurt into a corporate center.

## The United States

Before World War I, transportation was a local political issue under the sole authority of municipalities. Councilmen, mayors, neighborhood residents, and workers debated about franchise provisions, routes, fares, and public ownership. However, public and private actors continually subordinated public transit service to the interests of political machines, utility operators, and land speculators.

The fight for public control provoked a corporate response: the movement for urban reform and transit regulation. In averting municipalization of transit operations, the many new regulatory agencies provided a symbolic response to transportation conflicts. Effective, honest, and scientific management was the promised alternative to public ownership. Transit issues were shifted from the public arena to state and federal government agencies. This fragmentation of political authority insulated mass transit policy from public discussion, weakened local power, and gave corporate highway interests increased influence over policy formation.

Political fragmentation occurred in two ways: (1) through population dispersion and the creation of local governments competing with the metropolitan center and (2) through the establishment of regulatory activity and special governmental units concerning transportation.

Suburbanization prior to World War I was characterized by the dispersion of class, racial, and ethnic groups. As mobility studies of nineteenth-century cities show, geographical and social mobility were closely related. As older immigrant groups moved up the occupational ladder, they moved out of the city. By the turn of the century, these upwardly mobile groups opposed annexation and created independent local governments that competed with major urban centers for tax revenues and services.[2] These suburban governments demanded commuter service, competing with inner-city neighborhood demands for increased movement between residential and industrial areas. Private transit operators, connected with land and financial interests investing in suburbanization, responded more readily to the demands of the middle and upper classes. Route and fare preferences shifted away from the inner-city working-class neighborhoods – the bulk of the transit market. The creation of small but powerful suburban governments dissipated local autonomy.

In short, political fragmentation accompanied residential segregation by class. Interurban and commuter transportation service increased at the expense of intraurban circulation. Urban working-class groups mobilized to contest these new priorities and sought better transit service through public ownership. In response, regulation was imposed by state governments upon cities. Appointed regulatory bodies were a more accessible and stable means of control for corporate interests.

Long-distance travel routes increased; community-level, short-haul trips were ignored, and intraurban lines were abandoned. Access to the expanding regional transportation system was limited because regional and community-level transportation demands were not coordinated. Political fragmentation exacerbated this mismatch. Community transportation was usually confined to a single jurisdiction. As a result, local travel needs could not compete with the regional expansion goals of suburban communities and special governmental units. Inner-city travel needs suffered.

Other forms of government regulation also hurt public transportation. Building and zoning codes, traffic, and parking regulations all accommodated automobile traffic at the expense of transit speed and efficiency. As the case of Chicago demonstrates, the creation of special governmental units for bridge building, highway planning, and ultimately the coordination of all urban transportation served to promote highway transportation alone.[3] The creation of new governmental authorities further stymied popular demands and amplified corporation interests in highway transportation through governmental institutions.[4]

Federal business regulation also legitimized motorized transportation. As monopoly power increased the corporate car coalition of automobile, oil, rubber interests, production was diversified to include buses. As corporate strategists orchestrated the conversion to buses, transit performance declined. The failure to enforce antitrust regulations contributed to transit's decline. First, antitrust suits brought against the illegal elimination of rail transit failed because the government was unwilling to enforce judgments and reluctant to prosecute. Second, selective antitrust prosecution was directed at monopolistic behavior (price fixing, noncompetitive contracts, and the like) rather than the monopolistic structure of automobile, oil, and rubber corporations. Thus, although the government appeared to act, it really avoided attacking the fundamental sources of corporate domination over public transportation.[5] While the government's actions created the impression that it was limiting corporate interests, it was in fact promoting them.

Financial regulation, taxation, and traffic controls benefited private transportation at the expense of public carriers. After World War I, government involvement shifted to direct subsidization of highway transportation. This new state policy was cultivated between the world wars by the corporate powers that profited from it. By the start of World War II, corporate interests and highway technocrats had formed the highway lobby that has dominated transportation policy ever since.

Public investment in highways was not only the largest public works financing and construction project in history but also a successful political effort. Aside from the huge corporate investments in political campaigns and lobbies, highway financing created a mass highway constituency. Local, state, and federal highway officials, private construction firms, truckers, construction material suppliers, gasoline station owners, car insurance salesmen, and auto users created a political coalition that grew with each new highway appropriation. As we noted earlier, auto-related employment and factories were geographically distributed across the country.

Chicago provided a case study of how a city heavily committed to transit service succumbed to the national process of automobilization. Evidence of the economic and spatial changes in the city and of the methods by which corporate interests were translated into public policy at the local level have been examined. The continuity of corporate control over urban transportation planning, especially after the defeat of the popular opposition movement of the beginning of the century, is striking. In spite of the rise and fall of figures such as Yerkes and Insull, local corporate and financial power maintained ultimate control over transportation planning and subordinated it to their interests. Because of the pre–World War I defeat of the public ownership movement, fights against fare hikes and highway planning decisions were removed from the urban public agenda. As this happened, governmental power over transportation successively moved away from local control to state regulatory agencies, regional authorities, and federal highway planning agencies. Profit making through transit operation and investment, facilitation of housing and land speculation, downtown centralization, and the promotion of auto-related industries defined transportation politics in Chicago. Unlike Frankfurt, spatial functions of transportation often tempered, but never dominated, transit policy. This counterpoint of urban transportation as a planning instrument versus its use in serving narrow business interests occurs repeatedly in the two cases.

By the early sixties, urban mass transit faced extinction in the United States. More than 90 percent of the country's transit system were municipalized in a last-ditch effort to absorb growing deficits and maintain service. To contest the well-organized, well-financed highway lobby's transportation policy was considered politically impractical. Instead, public transportation officials opted for limited subsidization and were unwilling to call for a massive reinvestment in transit.

Since 1964, federal subsidization of public transportation increased to $3.4 billion, a fraction of the highway subsidy. Until 1976, subsidization was largely limited to capital expenditures for new equipment and construction. The long failure to support operating costs resulted in the construction of new and more costly systems with low ridership, while older, more heavily used systems received no subsidization at all. Past administrations subsidized transit construction, since it supported private industry; the upgrading of existing transit operations did not.

Limited subsidization failed to reverse the historic trend of declining transit use. Constrained by the public and private investment decisions of earlier decades, government has applied subsidies to highways at the expense of rail travel, "modernized" buses instead of light rail vehicles, and emphasized commuter travel instead of intraurban circulation.

Consequently, subsidized ridership has resulted in higher deficits. Abandoning rail routes and the promise of balanced transportation, federal subsidization of inefficient bus systems resulted in increased fiscal burdens and unpopular deficit financing. Ironically, buying buses through increased public debt supported monopoly corporations whose bus conversions had reduced transit in the first place.

Transit subsidies are a more visible source of public debt than highway construction. Transit deficits are a local budget item constantly in public view – the focus of labor negotiations, fare increases, and so forth. Thus, these expenditures are more readily perceived as a source of fiscal crisis than more hidden, although costly, highway deficits.

Reviewing the political and economic histories of Germany and the United States, we have seen how class and intraclass coalitions under historically determined conditions effect public transportation. Cross-sectional data on German and U.S. cities reveal the factors in transit decline – the interaction of politico-economic and ecological factors to reduce transit and promote highways. The historical evidence presented suggests how urban growth is influenced by special interest groups – class and corporate – who become involved in local and national politics. Corporate intervention occurs through these actors and organizations, whose profit-making interests are linked to the locational advantages gained by transit or highway development in the use of urban space. Depending upon the economic base of growth and its link to the national economy, the actions of these groups and individuals involve politically charged spatial conflicts that may be resolved through transportation planning. The evidence suggests that the organizations and activities of interest groups and state policymakers, and the development of modern capitalism, are causally connected and contribute to the decline of mass transit.

## Consequences of transit decline

This research into the macrosocial processes of urban transportation change informs us not only about the past but also about current policy debates. Every U.S. administration over the past forty years has celebrated the objective of safe, cheap, and efficient travel and assumed its achievement. As energy prices skyrocket, central cities continue to decline, the automobile industry faces market saturation and mass unemployment, and the rate of travel on major urban streets matches that of the pre-automobile era, the public finds it increasingly difficult to believe corporate, government, and transportation officials and researchers who state that our transportation system is the world's finest.[6] In focusing on the U.S. case, I would like to suggest the consequences of transit decline observed and explained in this study in three areas: (1) the fiscal crisis of mass transit; (2) the continuing highway versus mass transportation debate; and (3) the decline of transportation technology.

## Fiscal crisis

The financial decline of urban transportation is part of the larger fiscal crisis of U.S. cities, a crisis not merely of insufficient funds but of the city's ability to provide basic services and infrastructure for economic activity. Public and private budgets are both affected.

The initial subordination of transit construction and its use as an overhead investment for private developers prevented the even distribution of transit systems throughout urban regions. Capital flight from the transit industry after World War I represented disinvestment as public transportation became politicized in municipal government. This disinvestment and the flow of capital to the automobile sector were crucial in transit decline. Financial inanition in public transportation resulted in a vicious circle of rising fare, declining service, and declining ridership, which produced the fiscal collapse of most private transit systems by World War II. The establishment of receiverships and their dissolution through deficit-financed municipalization meant that from the beginning, public transit was overshadowed by past debt that gave lending institutions financal veto power over transit planning. Corporate control shifted from ownership to financial control. Banks added antitrust covenants to authority bonds, prohibiting their use for new rail construction.[7]

Ultimately, the tie-in arrangements involving auto, oil, and rubber manufactures and transit operating firms resulted in raised costs, reduced operating efficiency, and increased equipment and maintenance-related debt that drove public transit firms into permanent fiscal crisis.

Consequently, transportation costs were effectively socialized. Public rather than private investment became responsible for developing transportation infrastructure. Use of private automobiles, rather than investments in mass transit, became the thrust of transportation change. Ideologically, transportation was redefined as a private rather than a public issue. The role of the public budget was to accommodate private decisions. As transportation was removed from the public sphere, political mobilization was prevented; private transportation excluded public participation. By individualizing transportation and isolating competing modes, the range of choices for transportation policy was narrowed and dominated more easily by technocrats and corporations. The organization of transportation policy through political fragmentation and centralization exacerbated this trend and reinforced the redistribution of population within urban regions, making demobilization over transportation issues complete.

The results for consumers, as for taxpayers, are worth considering. With the decline of mass transit, personal and public costs of transportation have more than tripled in the past seventy years (from 5.1 percent of personal expenditures in 1909 to 17.2 percent in 1979) (U.S. Bureau of Census, *Historical Statistics of the United States*, 1976, Part 1:316–20; U.S Bureau of Census, *Statistical Abstracts of the United States*, 1979:Table 717, 444; Fuller, 1982:112–22).[8] Transportation became increasingly a private consumption item, with rising auto purchase, operation, and maintenance costs.

Moreover, public subsidy and investment policies have worsened steadily the fiscal crisis of local, state, and federal governments in transportation. Direct federal expenditures for the national highway program are currently between $200 and $300 billion; highway lobbyist Peter Koltnow, former president of the Highway Users for Safety and Mobility and currently head of the National Transportation Research Board, estimates that it will take more than that amount to maintain the interstate system and a similar level of funding for primary and secondary routes by 1990.[9] Since World War II, state and local highway debt has risen from $3.6 billion to $24 billion (*Historical Statistics of the United States*, 1976:Table 1006, 607).

Historically, the highway lobby has argued that money

spent on highways is a public investment, whereas that spent on public transportation is a costly subsidy. This interesting circumlocution ignores the general imbalance of modal subsidies: $15.8 billion for airways and airports compared to $1.3 billion for Amtrak in 1978; $216 billion for highways compared to $2.5 billion for public transportation. Overemphasis on highways causes many hidden fiscal burdens as well – police and safety services, local road construction and maintenance, and snow removal, to name only a few. In 1973, the Federal Highway Administration conservatively estimated that 30 percent ($7 billion in that fiscal year) of direct highway expenses were not covered by highway user revenues or tolls (U.S. Federal Highway Administration, 1975:IX–59). This estimate did not include indirect costs of auto accidents, energy waste, environmental damage, and urban sprawl. Nor does it cover the costs of expanded social services, declining urban taxes, and the abandonment of real estate that accompany low-density land use.

As public transit operations increased service during the sixties, deficit financing resulted in a growing antagonism between the operating authorities and the public faced with rising taxes and fares. Federal transit subsidies that were too little, too late were ineffective in reversing transit decline. At this writing, the Reagan administation proposes to phase out all operating subsidies (now about 15.7 percent of transit budgets) by 1984, eliminate new rail construction, and reduce capital expenditures between 15 and 30 percent. These proposals represent a historical watershed in the abandonment of mass transit. With reduced federal subsidies, public transit operating systems have raised their fares by 19 percent in the past year alone (American Public Transit Association, 1982). Although the systematic evidence is not yet in, local newspapers are reporting service, maintenance, and new capital expenditure cuts. Ridership continues to fall. The same conditions that precipitated the collapse of privately owned transit companies before World War II – lack of capital, reduced maintenance and modernization, rising fares, and declining ridership – now threaten the surviving public systems.

*Highways or mass transit: the future of urban
transportation policy*

As highway dependency grew, so did disillusionment with its
promise. Although motorization of urban transportation was
supposed to increase access to land by decreasing travel time,
it created instead land use patterns that imposed new spatial
limits on mobility. The average time required to travel to
work, which comprises much urban travel, remains the same
in spite of increasingly fast cars. Where public transit is largely
absent, the average travel time to work has increased. Moreover, the average blue-collar worker and the working poor,
consisting largely of minority populations, now take longer to
travel to work than they did after World War II. Projections
show average travel time to work increasing 15 to 20 percent
by the year 2000. Traffic congestion, parking costs and availability, and increased travel distances provide few transportation benefits. Extensive research concerning highways reveals
that new construction designed to relieve congestion failed to
do so.[10]

Concern over energy and natural resource depletion has also
provoked some rethinking of the highway solution. The motor
vehicle industry alone consumes a substantial amount of the
steel, aluminum, lead, iron, rubber, and zinc produced in the
United States.[11] Since auto production and profits are based
largely upon obsolescense (annual style changes and few years
of use), resource depletion has increased. The Environmental
Protection Agency indicates that resource reserves necessary
for current levels of auto production will dissipate by the year
2000 (Taebel and Cornhels, 1977:128). Costlier extraction processes and new technologies promise to escalate travel costs
further. Transportation's share of petroleum consumption has
increased to more than 50 percent since World War II. Cars,
trucks, and buses consume 80 percent of the gasoline used in
transportation – a tripling of use since 1950 (Office of Technology Assessment, 1975:17–24). In Western European countries,
only 25 to 30 percent of petroleum is used for transportation
because of more mass transit and more fuel-efficient cars, leading to lower per capita energy requirements than in the United

States.[12] As fuel economies declined, autos became the least energy efficient of all transportation modes for the daily journey to work (American Public Transit Association, 1974; Commoner, 1975:4–5; Office of Technology Assessment, 1975:21). Highways also used about twice as much energy in right-of-way construction as rail roadbeds.

Attempts to regulate highway vehicle fuel consumption have proved ineffective. If automobiles now receive better gas mileage than in the past, consumers also drive more. The media faults drivers for their travel behavior, but blaming the victim neither helps us understand the issues nor resolves the problems even in questions of urban transportation. Although mileage efficiency improves, consumers increasingly have more miles to travel because of land use patterns and increasing labor force participation of women. Increased highway construction has increased the number of places accessible solely by car.[13]

Although consumers have fought for seat belts, safer construction, and the like, the safety of urban travel has declined along with public transportation. Traffic accidents are a major cause of mortality and disability. Since mortality increased with decreasing auto weight and increased travel distance, the reduction of car weight and the increase in fuel efficiency ("downsizing") have resulted in increased mortality. Environmental safety, as measured by noise and air pollution, have been compromised by imbalanced transportation policy.[14]

The problems of safety, cost, and efficiency of highway dependency have been highlighted in the past decade's controversies over highways and mass transit. Political changes have also contributed to policy reconsiderations. Increased resistance to highway construction by a coalition of working-class whites and blacks whose neighborhoods were threatened and by middle-class whites whose sensibilities were offended by the steady bulldozing of their cities halted highway construction in some cities, beginning in San Francisco in 1965. Also, recent administrations have sought to replace earlier social welfare policies with an urban policy that would more directly benefit suburban commuters and their corporate employers. This policy would satisfy a conservative electorate while symbolically addressing urban problems. Urban transportation was, in the early seventies, a perfect centerpiece for a corporate-oriented urban policy.

To illustrate this shift in transportation policy and to understand its abandonment in the early eighties, the controversy over the Highway Trust Fund and rail versus bus transit modes should be considered.

*The Highway Trust Fund controversy.* For seventeen years, the Highway Trust Fund was the impenetrable coffer of the highway lobby. Established during the fifties, the Trust Fund guaranteed continued highway construction irrespective of economic conditions, transportation needs, and other financial priorities of government. During the late sixties, the Highway Trust Fund became a target of highway protest. It also came under attack by state and federal officials who sought greater flexibility in spending highway revenues. In 1968 twenty-eight states had approved the diversion of highway users' taxes for everything from welfare payments to mosquito control. Of $8.2 billion of state Highway Trust Funds used for purposes other than highway construction, only $80 million went to nonhighway transportation uses (*State Government News*, May 1970). State-level highway fund raids resulted from increased fiscal debt, not a commitment to new transportation policies.

Increasingly, some business leaders protested against the car coalition orthodoxy that corporate needs could be served only by the automobile. To maintain cities as centers of corporate administration and coordination, the problem of traffic congestion had to be solved. Within a few short months in 1971, support for transit alternatives began to be expressed. On September 23, President Richard Nixon announced before the Detroit Economic Club that "we cannot be rigid with regard to the Highway Trust Fund." That same year, the Highway Advisory Council of the American Road Builders Association advised support for a unified transportation trust fund, making the following tactical argument: "We feel it is in the cards that some modifications of the trust fund are coming up.

Consequently, we felt that we ought to take the lead in supporting a transportation trust fund."[15]

The corporate car coalition was split over the Highway Trust Fund controversy. GM, Exxon, Gulf, and the small highway contractors and suppliers opposed the pro-diversion proposals supported by Ford, Atlantic Richfield, Mobil Oil, and planning groups (e.g., the Regional Planning Association).[16] The hardline group sought unhindered highway construction. More moderate corporate elements argued for greater flexibility. The only way that corporations could legitimize their participation in mass-transit planning was to facilitate its financing through minor Trust Fund diversions. Those diversions would be limited by the federal government to transit construction costs only in large corporate metropolitan centers, leaving the rest of the country dependent upon highways.

An unlikely coalition including environmental groups (represented by the Highway Action Coalition), the Nixon administration, and moderate corporate leaders finally won congressional approval of limited Trust Fund diversions in 1973. Similar actions followed in those remaining state funds that had not heretofore permitted diversions.[17]

For mass-transit supporters, the victory was short-lived. The following year, the highway lobby succeeded in adding legislative provisions that permitted trust fund diversions to go to road repair rather than mass transit. Later congressional decisions allowed money eliminated from one interstate highway segment to be substituted for another segment elsewhere.

Little of the money potentially available for urban mass transit projects was used for that purpose. Of the $1.5 billion made available during the 1974–5 fiscal year, only $140 million was transferred to mass transit. Urban Mass Transportation Administration (UMTA) officials blamed this failure upon the "institutional bias" of city and state governments against public transportation (*Mass Transit*, May 1975). A 1977 study by the controller general explained that so little was spent on urban transportation because the highway lobby had managed to leave intact federal funding formulas that made highways less costly to state and local governments. This was accomplished by increasing the percentage of federal assistance for highways (in matching funds) over that for mass transit (Controller General of the United States, 18 March 1977).[18]

Transportation planning remained linked to road building. Nonlocal governmental units were still largely responsible for initiating all projects, and planners in those agencies had little expertise in transit planning.[19] Also, state governments delayed converting their highway departments to more general transportation planning needs; only seventeen states complied with federal directives to broaden transportation planning beyond highway modes.[20]

Although the Department of Transportation (DOT) was organized in 1967 to reduce the charge of federal highway bias by the Bureau of Public Roads, the Federal Highway Administration (FHWA) continues to dominate staff and funding within the department. Although UMTA appropriations have tripled in the past decade, they do not approach the spending level of the FHWA. Recent proposals to create a Surface Transportation Administration raised the suspicion that merging the FHWA and the UMTA would subordinate mass transit interests to an existing highway bureaucracy.[21]

The DOT *National Transportation Report* estimated that $530 billion would be spent on transportation by 1990, with 81 percent of that amount on highways (Demkovich, 1975:616). In terms of public investment, highways have not suffered from the limited diversions to mass transit. Current highway legislation has committed $10.2 billion annually for highway building, only $8.2 billion of which will come from trust fund receipts. Along with liabilities of $6.9 billion, this requires that $15 billion be paid from future revenues. Given this shortfall, pressures of increased gasoline taxes and reduced transit funding have occurred (*New York Times*, June 16, 1982).

Meanwhile, highway construction continues unabated. In 1978, highway construction was up 19.8 percent over the previous year.[22] Given guaranteed government contracts and lack of competition, the increasingly concentrated highway construction industry has little incentive to maintain lower costs, since the Highway Trust Fund is generally immune to budgetary politics.

## Conclusion

Despite changing circumstances requiring a more diversified and balanced transportation system, the highway lobby's dominance remains intact. The compromise over Highway Trust Fund diversions and a simultaneous increase in highway spending limited transit projects to a few major cities. Local transportation activists were satisfied by the symbolic raiding of the Highway Trust Fund. Local officials felt that success had been achieved simply through the criticism of highways, rather than by extended fight for transportation alternatives. They were unable to recognize the less perceptible shifts in corporate state policy, organization, and planning that have aborted a rebirth of mass transportation. With the demobilization of forces that encouraged transit in the seventies, the further abandonment of mass transit now proceeds.

*Bus versus rail transit: A technical controversy?* Throughout the seventies, urban rail transit was attacked in a series of studies (Congressional Budget Office, 1977; General Motors Corporation, 1979; National Transportation Policy Study Commission, 1979).[23] The Carter administration dismissed urban rail systems as "overdesigned," reduced Amtrak routes by nearly 43 percent, and partially dismantled the Conrail system. The Reagan administration, at this writing, seeks an additional 30 percent cut in the Amtrak budget (eliminating rail passenger service except for the Northeast corridor), a 60 percent decrease in urban rail capital expenditures, and elimination of any new route construction and existing operating subsidies (*Wall Street Journal*, March 20, 1977; *New York Times*, February 7, 1982; *Mass Transit*, February 1982).

Why is rail transit under siege? As in the rail/highway debates of earlier years, the superiority of motorized transportation over rail modes is broadly cited to support further highway construction. This reincarnation of the rail/bus debate heated up when transportation policy was reconsidered in the early seventies. Highway opposition movements and the emerging energy crisis renewed interest in and support for rail transit. Victories in local referenda supporting mass transit have outnumbered defeats in recent years.[24]

201

Because older producers of rail transit equipment disappeared with the advent of motorization, many aerospace firms saw rail transit as a possible path of industrial conversion after the Vietnam War. These firms became transit lobbyists.[25] However, these new entrants (e.g., Boeing and Rohr) into the transportation equipment market were no match politically for the more established highway lobby.

Business interest in rail transit was concentrated in growing corporate centers such as Los Angeles, San Francisco, Miami, Washington, D.C., and Atlanta. In these cities, local businesses dependent upon economic growth and increasing the valuation of declining central city properties joined with locally headquartered corporations to push for regional commuter rail systems that would revitalize urban centers and stimulate suburban growth (Adler, 1980). The creation of regional corporate centers required a rationalized urban land market made possible with fixed rail corridors. Growth locations and predictable land values would replace the helterskelter land use patterns of the automobile age. The coordinated development of land use and transportation facilities was advocated by city planners in fast-growing cities as a way to maximize their locational advantages (Zwerling, 1974; Adler, 1980).

However, there was no necessary coincidence between public support for mass transit and corporate needs for coordinated land use and transit corridor development. New rail transit planning was vested in regional authorities (e.g., Bay Area Regional Transit, Metropolitan Atlanta Regional Transit Authority, Washington Metropolitan Transit Authority) that served suburban commuters and corporate urban planners. Moreover, central-city or lower-class suburban dwellers not directly served by transit plans often resisted the burden of financing those systems through regressive sales and property taxes. In Houston, Los Angeles, and Seattle, rail transit proposals were defeated.

The rail systems that were constructed often failed to achieve the promised reduction of auto traffic. Since they were planned as commuter rail rather than mass-transit systems, they provided an alternative only to a limited segment of the population–upper-income commuters, who were likely to use their automobiles anyway (Webber, 1976). Confronted by continued federal motorization policies, local deficit spending grew in transit.

Cost, planning, and service limitations do not account for the negligible role of rail transit; corporate strategy does. Automobile and oil companies, presenting themselves as supporters of mass transportation, have promoted bus systems.[26] As one of the great highway builders, Robert Moses, exclaimed: "We are a motorized civilization . . . buses? More and more buses, not rail, are needed to meet the future needs of mass transit" (*Mass Transit*, April 1977:20).

Since 1971, GM has utilized government research funds to develop a bus of advanced design to rival the one earlier specified by government mandate, the Transbus. In an attempt to elimimate bus competition and circumvent DOT design specifications, GM in 1977 assembled a consortium of transit system buyers who agreed to contract specifications that only GM could meet.[27] Although these contracts violated antitrust and urban mass transportation laws and were contested in court, they were finally approved by the U.S. District Court in Houston. This drove American General, a remaining GM competitor, out of the bus market.

Transportation policy research uncritically supports bus systems. The corporate car coalition has monitored this research through government advisory panels.[28] The Office of Technology Assessment's $1.4 million report on the future of the automobile studiously avoided consideration of rail alternatives. The National Transportation Policy Study Commission, another congressional effort, was dominated from its inception by anti-rail commissioners and congressmen. GM, with the assistance of the National League of Cities, completed a comprehensive survey of public transportation research, concluding that bus systems and "people mover systems" (which compete with pedestrians rather than cars) are the only reasonable investment opportunities for public transportation.

The GM argument has been echoed in ensuing debates over public transportation. Both President Carter and Office of Management and Budget Director David Stockman have cited these cost–benefit studies to argue for transit budget cuts. However, this research is flawed because of the limited and selective data upon which its analysis is based. Projecting from largely pre-energy crisis ridership data, GM claims that public transportation will always account for only a small proportion of total urban trips (between 5 and 7.5 percent). Since low levels of government spending on public transportation are anticipated, buses are projected as the means of increasing transit use. The assumption is also made that transit ridership is limited to the poor, elderly, and handicapped. In GM's view, the lack of competition between public and private transportation is the result of demand by very different markets, and government expenditure on public transportation would interfere with market forces. Finally, utilizing questionable methods[29] of cost estimation, GM projects higher operating and energy costs for rail than for bus systems. As we have seen, these estimates belie actual operating data (St. Clair, 1981).

Faulty ridership extrapolations and cost estimations conveniently mask the concrete experience of other countries and U.S. cities that have encouraged balanced transportation. Since 1973, German, Swedish, French, and Canadian cities have inaugurated new suburban and regional rail systems as a response to the energy crisis, integrating them with expanded bus service along appropriate routes. Although these systems require massive infrastructural investment, they have increased the productivity of the transportation system as a whole and have reduced oil-generated balance of payments deficits (Commoner, 1975:Tables 11 and 13; Pisarski and de Terra, 1975; Organization for Economic Cooperation and Development, 1982). Other benefits included increased ridership, substantial reduction in city travel times, traffic safety increases, rising land valuations and employment multipliers in the regional economy, and environmental improvement (*Mass Transit*, July 1982:6, March 1982:12–13; Organization for Economic Cooperation and Development, 1978). In Germany, the proportion of public transportation travel increased to 19 percent for the country as a whole and up to 60 percent in major cities between 1973 and 1978. The argument that separate, noncompetitive transportation markets exists is hardly supported by such evidence, and it perpetuates a system of separate and unequal transportation access (American Public Transport Association, 1977:16–17).

The argument of bus superiority in energy conservation defies comparative experience. European transportation responses to the 1973–4 oil embargo included rail transit extensions to reduce dependency on autos and oil (Pisarski and de Terra, 1975; OECD, 1982). Energy savings result from land use patterns encouraged by rail transit (Stokes, 1977:16). Finally, in those few U.S. cities where rail transit survived, weekly gasoline consumption is about half that of nonrail cities (Stokes, 1977:17). Since the new GM-dominated bus fleet is less fuel efficient than earlier buses (*Wall Street Journal*, June 7, 1982), and since auto-generated gasoline consumption is rising, the role of rail transit should not be dismissed.

The car coalition's version of future public transportation limits options to bus systems that do not compete with the automobile market. If highways and rails are defined as mutually exclusive modes of transportation, public policy options are limited.[30] The planning issue is not buses *or* rail, but how to strike an optimal balance among a variety of modes, public and private, compatible with the widely varying physical forms of U.S. cities. The bus strategy has proved less the result of the asserted technical superiority of buses than another step toward transit abandonment. Unwilling to compromise their unchallenged control over ground transportation, and without competition from rail producers, the auto–oil–rubber complex has once again defined the national transportation agenda.

## The decline of public transportation technology

Corporate-directed transportation has not only destroyed transportation possibilities in the past but narrows future ones as well. Nowhere is this more apparent than in the devolution of public transportation technology. As in other areas of the economy, the patterns of capital investment in transportation left the United States with the most technologically backward and least efficient transportation system in the industrialized world, characterized by declines in investment, employment, cost efficiency, and productivity.[31] The absence of research, development, and technological innovation in rail car, roadbed, and tunnel construction has raised total transportation costs.

The decline of public transportation technology results from the interaction of (1) corporate failures in public transportation development, (2) political fragmentation and the failure of government regulatory agencies to stimulate technological innovation, and (3) government investment policies preserving existing transportation technologies.

For example, bus technology has been controlled almost exclusively by the monopoly power of GM (which has about 80 percent of the U.S. bus market). U.S. bus technology has fallen considerably behind its European counterparts, which introduced greater fuel efficiency, articulated buses, and newer suspension systems more than a decade before RTS-II was put into operation.

By putting the RTS-II into production prior to the release of federally approved standardized specifications, GM edged out all competitors. The supposed innovations of the RTS-II are questionable; some have referred to it as GM's old bus with more glass. The new suspension system, interior design, and construction are regularly criticized by transit operators. The small seating capacity, inflexible climate control system, additional weight, and defects in suspension and brake systems have led to higher operating and maintenance costs. The fuel efficiency is measurably less than that of older buses, and the purchase cost is about 50 percent higher.[32]

But if GM's bus innovation efforts are questionable, rail innovations are a disaster. With concrete highways covering many of the old rail rights-of-way, the cost of constructing new rail corridors is astronomical. In those few areas where old corridors have been preserved (San Diego, San Francisco, and Connecticut), the expense of purchasing the rights-of-way is also high. With roadbed construction and maintenance a declining occupation in the United States, labor training and management costs of roadbed construction are higher here than in other countries.

The electrical generating systems necessary for rail transit are in disrepair. When San Francisco recently assessed the capacity for its streetcar system, city consultants found that most of the generators, consisting of rotating machinery and mercury rectifiers, had been obsolete before the Depression.

Ironically, in the country where Richard Spague discovered electrical traction, that technology has not simply stagnated but disappeared. Designing the new San Francisco streetcar system, one city official reported, "there are not enough qualified engineers who work on this anymore." Electricians working on the project found that working with high-voltage direct current took considerably longer than in earlier days when traction construction was commonplace. Most signal and car-carried control systems for the new San Francisco streetcars had to be imported from Sweden and West Germany.

Similar problems exist for heavy-rail commuter and subway construction. Because of the lack of underground construction technology, tunneling costs in the United States are $140–160 million a mile as opposed to $6 million a mile in England. The lack of technological innovation, trained labor, and efficient management and labor practices have been cited by the DOT for these immense differences in construction costs.[33]

The quality of rail car equipment has also declined. Budd, now a subsidiary of Germany's Thyssen Steel, is the sole rail equipment producer in the United States. For a brief, unsuccessful period, Boeing Vetrol went from building Chinook helicopters to designing streetcars; Rohr Industries converted their jet fighter and missile production to subway car construction for the BART system.

Although such peacetime conversion was laudable, the direct application of high-powered military technology to rail transit by Boeing and Rohr was a disaster. As a Massachusetts Bay Transit Administration (MBTA) operations director noted, the resulting vehicles were far too complicated for transit use: "They were designed during the time when we all held the view that technology would save us all. So everything was redesigned. Nothing was kept from the old cars, even if it worked" (Hackney, 1978:8). In the new rail vehicles, wiring circuitry, drive control panels, generators, and door systems were constantly inoperative due to inappropriate design.

Government procurement policies worsened equipment problems. Each local governmental unit (usually a regional planning body) was able to specify options for rail supplies, which resulted in a complete lack of standardization. With each rail car and control system custom made, the cost savings necessary for rail industry development in the seventies were absent. The costs of new rail systems were exorbitant for all but the wealthiest cities (e.g., Washington, Atlanta, San Francisco). Also, the lack of local traffic regulations to facilitate higher-speed transit discouraged technological innovations for faster rail equipment. The lack of standardization also prohibited the future integration of rail systems. For example, Baltimore and Washington rail cars will not fit in each other's tracks or tunnels. Eventually, the DOT was convinced to mandate standardized specifications, but it failed to withhold capital grants from cities that failed to comply. Consequently, manufacturers who had retooled their plants to meet new standarized specifications were left without a market.[34]

Public investment policies bound transportation technology to the status quo. DOT investments in technological innovations have been anti-rail. Although $173 million was spent in research and development on buses and new automated pedestrian travel modes that do not compete with highway traffic (e.g., accelerated walkways and people movers), only about $40 million was spent on rail development (U.S. Department of Transportation, 1976). Multimillion-dollar research and development boondoggles abounded on such esoterica as the 300-mph Tracked Air Cushion Vehicle and the Gravity Vacuum Tube train, while subways and commuter rail vehicles could not maintain an average speed of 30 mph. More importantly, the combined UMTA research budget for all public modes was only a fraction of the billions spent on automotive and highway development.

The technological devolution of public transportation is representative of a pattern increasingly common in U.S. industry – the decline of productive technology.[35] Manufacturing not directly linked to the growth of the auto–oil–rubber coalition was not funded over the past decade. Without capital, technical capabilities faded that might have enhanced the viability of mass transit.

What has declined is not simply technical expertise but the industrial capacity to respond to changing conditions in politics, the economy, and the environment.

The costs of expenditure cuts in mass transit are reflected not only in reduced transportation productivity but in labor productivity in the urban system as a whole. The Federal Reserve Bank recently estimated the lost work time directly related to increased travel time and transit service deterioration (*Business Week*, March 21, 1981). "Cost savings" of budgetary cuts in preventive road and rail maintenance have exploded infrastructure repair costs and shortened the life of capital equipment.

Because of their overdependence upon highway travel in transportation planning, the industrial capacity of transportation suppliers to respond to changing market circumstances declined. United States rail suppliers have lost enormous national and international sales to foreign competitors constructing transit systems in the industrialized and developing world. Meanwhile, automobile corporations, protected from technological competition by other transportation modes, became less flexible in meeting international competition in the domestic and world markets.

With manufacturing capacity overdeveloped to change automobile styles annually, the ability to make more substantial improvements in transportation has withered. Public transportation remains an underdeveloped island in an overspecialized transportation industry dominated by monopoly firms controlling all forms of ground transportation. Moreover, the lead time necessary for developing a public transportation industry and constructing a balanced, efficient, and environmentally sound transportation system is rapidly running out. The long-term debts of a transportation system that promoted short-run corporate profits are now coming due.

## Transportation planning for whom?

The never-ending urban crisis, the failure of bureaucratic planning solutions, and the near ruin of public infrastructure, highways, and transit alike force a rethinking of transportation policy. If the past creates the present, the hope of this study is that observation of the past may help change the evaluation of present and future circumstances. Urban transportation has reached an abrupt dead end in the United States. We are begining to sense the wall at the end of the tunnel. There is only one way out of a dead end. Looking backward can always be considered romantic or utopian, but in the case of urban transportation, nothing is more impractical than perpetuating the status quo at a higher cost in the face of the energy, employment, and economic limits that our cities face. There are no quick fixes for urban transportation; offered here are only a few directional signposts for a retreat from obsolescence.

Political centralization and economic concentration are the core processes of twentieth-century social organization; they are also its undoing. Centralized planning policies, drained of democratic participation, have promoted monopoly economic power. Both political and economic bureaucracies, separately and together, have lost the flexibility of more adaptable, competitive, and democratic organizational forms to cope with drastically changed urban economic conditions. The reconstruction of mass transit and the cities it serves faces three areas of policy challenge: (1) bureaucratic planning centralization, (2) public investment and subsidy policy, and (3) the shared monopolization of the ground transportation industry.

The largest planning bureaucracy of the modern state was created by federal, state, and local highway building. After the defeat of urban populism, transportation came to be defined as a purely technical problem that only experts could solve; public participation was accordingly excluded. The technical definition of urban transportation also dominated the appointed, corporate-directed regional planning authorities and resulted in large, costly, and ambitious transportation proposals. Addressing private development (central business district renewal or suburban commuting) and corporate goals in isolation from more general travel needs, new rail systems failed to tap the greatest source of ridership. The greatest economic benefits of new infrastructural investment were never realized.

The pitfalls of centralized bureaucratic planning can be avoided by decentralization. Currently, localities enforce national transportation policies. Instead, they should be empowered to plan their own systems, integrated at a regional level. Rather than following suburban sprawl, local planning could stabilize and link urban, suburban, and polycentric travel. National transportation agencies should serve as a technical and information resource for elected neighborhood and metropolitan planning boards, rather than providing preordained plans. Experiments in some U.S. cities (e.g., San Diego, Madison, and Portland), as well as in Italy and France, indicate that increases in ridership, auto travel speeds, cost effectiveness, and environmental quality have resulted.[36] The democratic decentralization of transportation planning would allow consumers to become the planners rather than the planned. This is quite different from current "New Federalism" proposals, which are masking massive public disinvestment and abandonment of transit.

Economic concentration in the ground transportation industry and its resulting imbalance can be eliminated by introducing competition between travel modes and their supplier industries. Both the supply and operating transit industries require effective governmental intervention and coordination. Public investment and economic policy should interact to revive transportation markets. During the most recent oil crisis, whose repetition can safely be predicted, the rising demand for public transportation equipment remained unmet, furthering breakdowns and productivity losses in transit services (*New York Times*, October 28, 1979). Productive capacity atrophied under monopoly control. Public subsidization of research and development could create many benfits in enhanced productivity and employment. As part of a general reindustrialization effort, abandoned and underutilized plant, equipment, and labor could rebuild the transportation industry and inject new competition into a currently monopolized market.[37]

Heretofore, transportation has been financed through sales

and property taxes, deficit spending, and highway trust funds. These fiscal instruments are as regressive as they are overused, resulting in negative income distribution impacts and insulation from public control and market forces. Financing highways through designated rather than general revenues has prevented flexible planning, sheltered highway planners from fiscal pressures, and satisfied large corporate interests in preventing transit viability. Robbing future revenues through highway and transit deficit spending to pay for past mistakes is neither viable nor responsible.

Public transit can be financed through a widely accepted although underutilized principle of public finance: Public infrastructural investment in the urban transportation industry is a social expenditure with many private benefits: enhanced value of real estate close to transit corridors; publicly subsidized markets and overhead for auto, oil, and rubber product revenues; increased savings in travel time and costs by auto drivers or commercial goods transport through congestion relief; and wage subsidies to private employers through low transit fares. The regressive edge of current deficit financing can be removed. San Francisco is experimenting with special assessment districts rather than property taxes to finance transit improvements. New York and Connecticut have tried, albeit unsuccessfully due to the lack of federal legislation, to tax gross oil company receipts. France and Italy both tax large employers for the benefits of low-cost transit. Such taxes are neither expropriatory nor unjustified, but reflect the need for beneficiaries to pay their fair share of public costs. The current focus on user taxes ignores the free ride that nonusers get from infrastructural investment.

Indirect public savings are also worth considering. Transportation research indicates that transit's decline was not merely a physical but also a social barrier to income and employment mobility. Decent transit is an incentive for social participation rather than isolation, giving workers, unemployed persons, women, and youth entering the labor force access to employment opportunities.[38] Urban services for the elderly and children could also improve. These changes could reduce overall social welfare expenditures.

But innovative public financing or decentralized planning alone will not address the fundamental problem revealed in this research – the political and economic power of large corporations. New subsidies creating a demand for transit equipment and services would not ensure a supply as long as production remains under monopoly control. Vigorous antitrust enforcement is a thing of the past, yet it must be restored to break the ties that bind industrial groups. No transportation policy will succeed unless it considers the network of automobile and oil firms in the ground transportation industry.

Interlocks, informal association, and collaboration between automobile, oil, and rubber firms should be made illegal. Rigorous enforcement of antitrust laws and further enabling legislation to control corporations and force them to disclose legally binding information about public impacts of their private decisions would contribute to transit's rebirth.

The constituency for these changes is increasingly clear as major industries decline, consumers suffer, and small businesses fail. Consumer boycotts against monopoly firms occur more frequently, and trade union, consumer, and business calls for industrial policy grow. If past hopes for an accessible and participatory city are to be harbingers of future urban life, new structures of politics and economics await design.

Urban congestion, gas station lines, crumbling bridges, abandoned neighborhoods, and isolated suburbs are part of what our cities have become. The issue facing urban transportation policy is how to bridge the gap between city and town, suburb and countryside, not to see which wins on a demographic scorecard. Balanced transportation systems serving cars *and* trains, buses *and* streetcars can provide the links between our residences and our workplaces. If, however, we continue to isolate our living from our work, the spatial gaps in our social lives will diminish our cities and our lives within them.

# Statistical appendix

Tables 1 and 2 list the thirty German cities included in the statistical analysis and the thirty-one U.S. units used. In order to construct comparative data for 1900 and 1970, only that subset of the most important German cities in 1900 that survived in the Federal Republic of Germany after World War II was included. The unit of analysis for those 1900 and 1970 cities is the *Gemeinde*. All data was coded directly from statistical volumes mentioned in Tables 3 and 4 concerning the operationalization of the measures. All of the data for the German cities are extracted from relevant German census information and data reported by local governments to the *Deutsche Städtag* (German League of Cities). Corporate location data for 1900 were provided by Professor Juergen Kocka and Hannes Siegrist from the unpublished study of the 100 largest business enterprises in late-nineteenth and early-twentieth-century Germany. Corporate data for 1970 were coded from the directory of top 500 German industrial corporations (Schmacke ed., 1972).

For the United States and Germany, data were collected and organized as panel data for 1900 and 1970 (Madala, 1977; Bielby and Hauser 1977). The unit of analysis for the United States for 1900 is the urban center, which was an early census unit that included the central city and immediately adjacent suburbs and communities. Thus it is comparable to the 1970 unit of analysis, the urbanized area. To compare the census definitions of urban center and urbanized area, see U.S. Bureau of the Census (1905: 24; 1972). Urban centers included cities with a core population of 50,000, and their immediately adjacent suburbs gave them a population of more than 100,000. The thirty-one urban centers defined by the U.S. Bureau of Census had adequate data gathered on public transportation. By 1907, the Census Bureau reported public transportation data only by geographical division and not by urban unit. The variables were operationalized in the order mentioned in Tables 3 and 4. Ridership data were recorded from the U.S. Census of Street Railways and Electrical Railways (1905) and the U.S. Department of Transportation National Transportation Survey (1972); additional data were provided to the author by the American Transport Association (1971). Tables 5 and 6 provide the descriptive statistics for the aforementioned variables. Tables 7–10 include the correlation matrices for the different variables in both sets of cities for 1900 and 1970. Tables 11–20 include the regression models of the data

214

discussed. The urbanization index was constructed by computing an orthogonally rotated factor matrix for the above variables. Factor weight for those variables is converted into a factor score by multiplying these coefficients by the standardized value of each city and adding the products of that operation. This procedure is described in Kim (1978). The rotated and factor matrices for these operations are presented in Tables 21–25.

The models that confirm the regression analysis for earlier equations by taking into account residual disturbances indicated by the pre–World War I data and assumptions about the distribution of independent variables, using change scores as dependant variables, are presented in Tables 26–28. Table 29 summarizes the extent of rail transit abandonment.

# Statistical appendix

### Table 1. *30 German cities included in statistical analysis*[a]

| | |
|---|---|
| Aachen | Freiburg |
| Augsburg | M-Gladbach |
| Berlin | Hamburg |
| Bochum | Hannover |
| Braunschweig | Karlsruhe |
| Bremen | Kiel |
| Cassel | Lubeck |
| Cologne | Mainz |
| Crefeld | Mannheim |
| Darmstadt | Munich |
| Dortmund | Munster |
| Dusseldorf | Nurnberg |
| Duisberg | Stuttgart |
| Essen | Wiesbaden |
| Frankfurt am Main | Wurzburg |

[a]In order to construct comparative data for 1900 and 1970, only that subset of top fifty-five cities in 1900 that survived in the Federal Republic were included in the analysis.

## Table 2. *31 U.S. urban units used in statistical analyses*

Albany–Schenectady–Troy, New York
Baltimore, Maryland
Boston, Massachusetts
Buffalo, New York
Chicago, Illinois–northwestern Indiana
Cincinnati, Ohio–Kentucky–Indiana
Cleveland, Ohio
Columbus, Ohio
Denver, Colorado
Detroit, Michigan
Indianapolis, Indiana
Kansas City, Missouri–Kansas
Los Angeles–Long Beach, California
Louisville, Kentucky–Indiana
Memphis, Tennessee–Mississippi
Milwaukee, Wisconsin
Minneapolis–St. Paul, Minnesota
New Orleans, Louisiana
New York–northeastern New Jersey
Omaha, Nebraska–Iowa
Philadelphia, Pennsylvania–New Jersey
Pittsburgh, Pennsylvania
Providence–Pawtucket–Warwick, Rhode Island–Massachusetts
Rochester, New York
Saint Joseph, Missouri–Kansas
Saint Louis, Missouri–Illinois
San Francisco–Oakland, California
Scranton, Pennsylvania
Syracuse, New York
Toledo, Ohio–Michigan
Washington, D.C.–Maryland–Virginia

Table 3. *Operationalizations for examining structural determinants of German public transportation change, 1900, 1970*

| Variable | Operationalization | Source |
|---|---|---|
| Public transportation | Passengers per inhabitant (passengers/population) | SJDS, 1903, BD.11:214–17 SJDG, 1971, 1972, BD.59, 60: 122, 316 |
| Urbanization index | Population size, population density, city age, number of establishments | SJDS, 1903, BD.11:48, 72, 275 SJDG, 1971, BD.59:8, 220 |
| Tertiary employment | Government administration, business and educational services, trade and transportation | SJDS, 1903, BD.11:275–80. SJDG, 1971, BD.59:421 |
| Industrial employment | | |
| Old industry | Mining and mining products, iron and steel, metals, electrical manufacturing | SJDS, 1903, BD.11:276–80 SJDG, 1972, BD.60:78–82 |
| Auto–oil–rubber complex | Oil processing, automobile and parts manufacturing, rubber processing and manufacturing, highway construction | SJDG, 1972, BD.60:78–82 |
| Corporate power | Total number of corporate headquarters for top 100 corporations in 1907 and top 500 industrial corporations in 1970 | Schmake Hrsg. (1972); Kocka and Siegrist (1978) |

Table 4. *Operationalizations of variables used in regression analysis of U.S. public transportation systems in 31 cities, 1900, 1970*

| Variable | Operationalization | Source |
|---|---|---|
| Public transportation | Total transit passengers/population | U.S. Census of Street and Electrical Railways (1905); U.S. Department of Transportation National Transportation Survey (1972); American Public Transportation Association, Transit Operating Report (1971) |
| Public transportation decline | 1900–1970 public transportation | Same as above |
| Urbanization index | Factor scale for population size, density, city age, number of economic establishments, rank in national dominance in 1890, value added in manufacturing (1970), total retail sales (1970), volume of wholesale sales (1970). | U.S. Census of Population (1908, 1972); City–County Data Book (1972); Abrahamson and DuBick (1977) |
| Tertiary employment | Percent employment in personal, business, government, educational, trade, and transportation services | U.S. Census (1902, 1972) |
| Auto–oil–rubber sector employment | Percent local employment in auto, oil, and rubber industries | U.S. Census of Manufacturing (1910); U.S. Census of Population (1972) |
| Corporate power | Number of corporate headquarters of top 500 industrial firms | Navin (1970); *Fortune* (1971) |
| Corporate intervention | National City Lines-owned transit or sole supplier contracts with GM, SOCAL, Phillips, Firestone, or Mack | U.S. District Court-N. Illinois 49 C 1364, U.S. v. National City Lines, et al., Appendix to Transcript 75-4 to 76-3 |
| Public ownership | Municipalized transit operation | American Public Transit Association, File No. 073.1 |

Table 5. *Structural determinants of German public transportation, 1900–1970: descriptive statistics*

| Variable[a] | 1900 (n = 30) | | 1970 (n = 30) | |
| --- | --- | --- | --- | --- |
| | Mean | S.D.[b] | Mean | S.D. |
| Corporate power | 1.633 | 3.253 | 10.933 | 11.6232 |
| Urbanization index | .000 | 1.000 | .000 | 1.000 |
| Tertiary employment | 28.12 | 8.11 | 50.1867 | 6.2917 |
| Old industrial sector employment | 27.302 | 14.4356 | 36.70 | 15.33 |
| Auto sector employment | – | – | 42.18 | 14.6621 |
| Auto sector corporate power | – | – | .400 | .4983 |
| Public transportation | 67.6873 | 36.5743 | 208.483 | 48.4251 |
| Transportation decline | – | – | –12.2165 | 94.9363 |

[a]See Table 3.
[b]S.D. = standard deviation.

Table 6. *Structural determinants of U.S. public transportation, 1900–1970: descriptive statistics*

| Variable[a] | 1900 (n = 31) | | 1970 (n = 31) | |
|---|---|---|---|---|
| | Mean | S.D. | Mean | S.D. |
| Passengers per inhabitant | 205.842 | 91.53 | 44.581 | 32.039 |
| Corporate power | 1.23 | 1.38 | 1.471 | 1.368 |
| Urbanization index | .000 | 1.00 | .000 | .9795 |
| Economic structure (percent employment in auto, oil, rubber) | 2.62 | 3.76 | 11.88 | 5.03 |
| Tertiary employment | 32.09 | 5.43 | 51.76 | 6.41 |
| Transit decline (1900–70 passengers per inhabitant) | – | – | −160.967 | 9.125 |
| Corporate intervention (auto–oil– rubber supply contracts) | – | – | .55 | .50 |
| Public ownership | – | – | .87 | .71 |

[a]See Table 4.


Table 7. *Correlation matrix among urbanization, politicoeconomic, and transportation variables for 30 German, cities, 1900*[a]

| | 1 | 2 | 3 | 4 | 5 |
|---|---|---|---|---|---|
| 1 Public transportation | | .56 | .26 | .15 | .64 |
| 2 Urbanization index | | | .03 | −.09 | .89 |
| 3 Tertiary sector | | | | .42 | .06 |
| 4 Old industry employment | | | | | .48 |
| 5 Corporate power | | | | | |

[a]See Table 3 for variable operationalizations.

Table 8. *Correlation matrix among urbanization, politicoeconomic, and transportation variables for 30 German cities, 1970*[a]

| | 1 | 2 | 3 | 4 | 5 | 6 | 7 | 8 |
|---|---|---|---|---|---|---|---|---|
| 1 Public transportation | | .29 | .55 | .09 | .01 | .05 | -.11 | -.08 |
| 2 Transportation decline | | | -.15 | -.30 | -.20 | -.58 | -.14 | -.49 |
| 3 Urbanization index | | | | -.07 | -.38 | .48 | .21 | .35 |
| 4 Tertiary sector | | | | | .39 | .48 | -.06 | -.27 |
| 5 Old industrial employment | | | | | | .16 | -.29 | -.04 |
| 6 Corporate power | | | | | | | .15 | .60 |
| 7 Auto–oil–rubber employment | | | | | | | | -.02 |
| 8 Auto–oil–rubber corporate power | | | | | | | | |

[a]See Table 3 for variable operationalization.

Table 9. *Zero-order correlation coefficients among urbanization,*
*politicoeconomic, and transportation variables for 31 U.S. Cities,*
*1970*

|  | 1 | 2 | 3 | 4 | 5 |
|---|---|---|---|---|---|
| Public transportation |  | .52 | .64 | .08 | .13 |
| Urbanization index |  |  | .84 | −.22 | −.19 |
| Corporate power |  |  |  | .25 | .11 |
| Tertiary sector |  |  |  |  | −.01 |
| Economic structure |  |  |  |  |  |

Table 10. Zero-order correlation coefficients among urbanization, politicoeconomic, and transportation variables for 31 U.S. Cities, 1970

|  | 1 | 2 | 3 | 4 | 5 | 6 | 7 | 8 | 9 |
|---|---|---|---|---|---|---|---|---|---|
| Public transportation |  | .46 | -.19 | .07 | .56 | -.14 | .17 | .52 | .14 |
| Corporate power |  |  | -.36 | .31 | .65 | .46 | -.41 | .70 | -.10 |
| Centrality |  |  |  | -.51 | .03 | -.29 | -.21 | -.27 | -.03 |
| Economic structure |  |  |  |  | .18 | .64 | -.14 | .31 | .08 |
| Urbanization index |  |  |  |  |  | .27 | -.50 | .69 | -.07 |
| Corporate intervention |  |  |  |  |  |  | .10 | .27 | .29 |
| Public transportation decline |  |  |  |  |  |  |  | -.46 | .24 |
| Early corporate power (1917) |  |  |  |  |  |  |  |  | -.19 |
| Public ownership |  |  |  |  |  |  |  |  |  |

Table 11. *Urbanization and public transportation, simple bivariate model, 1900* (Germany)

| Dependent variable: public transportation passengers per inhabitant | | | | |
|---|---|---|---|---|
| Independent variable | $B$ | $\beta$ | S.E. | F |
| Urbanization index[a] | 20.60 | .560 | 5.72 | 12.985* |
| $\alpha = 67.697$[a]Adj. $r^2 = .292$   S.E. $= 36.765$   $F = 12.985$ | | | | |

[a]Includes population size, density, city age, and number of economic establishments.
*Significant at .05 level.

Table 12. *Corporate power, urbanization, tertiary employment, old industrial sector employment, and public transportation: additive regression model, 1970* (Germany)

| Dependent variable public transportation passengers per inhabitant | | | | |
|---|---|---|---|---|
| Independent variable[a] | $B$ | $\beta$ | S.E. | F |
| Corporate power | −2.03 | −.49 | .76 | 7.08* |
| Urbanization index | 47.954 | .96 | 9.72 | 24.36* |
| Tertiary employment | −.41 | −.05 | 1.22 | .11 |
| Old industry sector | .15 | .47 | .60 | 6.08* |
| $\alpha = 197.15$   Adj. $r^2 = .421$   S.E. $= 36.85$   $F = 6.267$ | | | | |

[a]See Table 3 for operationalization.
*Significant at .10 level or below.

Table 13. *Auto–oil–rubber corporate power, urbanization, tertiary employment, auto–oil–rubber industrial employment, and public transportation: additive regression model, 1970* (Germany)

| Dependent variable: public transportation passengers per inhabitant | | | | |
| --- | --- | --- | --- | --- |
| Independent variable[a] | B | β | S.E. | F |
| Corporate power[b] | −32.803 | −.32 | 16.91 | 3.76* |
| Urbanization index | 41.36 | .79 | 8.59 | 23.19* |
| Tertiary employment | 1.48 | .15 | 1.57 | .90 |
| Auto–oil–rubber employment | −.92 | −.28 | .50 | 3.34* |

$\alpha = 187.40$   Adj. $r^2 = .46$   S.E. $= 38.55$   $F = 6.15$

[a]See Table 3 for operationalization.
[b]Includes only auto–oil–rubber group.
*Significant at .10 level or below.

Table 14. *Regression analysis on the decline of public transportation in German cities, 1929–70* (Germany)

| Independent variable: change in passengers per inhabitant, 1929–70 | | | | |
| --- | --- | --- | --- | --- |
| Independent variable[a] | B | β | S.E. | F |
| Corporate power | −5.63 | −.69 | 1.58 | 12.64* |
| Urbanization index | 11.10 | .11 | 20.15 | .30 |
| Tertiary employment | .46 | .03 | 2.53 | .033 |
| Old industrial sector | −.27 | −.04 | 1.24 | .05 |

$\alpha = 51.54$   Adj. $r^2 = .34$   S.E. $= 76.4$   $F = 4.81$

[a]See Table 3 for operationalizations.
*Significant at .05 level.

Table 15. *Regression analysis of residuals from regressing 1970 public transportation on 1929 public transportation* (Germany)

Dependent variable: transportation residuals

| Variable | B | β | S.E. | F |
|---|---|---|---|---|
| Corporate power | −2.84 | −.65 | .85 | 11.12* |
| Urbanization index | 49.05 | .96 | 10.62 | 21.33* |
| Tertiary employment | .58 | .06 | 1.73 | .12 |
| Old industrial employment | 1.27 | .42 | .65 | 3.83** |

$\alpha = -42.71$   Adj. $r^2 = .44$   S.E. $= 37.96$   $F = 5.68$

*Significant at .05 level or below.
**Significant at .10 level.

Table 16. *Ecological factors and public transportation: a simple bivariate regression model, 1900* (U.S.)

Dependent variables: public transportation passengers per inhabitant

| Independent variable[a] | B | β | S.E. | f |
|---|---|---|---|---|
| Urbanization index (Population size, age, density, dominance, number of industrial establishments) | 47.78 | .524 | 14.4 | 10.985* |

$n = 31$   Adj. $r^2 = .249$   $F = 10.985$   $\alpha = 205.54$

[a]See Table 4.
*Significant at .05 level or below.

Table 17. *Corporate power, tertiary employment, and public transportation: additive regression model, 1900* (U.S.)

Dependent variable: public transportation passengers per inhabitant

| Independent variable[a] | B | β | S.E. | F |
|---|---|---|---|---|
| Corporate power | 48.69 | .71 | 20.87 | 5.44* |
| Tertiary employment | 4.49 | .27 | 2.41 | 3.45* |
| Auto–oil–rubber sector | 1.264 | .052 | 4.048 | .098 |
| Urbanization index | .085 | .000 | 27.72 | .00 |

$n = 31$    Adj. $r^2 = .405$    $F = 6.1$    $\alpha = 1.10$

[a]See Table 4.
*Significant at .10 level.

Table 18. *Regression of public transportation on ecological and political economic variables, panel data, 1970* (U.S.)

Dependent variable: public transportation passengers per inhabitant

| Independent variable[a] | B | β | S.E. | F |
|---|---|---|---|---|
| *Model 1* | | | | |
| Corporate power | 11.02 | .47 | 4.3 | 6.561* |
| Tertiary employment | −.39 | −.08 | 1.01 | .149 |
| Auto–oil–rubber sector | −.71 | −.11 | 1.27 | .310 |

Adj. $r^2 = .139$    S.E. $= 29.72$    $F = 2.6$    $\alpha = 57.00$

| Independent variable[a] | B | β | S.E. | F |
|---|---|---|---|---|
| *Model 2* | | | | |
| Corporate power | .79 | .03 | 5.41 | .021 |
| Tertiary employment | −1.48 | −.30 | .997 | 2.195** |
| Auto–oil–rubber sector | −1.25 | −.20 | 1.16 | 1.170 |
| Urbanization index | 19.38 | .59 | 7.17 | 7.314* |

Adj. $r^2 = .303$    S.E. $= 26.76$    $F = 4.25513$    $\alpha = 134.77$

[a]See Table 4.
*Significant at .10 level.
**Significant at .10 level one-tail.

Table 19. *Regression analysis of the decline of public transportation in the United States, 1900–70*

Dependent variable: change in passengers per inhabitant, 1900–70

| Independent variable[a] | $B$ | $\beta$ | S.E. | $F$ |
|---|---|---|---|---|
| *Model 1 (with corporate intervention)* | | | | |
| Corporate power | −30.74 | −.461 | 16.601 | 3.429* |
| Tertiary employment | −6.95 | −.48 | 2.914 | 5.693* |
| Auto–oil–rubber sector | −6.72 | −.37 | 4.14 | 2.63** |
| Corporate intervention | −45.64 | −.25 | 39.29 | 1.35 |
| Urbanization index | −17.63 | −.19 | 20.7 | .726 |

$r^2 = .292$   S.E. = 76.74   $F = 3.484$   $\alpha = 298.85$

| | | | | |
|---|---|---|---|---|
| *Model 2 (with public ownership)* | | | | |
| Corporate power | −.22 | −.33 | 15.55 | 2.22** |
| Tertiary employment | −6.23 | −.44 | 2.85 | 4.78* |
| Auto–oil–rubber sector | −4.23 | −.23 | 3.33 | 1.62 |
| Public ownership | .24 | .19 | 19.7 | 1.5 |
| Urbanization index | −.20 | −.22 | 20.50 | .98 |

$r^2 = .30$   S.E. = 26.5   $F = 3.53$   $\alpha = 223.65$

[a]See Table 4.
*Significant at .10 level.
**Significant at .10 level, one-tail.

Table 20. *Regression model of 1970 public transportation, including 1900 transportation as an independent variable, United States*

Dependent variable: 1970 passengers per inhabitant

| Independent variable | $b$ | $\beta$ | S.E. | $F$ |
|---|---|---|---|---|
| Corporate power | 4.41 | .18 | 5.53 | .64 |
| Urbanization index | 25.22 | .77 | 7.53 | 11.23* |
| Tertiary employment | −.767 | −.15 | 1.03 | .56 |
| Auto–oil–rubber sector | −.87 | −.14 | 1.12 | .60 |
| 1900 passengers per inhabitant | −1.47 | −.42 | .08 | 3.48* |

$\alpha = 118.394$   Adj. $r^2 = .36$   S.E. = 25.56   $F = 4.443$

*Significant at .10 level or below.

Table 21. *Factor analysis for data reduction in construction of urbanization index, Germany, 1900*

Factor 1 (urbanization)

| Variables | Varimax rotated factor matrix | Factor score coefficients | Communality |
|---|---|---|---|
| Employment/residence ratio | .18005 | .10859 | .30910 |
| Governmental administration employment (%) | .23712 | −.06488 | .74009 |
| Workers (%) | −.09419 | .01730 | .56297 |
| Business and educational services (%) | .11940 | −.12577 | .74955 |
| Trade and transportation (%) | .20103 | .01653 | .68796 |
| Number of economic establishments | .97394 | .25749 | .99690 |
| Population size | .97632 | .90698 | .99380 |
| Population density | .82941 | −.07087 | .73935 |
| City age | .62336 | −.11212 | .69648 |

Eigenvalue = 3.98; Percent of variance = 61.0.

230

Table 22. *Factor analysis for data reduction in construction of urbanization index, Germany, 1900*

Factor 1 (urbanization)

| Variables[a] | Varimax rotated factor matrix | Factor score coefficients | Communality |
|---|---|---|---|
| Population size | .89600 | .54036 | .81907 |
| Population density | .53700 | .03369 | .30236 |
| City age | .85094 | .26771 | .76604 |
| Housing age | −.12053 | −.12823 | .79409 |
| Government-subsidized housing | .054019 | .27925 | .78925 |
| Number of economic establishments | .53709 | .24828 | .99590 |

Eigenvalue = 2.4758; percent of variance = 47.9.
[a]Eliminated from this factor analysis due to communality .30 were the following variables: tertiary employment, owner occupancy, and employment residence ratio.

231

**Table 23.** *Factor analysis for urbanization index, United States, 1900*

| Variable | Rotated factor matrix | Commu-nality | Factor score coefficient |
|---|---|---|---|
| Log population | .98 | .96 | 1.00 |
| Log density | .67 | .51 | −.07 |
| City age | .78 | .61 | .08 |
| Percent manufacturing employment | .20 | .84 | −.18 |
| Percent owner-occupied dwellings | −.49 | .38 | .01 |
| Percent residential employment | −.44 | .60 | .11 |
| National dominance score | .95 | .92 | .49 |
| Percent service employment | −.22 | .97 | −.24 |
| Log economic establishments | .88 | .79 | −.47 |

Eigenvalue = 4.25; percent of variance = 64.4; cumulative percent = 49.8.

**Table 24.** *Factor analysis for urbanization index, United States, 1900*

| Variable | Rotated factor matrix | Commu-nality | Factor score coefficients |
|---|---|---|---|
| Log population | .88 | .97 | .86 |
| Log density | .87 | .83 | .46 |
| City age | .68 | .50 | .12 |
| Percent manufacturing employment | −.05 | .84 | −.02 |
| Percent service employment | .02 | .92 | −.11 |
| Percent residential employment | .02 | .32 | −.00 |
| Percent owner occupancy | −.56 | .53 | .23 |
| Number of economic establishments | .74 | .57 | −.21 |

Eigenvalue = 3.04; percent of variance = 55.1; cumulative variance = 41.3.

Table 25A. *Factor analysis with inclusive measures of urbanization and centrality, United States, 1970*

Factor 1: urbanization index

| Variable | Communality | Rotated factor matrix | Factor score coefficient |
|---|---|---|---|
| Log population | .89 | .58 | −.31 |
| Log density | .92 | .44 | −.18 |
| City age | .53 | .40 | .13 |
| Percent manufacturing | .83 | .05 | .01 |
| Percent service employment | .93 | −.16 | .00 |
| Percent residential employment | .75 | −.08 | .02 |
| Residential employment ratio | .44 | −.27 | −.06 |
| Owner occupancy | .60 | −.42 | .08 |
| Value added in manufacturing | .93 | .94 | −.06 |
| Total retail sales | .99 | .97 | 1.58 |
| Volume of wholesale sales | .77 | .86 | −.26 |

Eigenvalue = 4.91; percent of variance = 54.7; cumulative percent = 42.6.

Table 25B.

Factor 2: centrality

| Variable | Rotated factor matrix | Factor score coefficient |
|---|---|---|
| Log population | −.10 | .07 |
| Log density | −.30 | −.04 |
| City age | −.15 | −.10 |
| Percent manufacturing | .90 | .22 |
| Percent service | −.94 | −.66 |
| Percent residential employment | .11 | −.08 |
| Residential/employment ratio | .54 | .02 |
| Owner occupancy | .60 | .01 |
| Value added in manufacturing | .15 | .30 |
| Total retail sales | −.08 | −.37 |
| Volume of wholesale sales | −.12 | −.02 |

Eigenvalue = 4.91; percent of variance = 26.6; cumulative percent = 63.9.

Table 26. *Regression model of 1970 public transportation, including 1929 public transportation as an independent variable, Germany*

Dependent variable: passengers per inhabitant

| Variable | B | β | S.E. | F |
|---|---|---|---|---|
| Corporate power | −2.31 | −.51 | .88 | 6.85* |
| Urbanization index | 56.87 | 1.08 | 11.29 | 25.39⁻ |
| Tertiary employment | .86 | .90 | 1.67 | .26 |
| Old industrial employment | 1.56 | .50 | .65 | 5.80* |
| 1929 transit | −.04 | −.06 | .11 | 1.00 |

$\alpha = 142.24$   Adj. $r^2 = .52$   S.E. $= 36.50$   $F = 6.15$

*Significant at .05 level or below.

Table 27. *Regression analysis of residuals from regressing 1970 public transportation on 1900 public transportation*

Dependent variable: transportation residuals

| Independent variables | B | β | S.E. | F |
|---|---|---|---|---|
| Corporate power | −.80 | −.03 | 5.75 | .019 |
| Urbanization index | 16.83 | .52 | 7.62 | 4.88** |
| Tertiary employment | −1.79 | −.36 | 1.06 | 2.84* |
| Auto–oil–rubber sector | −1/42 | −.23 | 1.23 | 1.33 |

$\alpha = 110.559$   Adj. $r^2 = .1842$   S.E. $= 28.44629$   $F = 2.694$   $n = 31$

Significant at .10 level or below.
**Designates two-tail test.
*Designates one-tail test.

Table 28. *Structural determinants of urbanization: a regression model of the urbanization index on politicoeconomic variables, 1970*

Dependent variable: ecological factor

| Independent variable | $b$ | $\beta$ | S.E. | F |
|---|---|---|---|---|
| Corporate power (1900) | .345 | .468 | .124 | 7.71* |
| Centrality | .047 | .309 | .019 | 5.77* |
| Corporate power (1970) | .309 | .431 | .125 | 6.14* |

Adj. $r^2$ = .568   S.E. = .643   F = 14.167

*Significant at .10 level.

Table 29. *Summary of rail abandonments in the United States 1915–57*

| | |
|---|---|
| *Total companies* | |
| Number of companies | 815 |
| Miles of track | 18,082.54 |
| *City companies* | |
| Number of companies | 334 |
| Miles of track | 4,772.77 |
| *Interurban companies* | |
| Number of companies | 319 |
| Miles of track | 8,527.57 |
| *City and interurban companies* | |
| Number of companies | 162 |
| Miles of track | 4,782.20 |

*Source:* American Transit Association, November 18, 1958, mimeo; APTA, File No. 900.013.

# Notes

## 1. Introduction

1 Technological determinism as the explanation of urban spatial structure appears quite early in the writings of human ecology (Park, 1952:171–7; McKenzie, 1968:9–18). A classic summary of this position is found in Hawley (1950:382–5;1971:242–5). An excellent criticism of human ecology from the perspective of urban political economy is found in Harvey (1973:131–2, 173–6) and Castells (1979:33–59, 50–84). The reduction of the explanation of urban change to technical or spatial conditions is discussed in further depth in Yago (1983).

2 Ecological theories about transportation have been largely incorporated into urban and transportation planning. Ecological and spatial structure of cities assumably prescribes transportation solutions, thereby reinforcing existing travel patterns and promoting highway solutions to congestion. A recent report on transportation planning studies commissioned by the U.S. Department of Transportation (DOT) discussed the theoretical and methodological weaknesses of this perspective: "Even though an impressive amount of effort has been spent on this type of research, the results have been meager in view of the standards called for by the purposes and objectives stated in the studies. The technical reasons why an unsatisfactory amount of knowledge has come from these studies stem from their completely inadequate theoretical foundations and methodological approaches. These problems have crippled attempts to establish and evaluate transportation impacts" (Charles River Associates, 1972:4–5). For examples of the incorporation of ecological propositions in planning studies, see Hansen (1959), Daniels (1972), Peat, Marwick, Mitchell and Company (1975), and Putman (1976). For further review of transportation planning and metropolitan development, see Cheslow and Olsson (1975).

3 A great deal of research predicting transit and locational decisions on the basis of income, car ownership, the presence of public transportation, and other factors exists. See Lansing et al. (1964); Kain and Beesley (1965:163–85); Meyer, Kain, and Wohl (1965); Kain (1967:161–92); Lansing and Hendricks (1967). Again, this body of literature is largely descriptive. It fails to pose relational questions about the historical competition between technical modes of transportation, cities within their national urban systems, and classes whose political and economic interests are spatially linked to patterns of urban development. This research on the determinants of transportation demand is even more unconvincing when we look beyond the limited choices upon which market behavior is based for evidence of not only current but also potential consumer preferences. The notion that consumers vote with their wheels (Altschuler, 1980) fails to consider the narrow range of options they are offered. Substantial survey research indicates widespread public support for increased transit services, deemphasis of the automobile, improved nonprofit public transportation, and renewed rail service (Simpson and Curtis, 1969; King, 1975; APTA, 1982).

4 Both the multivariate statistical procedures described in Chapter 2 and the comparative historical case presentations in Chapters 3–6 attempt to order the concatenation of events in both countries, cities, and time periods to delineate the social forces that constrain, promote, or eliminate available technical solutions to transportation problems. See also Bonnell (1980) for a discussion of methodological issues in comparative cross-national studies.

5 The comparisons in Chapters 3 and 4 should be noted. Concerning the comparisons between growth patterns of large firms in Germany and the United States, see Chandler and Daems (1974:1–34), Kocka (1975:203–6), and Chandler (1968:225–98).

## 2. Twentieth-century mass transit in German and U.S. cities

1 It is worth noting that the tendency toward transit decline was abruptly reversed in Germany after the entrance of the Social Democratic party into the national government. Legislation passed in 1967, 1971, and 1973 promoted vast expansion of German transit systems. Between 1970 and 1980, transit ridership patterns in Germany and the United States diverged again; Germany experienced massive increases in ridership, while U.S. transit systems further eroded. Although these developments are beyond the scope of the present analysis, the ability of German cities to respond more effectively to problems of highway dominance and the energy crisis are probably related to the factors of industrial diversification and institutionalized transit support described in this study.

2 An emerging social history of automobile usage is represented in the work of Flink (1975) for the United States and Krämer-Badoni et al. (1971) for Germany.

3 The massive collapse of U.S. mass transit makes it methodologically difficult to ascertain unique causes of decline statistically. The amount of variation in transit ridership between U.S. cities decreased drastically over this period (the standard deviation declines from 91.53 to 32.09 between 1900 and 1970). Statistically, it is like trying to explain the causes of homicide when the entire population dies. Nevertheless, these limits do not paralyze this exploratory research, which can be elaborated with other historical evidence in later chapters. It is hoped that this explanation will suggest useful avenues of historical research for later efforts.

4 Basically, this means that there is some source for the redundancy between independent variables and the dependent variable. The fact that these ecological variables are substantially correlated with each other means that the resulting regression coefficients are misleading. See Cohen and Cohen (1975:115–17).

5 It should be noted that the urbanization index suppresses the effect of corporate power and tertiary sector employment in the correlation matrix. For the United States the $r^2$ for corporate power is .64, whereas its regression coefficient jumps to .71. More dramatically, the $r^2$ for tertiary employment is .08, whereas in the multivariate model, its impact increases considerably ($\beta = .27$). See the correlation matrices in Appendix 1 for further details. This is a case of classic suppression effect in multivariate statistical analysis.

6 For further details on the relationship between urbanization and industrialization in Germany and the growth of tertiary sector employment, see Kölmann (1976), Mazerath (1970), Rüleke (1977), and Holzner (1978).

7 There has been a continuous tension within German industry between old (early) and new (later) industries (Brady, 1934:129–34; Kocka, 1973). This conflict erupted between pro-rail and pro-automobile industries, as will be discussed in Chapter 3.

The growth of the auto-related sector is recounted in Busch (1966) and König (1960).

8 The findings of the statistical models for Germany and the United States concerning transit decline require some qualification. Using the difference between 1900 and 1970 ridership confirms the direct effects of politicoeconomic variables of urban structure upon transit decline. However, statistical assumptions about this model may arbitrarily set the constant value of independent variables equal to 1, thereby falsely ascribing negative direct effects whose impact may be indirect by introducing an upward bias. Moreover, the model assumes a linear path of transit decline, although the nationally aggregated data (city-level data over time being unavailable) suggest that it may have been nonlinear, with changes in ridership being distributed unequally over time (details of these statistical problems are discussed in Grunfeld, 1961; Sorenson, 1974; and Halaby, 1980).

By using the earlier transit ridership as an independent variable, some of these restrictive statistical consumptions are removed. Unfortunately, this model is much less intuitively meaningful and impenetrable to meaningful interpretation. In the German case, this model results in almost no change. In the U.S. case, the apparently direct effects are absorbed by urbanization and 1900 transit, making those effects largely indirect (Appendix, Table 20). This shift can be interpreted as follows: (1) the effect of 1900 transit on 1970 transit robs the other variables of their negative effects since the error terms of the two are correlated, suppressing the effects of other variables; (2) the decline in variation of the dependent variable is too great; (3) sampling error in the U.S. data misses shifts in economic structure and corporate power between a geographically distributed set of cities; (4) measurement error of the theoretical constructs of local economic structure, corporate power, and urban centrality exists.

This is evidence for the adage about statistical analysis in the social sciences: "There are no compelling statistics, only compelling interpretations of statistics." With these qualifications, the interpretation should be understood and should offer suggestions for future avenues of investigation.

9 The role of corporations and business elites has been considered extensively in community power studies (Aiken and Mott, 1970: chaps. 4–7). See also Mills (1946), Kefauver (1962), Caro (1974), Green (1976), Lincoln (1972), and Friedland (1982).

10 The coordinating function of corporate headquarters is demonstrated in Lincoln (1972), Pred (1976), Aiken and Martinotti (1981), and Friedland (1982).

11 The early process of economic concentration, the emergence of finance capital, and the development of intracapitalist class conflicts in Germany are topics with a long tradition in German economic history. Concerning the process of monopolization and its impact upon German industrial development, see Hilferding (1910) and (1947), Mashke (1970), Neumann (1942) and Lenin (1968). For the effects of economic concentration upon class structure, see Hardach (1977:503–24). The best discussion of the relationship between economic concentration in various sectors and political conflicts within and between classes is in Abraham (1981).

12 The order and magnitude of the relationships between urbanization and other urban structural characteristics considered here are not significantly changed when we adjust for the influence of transit ridership before 1970. To isolate the effects of variables that are independent of earlier transit ridership, regression analysis into the residual effects of 1970 transport over 1900 or 1929 ridership (Tables 15, 27, 28) was performed; it yielded insignificant changes in the other independent variables. For details on the estimation procedure, see Wonnacott

and Wonnacott (1970:375–8). By taking into account the residual disturbances of earlier transit ridership and the distribution of independent variables when using change scores as a dependent variable, this analysis of residual effects confirms the more intuitively meaningful models discussed in the text (Halaby, 1980).

13 Corporate intervention was coded for each U.S. city on the basis of court records from the National City Lines (NCL) and GM bus cases discussed in Chapter 4. A dummy variable was constructed to classify cities that had transit systems purchased by NCL or systems with noncompetitive supply contracts with those firms. Public intervention was also coded as a dummy variable to classify transit operations by public or private ownership (where both existed, the largest firm was used). Admittedly, this variable captures very poorly the type of state intervention that maximizes public accountability.

14 Data on public ownership were gathered from the American Public Transit Association file on "Publicly Owned Transit Systems in the United States," APTA File No 073.1. For a discussion of early municipalizations and popular campaigns for public ownership, see Thomas (1925). An analagous comparison of public and private performance of electrical utilities is found in Mather (1976).

### 3. The formation of national transportation policy: the case of Germany

1 This concentration has been repeatedly discussed in German economic history. Associated with that level of concentration have been various manifestations of monopolization through cartel agreements, trade restraint agreements, and the like. For a fuller discussion, see Hilferding (1910) and (1947), Neumann (1942), Lenin (1968), Mashke (1970). For the effects of this structure on the German class structure, see Hardach (1977:503–24).

2 Family ownership remains a declared form of business ownership under German law.

3 Until the 1920s, German industrial capital was unable to overcome the overwhelming protectionism of German agriculture that was supported and politically ensured by the Junkers. Although attempting to overcome higher wage costs through the high costs of agricultural products, the German bourgeoisie was unable to break the Junkers' hold on large agricultural areas in the east and their political hold over middle-sized landowners in other areas of Germany who sought cooperation with the Junkers through various political parties and organizations such as Zentrum, the Conservative party, and the Bund der Landwirte.

4 The first group of auto manufacturers, Daimler and Benz, originated in the motor industry; the second group, Alder and Durkopp, came from the bicycle industry. The two groups of manufacturers exchanged motors and chassis on a cooperative basis (Siebertz, 1943; Schildberger, 1976).

5 The growth and concentration in the automobile market began under fascism and continued after World War II (König, 1960:303–31; Busch, 1966:15–20).

6 I have relied upon a number of excellent discussions regarding development of public policy at the national and local levels. For further reference, see Rowe (1906), Schott (1912), Baugert (1937), Andic and Veverta (1964:180–6), Lane (1968), Croon et al. (1971), and Logan (1972).

7 The summary of the above-mentioned elements of rail-related policy during the Weimar period and the *Schiene/Strasse* debate is based upon records of the Eisenbahn/Kraftwagenverkehrs Ausschuss (EKA-Rail/Motor Traffic Commission) of the Deutsche Industrie und Handelstag (DIHT), BA, R11/1516). A particular point of

dissension between older industries and new growth industries concerned the complicated licensing arrangements that the state required of private motor transportation. For a discussion of these and other issues, see Niederschrift über die Sitzung des EKA, Confidential (June 16, 1932; April 14, 1932; BA, R11/1516).

8 In commenting on the rail motor traffic debate, Carl Schippert of the Reichsverband der Automobilindustrie (RDA), wrote: "The actions in the structure of our economy were naturally of penetrating influence in the formation of the traffic situation of the railways" (Schippert, 1933:19). He went on to note that the rail bias benefited the continued regional concentration of economic growth in the Ruhr and Silesia industrial areas, thereby neglecting the dispersion of economic benefits (*Vossische Zeitung*, 17 February 1933). The RDA's statements were directed primarily against the Verband der Eisen und Stahl Industrie, an industrial association representing the core of the earliest wave of German capital accumulation, whose monopoly character and geographic concentration had made it possible to dominate many of the rail/motor debates in the DIHT and in the Transportation Ministry (EKA papers, BA, R11/1516; Vorwig, 1970:6–10; Feldman and Nocken, 1975:419–20). The tension between old and new industries in such issues as industrial production, cartelization, and so forth are discussed by Levy, (1966:20–2, 126–33); see also, (Köhne, 1931:44–7).

9 There was a crisis in the rising costs of commodity and personal transportation. The price of transporting industrial goods was rising, and state subsidization of transit was an increasing fiscal burden. Therefore, there was a desire to externalize those rising costs to individuals through automobilization. Concerning these problems of industry, former Chancellor Heinrich Brüning recalled that "particularly difficult was the position of the Iron/Steel and Cement industries. They suffered not only from the effects of an over-speedy rationalization, but also under the fact that the railroad . . . could not provide any further commitment. A way out for both industries was only through the building of new streets with numerous bridges . . . Already as a member of the Reichstag, I supported the propositions of the Hafraba . . . I was always informed by their business manager Willy Hof concerning the progress of their work and created with Hafraba the necessary connections." (Quoted in Kaftan, 1956:132)

10 Among them was Louis Renault, one of the founders of the French automobile industry. Renault was also well informed about converting automobile manufacturing equipment to artillery shell production. During World War I, he had produced an innovative lightweight tank that was primarily responsible for repelling Ludendorff's offensive (Landes, 1969:446–8).

11 Aside from the measures mentioned in the text, other legislation effectively resolved the rail/street debate in favor of streets. The Law for the Preparation of the Organic Construction of the German Economy allowed motor transportation numerous advantages (April 21, 1934, BA, R4311/748). Similarly, the Law for Passenger and Freight Traffic (April 12, 1934) placed all transportation modes under a unified set of regulations. On May 19, 1934, the Law for Freight Discounts of Commodities as Part of the Work Creation Program granted rate subsidization to the motor transport industry.

12 We find an illuminating memorandum in the records of the Reichwirtschaftsministerium concerning "Transportation Education in National Socialist Schools" (5.11.34, BA, R11/1540); similar financial support by the auto-industry, the commercial trucking industry, and the government for a Transportation Institute was forthcoming (5.4.35, BA, R11/1542).

**13** The auto industry contributed generously to motorization propaganda within the Nationalsozialistisches Kraftfahr Korps (NSKK) and the SS (Hilgard to Lammers, 14.2.39, BA, R4311/749a); the integration of the German Auto Club (DDAC) into the NSKK (Memo 15.5.34, BA, R4311/753); and monetary support and technical assistance to the NSKK [Huhnlein, quoted in Müller, 1936:194; Baugart (Opel) and Nordhoff (Opel) to Krauss (NSKK) 14.7.34, 4.6.37, BA, NS24/145; Scholtz (RDA) to Lammers (Reichskanzlei) 7.1.39]. For a full account of the benefits that accrued to the auto industry through the motorization program, see *Statistisches Reichsamt* (1938:3–31).

**14** The military importance of motorization was widely recognized and discussed by the Nazis. In 1935, an editorial in *Die Strasse* noted: "The trade highways serve the military only for advance and retreat. Since these routes are no longer sufficient, a new transportation network must be laid over the whole countryside" (*Die Strasse*, May 1, 1935). The Berliner Police president noted that even automobile inspection was necessary in order to determine the number of cars that could be eventually "mobilized for military purposes" (*Berliner Börsenzeitung*, October 30, 1935). Motorization was also critical for plans of consolidating the Reich, RVM Staatsekretär König noted: "The automobile is . . . like no other means of transportation, uniquely suited to take over the task of providing transportation connections with economically poor border areas" (König, BA, R11/1542). Motorization and road building were therefore critical in connecting Silesia, East Prussia, and other outlying areas of the Reich. In discussions of the Reich Transportation Council, this was often referred to as the *Ostraumproblem* (Hay memo, November 26, 1934, Reich Transportation Council, BA, R11/1540). At the direction of the military, the Reich Transportation Ministry became very cooperative with the Polish government during 1935 in preparing construction for a Warsaw–German border autobahn (*Die Strasse*, January 1, 1935).

**15** As the Frankfurter Stadtbaurat G. Schröder noted: "The demands of the Automobile Industry are well known [in suggesting] the enclosing effect of the Autobahn on unpopulated areas thereby loosening the pressures [of population] on the big cities thus encouraging the settlement program of the German people" (FSA, Akt. 3416/1, Stadtkanzlei). Concerning the relationship between this policy and its expression in the Deutsche Gemeindetag, government, and party organizations, see the Lingnau papers (FSA, Stadtbaurat FFM, 1934–5, Akt. 3416/1–4; and BA, R4311/748).

**16** The autonomy of local politics was abolished with the Municipal Government Act of 1935. However, in major cities such as Frankfurt/Main, this centralization of power affected the rapid mobility of local planners and businessmen into the NS–urban policy organizations (Mazerath, 1970).

**17** The EKA, as noted earlier, was the major location of the rail/motor traffic debate; since the DIHT was an umbrella organization of German industry and commerce, that debate reflected various capital factions. As an organization made up of decentralized units, the EKA made the regional as well as the old/new split of German capital more apparent. For instance, the Essener DIHT (center of much heavy industry and old capital) was responsible for the stipulations preventing motor tax usage for highway construction. During 1932, the possibility of a Reichbahn monopoly over trucking was raised before the EKA as a way to allow the Reichbahn to contain competition so as to maintain a level of business on the rails that would keep rail costs from rising (Niederschrift des EKA, June 16, 1932, BA, R11/1516; Ducker, EKA, November 1, 1932, BA, R11/1516). Others felt that allowing the Reichbahn to diversify into motor transport would be setting a dangerous precedent that would place a "strong restraint upon the motorization of Germany" (April 14, 1932, EKA, BA, R11/1516). The final resolution of the EKA was to create a *Zwangsyndikat* (forced association) that coordinated prices and competition in the interest of industries seeking to transport their goods. Later, members of the DIHT felt that the RDA was obtaining too much influence over this syndicate and sacrificing the desire of corporate transport consumers for cheap service to the automobile and trucking interests for motorization (König to Von Renteln, March 13, 1934, BA, R11/1540; *Deutsche Wirschaftszeitung*, December 14, 1933; Hay memo, undated 1933, BA R11/1540). The basic opposition was between representatives of heavy industry, who were interested in lower rail rates, and the RDA, which was interested in motorization. There were periodic complaints about the lobbying efforts of these two groups within the RVM (Referat Vekehrsarbeit, 1934, BA, R11/1540).

18 Most, Hilland, and Ducker of the DIHT met often with their sympathetic colleague in the (RVM), Staatskretär König, in an attempt to avoid subsuming all business interests under one state organization – the Reichsverkehrsrat. The RV minister, Eltz von Rubinach, had, however, already made his commitments to the RDA (*Berliner Börsenzeitung*, March 11, 1934). Through König, they attempted to present a more "general" business interest as opposed to the "particular interest of the auto industry" (28.1.33, BA, R11/1540).

19 Through the influence of the DIHT, the RVM promoted the idea of decentralization of transportation planning through the various chambers of the DIHT. Schacht (economics minister) and others were opposed, however, to maintaining contact with local and regional chambers. Instead, they preferred to deal directly with producer industry associations such as the RDA (auto industry). The RWM's final decision had priority over that of the RVM since it coincided with Hitler's program to centralize and reorganize the economy (Memo on How to Prepare for the Organic Construction of the Economy, 27.2.34, BA, R4311/748). After this law was passed, all industrial associations were organized in "economic groups" within the state. This did not mean that any significant change occurred. The Economic Group Motor Vehicle Ministry (Wirtschaftsgruppe Fahrzëugindustrie-Wigrufa) operated with the staff and out of the building of the RDA (Wigrufa Bericht, BA, R13/IV; Vorwig, 1970:11; Weger, 1976:34). As Hilland of the DIHT noted in his meeting with Brandenburg, director of the Reichsverband der Deutschen Industrie (RDI): "One can see in the RWM . . . something that appears now in the negative form of the RDA, which until now has followed its own crass interest in politics whereby it has raised in first place as a physiological [sic] demand [of government policy] the promotion of the motor car" (May 7, 1934, BA, R11/1542).

20 Germany's ruling class has a remarkable ability to survive wars, fascism, and economic collapse. This resilience is particularly notable in the post–World War II period. The continuity of German cpaitalists in positions of political and economic power, and the restoration of German capital, have been well discussed in Badstübner (1965), Zapf (1965), Huffschmid (1969), and Jäggi (1973). For example, in 1947 the VDA was able to revise the Allies' industrial recovery plan so as to increase auto production from 40,000 to 250,000 units and the amount of steel used from 200,000 to 460,000 tons. They also encouraged advantageous trade policies for auto exports (Weger, 1976:60).

21 Aside from Marshall Plan funds and the like, by 1967 GM had received $33 million

in reparations and tax benefits for damages to its war plane and motor vehicle plants (Snell, 1974:A22). GM's Hoglund directed auto-related matters through the U.S. military.

22 Coming from the building trades union, Leber, the SPD transport minister, whose plans for highway construction were the dominant fixture of recent transportation policy, was representative of the more conservative wing of German trade unions (see Linder, 1975:239). The automobile industry also managed to mobilize the support of broader industrial interests for legislation favoring the continued motorization of Germany (Deutscher Industrie und Handelstag, 1968; Braunthal, 1972; Willeke, 1975). The amount of state investment in highway building quadrupled from 1949 to 1970. More importantly, the highway share of total state investment increased from 59.4 percent (1955) to 77.2 percent (1969) (Jurgensen, 1968:200; Sandhäger, 1967:Table 3, 19). For a more recent appraisal of the paving of Germany, see *Der Spiegel* (April 3, 1978:41–57).

23 One characteristic of the shift in orientation was the beginning of renewed subway building (U-Bahn) as opposed to further streetcar construction (S-Bahn). This represented the reorientation of urban traffic toward suburban commuting rather than intracity circulation (Guhl, 1975:56–7). Linder (1973:58) had noted well the inadequacy of current German transportation policy:

Although this goal [of public transportation] declaration of Brandt's administration still stands on paper, the actual transportation policy is totally unreformed. The amount of budget allocated to cities for public transportation stagnates. In 1974, the first "special program" for public transportation for 200 million DM fell victim to budget cuts. Meanwhile, the long-distance highway budget was increased by a similar amount.

Further explication of corporate intervention into transportation policy in the Federal Republic was obstructed by the still closed files of the Transportation Ministry at the Bundesarchiv. Nevertheless, it seems clear that such intervention has continued. Although public transportation subsidies have grown considerably, their function was directed toward relieving auto congestion rather than seriously providing an alternative to automobile transportation and competition between modes. This attitude is revealed in an interview with Transport Minister Kurt Gescheidle (*Der Spiegel*, March 21, 1977:100, 102). For more discussion of the subsidy programs, see Dunn (1981).

## 4. The formation of national transportation policy: the case of the United States

1 Many authors have suggested that the United States had an advantage in building capitalism because it was not faced with the residues of feudalism (Baran and Sweezy, 1965; Moore, 1966). In nineteenth- and early twentieth-century Germany, on the other hand, centuries of autocratic rule had an impact upon the emerging economic and political structures of capitalism (Hilferding, 1910; Neumann, 1942).

2 Kolko (1976:2–12) has argued convincingly that rapid economic growth occurred in the United States without the existence of centralized financial and capital control, as many have assumed. He maintains that decentralization and local and regional authority were far more characteristic of the U.S. economy prior to 1900.

3 In the case of both electrification and automobilization, the pace of innovation was faster in the United States than in Germany. Public transportation was fully elec-

trified in the United States by 1895, whereas full German electrification did not occur until the turn of the century (McKay, 1976:35–84). Similarly, in speaking of automobilization, the same process appears to have occurred (Krämer-Brdoni et al., 1971:19–24).

4 The growth of electrification in public transportation was part of the electrical industry's major growth as a central accumulation industry during this period. Thomas Edison was the first to see electrical railways as a way to even the load factor for electrical generating plants. Thus, electrical traction was important in the generation and consumption problems of the electrical industry (see Passer, 1953:250–5).

5 It was also a convenient way to displace social conflict. Henry Ford was noted for the aphorism, "We shall solve the problems of the city by leaving the city." The point is that technological changes in transportation equipment made possible more rapid capital accumulation and disorganized the working class over commonly conceived problems of production and consumption. The spatial dislocation of the working class through transportation and urban physical changes separated the areas of production and consumption struggles, thus diminishing the class struggle over such issues (Katznelson, 1976:28). This is further discussed in Chapter 7.

6 The expansion of the electrical transit system was often not in the interests of rational transportation development, but it increased profits for transit operators, land speculators, and banks. Ralph S. Bauer's testimony before the Federal Electrical Railroad Commission (1919:1622) illustrates this point. Bauer, president of the Lynn, Massachusetts, Board of Trade noted:

I found that a little later on in the nineties, banking interests in the Northeast became interested in the street railway problem, and believed that by consolidating these competing companies there could be evolved from such consolidation a unit system which would pay tremendous profits . . . I further found that the ground hogs in the different communities – the land speculators – had brought certain influences to bear on the local governments which compelled the street railway to build extensions into property for the sake of adding rental and sales values to pasture land, and the politicians in charge of the localities in those times brought sufficient influence to bear on the railway to compel them to build the kind of extensions *which were never profit producing lines.*

7 Contrary to some current interpretations, the movement for public ownership of transit, utilities, ice manufacturing, and so on at the turn of the century was not simply a petit-bourgeois movement of the Progressive era. My archival research concerning the traction question in Chicago indicates working-class community mobilization (of community groups, Socialist and People's parties, religious groups) in alliance with many small business interests in the community against what was called "the exploitation of people's needs" (food, transportation, electricity, etc.) (Vickers, 1934; Goodwyn, 1976). For information on popular oppositional movements regarding transit during this period for San Francisco, see Bean, 1968; New Orleans (Jackson, 1969); Baltimore (Crooks, 1968); Detroit (Holli, 1969); Cincinnati (Miller, 1968); Philadelphia (Warner, 1968); Milwaukee (MacShane, 1974). Cheape (1980) presents additional evidence of these referenda and mass protests in Boston, New York, and Philadelphia and how these demands were transformed into regulatory management procedures in a bureaucratic framework.

8 The most important social science statements on the decline of rail service have been made by Hawley (1950), Rae (1965); Meyer et al. (1972), Berry and Neils (1969), Holt (1972), and Owen (1965).

9 The usual interpretation of the twenties as the death knell of public transit is due in part to the aggregation of national figures, which obscures gains made in transportation in specific cities.

10 Figures concerning comparative operating costs of bus versus rail operations are found in Dewees (1970:560–70) and Henry D. Quinby (*Modern Transit Report*, 1950, APTA File No. 900.01). As Snell notes:

> Engineering studies strongly suggest that conversion from electric trains to diesel buses results in higher operating costs, loss of patronage, and eventual bankruptcy. They demonstrate, for example, that diesel buses have 28% shorter economic lives, 40% higher operating costs, and 9% lower productivity than electric buses. They also conclude that the diesel's foul smoke, ear splitting noise, and slow acceleration may discourage revenues and contribute to the collapse of hundreds of transit systems (Snell, 1974:37).

11 Regarding descriptions of the market saturation problems of the major growth industries of this period (auto–oil–rubber, etc.) see Sloan (1962:208), Weiss (1962), Flink (1975). This represented the first crisis of "Fordism." Before the mid-twenties, demand for products in the oligopolized growth industries was not problematic. As Davis (1978:223) notes, "the initial demand for the new-fangled necessities was provided by the increasing strata of the 'new middle classes' who grew apace with monopolization and the new expansion of corporate bureaucracies. This 'golden circle' of rationalization + consumer durables + the new salariat fueled and sustained the great boom from 1919 until 1926." Work process changes affecting production costs and wage policy were not sufficient to explain the curbing of demand for automobiles. The challenge of competing transportation technologies was then confronted. Horizontal diversification became the corporate strategy to ensure market control both economically and politically.

12 The most important break in the story of the decline of public transit has been the investigation by Bradford Snell (*American Ground Transport*, Hearings before the Subcommittee of Antitrust and Monopoly, U.S. Senate, Washington, D.C., 1974). Much of the present discussion is based upon Snell's thorough study. Snell has pointed the way to the critical questions concerning transit's decline in the United States. Snell's hypothesis has been widely contested. It is astounding how regularly unsubstantiated claims about the technological superiority of highway transportation were made in both popular and scientific works. Dunn (1981:75) states: "But the economics of the declining transit industry would have dictated much of this switch [from streetcars to buses] in any case, since buses were cheaper to purchase and operate [in the short run] than trolleys." Concerning automobiles, Altschuler (1980:21) argues: "In the course of achieving this overwhelming dominance, the automobile appears to have become the less expensive mode for most purposes, as well as the more rapid, convenient, and flexible." Neither Dunn nor Altschuler seems disposed to provide any evidence for these claims. What evidence exists suggests the opposite, as we have indicated in the studies of Germany and the United States (in Chapter 2). Most recently, David St. Clair (1981:579–600) examined aggregate data from trade sources to compare the costs and profits of motor buses, electric buses, and electric streetcars for the years 1935–1950. He concludes, "motor buses were consistently the least economical

transit vehicle during the period 1935–1950" (St. Clair, 1981:600). This includes consideration of both capital and operating costs and is the most definitive study of comparative modal costs.

13 Greyhound officers such as Glenn Traer, Ralph Bogan, and George Stevens were involved in setting up City Coach Lines in Michigan to conduct conversion operations there. City Coach was later absorbed in the creation of National City Lines (FBI Field Office Report, Detroit, April 20, 1956). For other background on Greyhound, see Murphy (1955:3–10). The GM connection was ever present. Assistant Attorney General Stanley Barnes wrote to FBI Director J. Edgar Hoover: "It is believed that GMC may have given financial and other assistance to operating companies other than NCL during their early days in return for which it has received the bus business of such companies. It is believed that Greyhound Corp., Chicago Motor Coach, and New York Omnibus Corporation are among the companies in this category" (Memo: Investigation of Motor Bus Industry, December 1, 1953, FBI Files). There were other ownership ties that bound operating firms to GM prior to the NCL episode. The Public Service Corporation of New Jersey had purchased GM buses exclusively since the twenties. It was influenced in these purchases by J. P. Morgan and Company, a large owner and early source of finance for GM. Assistant Attorney General Stanley Barnes wrote to FBI Director Hoover: "Public Service Transport (Newark) operated as subsidiary of Public Service Corporation of New Jersey which was controlled by United Corporation and United Gas Improvement Co. of Philadelphia (owned by J. P. Morgan and Co.) since the early twenties purchased on an exclusive basis" (Barnes to Hoover, July 5, 1955, 60-107-42, FBI Files).

14 Henry P. Bruner, himself a private consultant and transit operator, surveyed many properties for NCL and GM (see Government Exhibit No 77, NCL Case). Bruner noted that GM was often ready to assist in financing transit and equipment purchases as a way of developing its business (interview with author, May 19, 1978).

15 "Noncompetitive supply contracts" were contracts granted to GM and the other firms involved in the NCL enterprise without bids. They had the same effect of locking transit systems into bus technology without the additional cost to the corporations of their investment. GM tied these exclusive supplier contracts of buses to parts as well. After the NCL case was tried, such noncompetitive arrangements became a major way in which GM dominated the transit market (Case Report, Motor Bus Industry, Los Angeles, March 9, 1954, FBI Files).

16 U.S. vs. NCL et al., Civil Action 49 C1364, Appendix to Transcripts, 47-1:47-7; also Supplementary Information Regarding Interrogatories No. 6, 9, 10, 11, and 12, Transcript Appendix 74-4:76-3 listing supplier, parties to contracts, etc.; also 344-1: 344-11.

17 In many other cities, such supplier contracts of surveyed properties were involved. This was an important way to develop and stabilize markets for the oil, rubber, and automotive products of these major corporations. This same process occurred with Standard Oil of California's ownership and development of United Airlines (interview with H. Templeton Brown, SOCAL Defense Lawyer in NCL case, May 18, 1978). This defies the usual organizational and economic theories that corporations "respond" to markets. Instead, they create and manipulate them when possible (Fitzgerald, NCL, to. Babcock, GM, June 8, 1944, NCL Case, Government Exhibit, No. 165).

18 In general, the transit acquisitions were directed by the supplier firms. For ex-

ample, Russell A. Firestone, assistant treasurer, after negotiations with H. C. Grossman of GM, directed Jesse Haugh of Pacific City Lines to purchase Sacramento and Salt Lake streetcar lines (R. A. Firestone to J. S. Haugh, September 6, 1943, FBI Files, 60-3275). Numerous examples of similar correspondence can be found in the FBI records of both the NCL and motor bus industry investigations released to this author under the Freedom of Information Act. Other relevant evidence was either destroyed by the government "for lack of historical significance" or returned to GM (see Yago, 1979).

19 For example, J. G. Campbell, president of the Jamestown and Buffalo Transit Companies, got into the transit business in 1937 after working for eighteen years at the motor coach division of GM (APTA, 900.01 Buffalo Transit; Passenger Transport, August 18, 1961). J. C. "Smiling Johnnie" Blaine of New Orleans and later St. Louis transit systems was also active in conversions. He later became a vice-president of NCL. Finally, one of the more colorful figures, Benson M. "Barney" Larrick, was an NCL manager and a master at converting systems quickly in Los Angeles, Miami, Tampa, Mobile, Tulsa, Tucson, Buffalo, and other cities. He was dubbed "General Manager in Charge of Conversion to Buses" (*Mass Transit*, April 1952:31). His downfall came when he left NCL and took charge of the Minneapolis conversion. By 1956 he had been convicted of fraud, along with other Minneapolis figures involved in a transit-organized crime menage over the conversion to buses (*Colliers*, September 19, 1951).

20 Sam Schreiber, an independent operator, later became a consultant for other conversions throughout the country. He often appeared at Public Service Commission hearings, testifying in favor of bus conversions as an expert witness on NCL's behalf. Ultimately, he was absorbed within the NCL directorate. Other pro-GM consultants active at the time were Dr. Martin A. Ellicott of the Illinois Institute of Technology and engineers from GM's truck and coach division, who often testified about the "harmlessness" of bus emissions.

21 In Rochester, New York, the ATA was fored to suppress a pro-rail promotional film that was being distributed to civic groups. B. E. Tilton, head of the Syracuse, Rochester, and Utica properties, threatened to resign from ATA unless these films were stopped (Wingarter to Gordon and Hecker, 2/15/1940, APTA, 900.01, Syracuse). Similarly, in Newark: "Public Service has continually fought to suppress all information about these modern rail vehicles" (Modern Transit Report to the Board of Public Utility Commissioners, State of New Jersey, December 6, 1950). Public Service of New Jersey was later a defendant in the GM–bus antitrust case. In Buffalo, "it is only fair to point out that the people . . . did not choose the bus in preference to modern streetcars, for the . . . public, in general, never had an opportunity to see, ride, or experience the service which the modern P.C.C. cars and Brilliners could furnish" (Gordon, 1970:38).

22 Usually, transit and urban historians maintain that the lack of public transit innovations was the cause of its demise (Holt, 1972). This ignores the developments of aluminum, lightweight cars, newer electrical and more efficient motors, and so on (Cavin, 1976).

23 Stockholder suits against bus conversion occurred in Baltimore, Los Angeles, Minneapolis, and St. Louis (APTA Files No. 900.01, for the respective cities).

24 Various better transportation committees, modern transit committees, democratic party clubs, and others were involved in opposing bus conversions (*Bus Transportation*, March 1954:57).

25 See statement of J. M. Elliott, international president, Amalgamated Transit

Union, AFL–CIO, before the hearings of the Committee on Banking and Currency, House of Representatives (1970:523).

26 For instance, GM's licensing of repair and dealerships, financing of used-car purchases, and involvement in road construction through subsidiaries (NA, 60-107-09, 60-107-14, 60-107-27).

27 The USHC represented the first serious foray of government policy into providing the social infrastructure for housing. The "Own Your Own Home Campaign" was the first federal experiment in financing home ownership (NA, RG3/407). The municipal and transportation loans division was active in providing money for transit extensions during a period of capital shortage (NA, RG3/409, 401, 411, 408).

28 This shift, as we have noted, meant no increase in public transportation ridership. Buses were still basically feeder lines to still-existing rail facilities. The small, smelly buses of the period, which required the consumer to have transfer money and spend more time on the road, led many people to buy cars.

29 The Reconstruction Finance Corporation was quite active in supporting bus conversion programs during the 1930s (APTA Files, No. 900.01, 308.01, various city files). As part of modernization and public service, the use of these subsidized loans aided the corporate strategy of bus conversions. See also U.S. National Resources Committee (1940).

30 The Highway Act of 1944 granted the largest single amount for road building, $124 million. Later, President Dwight Eisenhower oversaw the great highway-building efforts of the fifties. His military experience greatly influenced his desire to see such a program fully funded. See his recollections on this period (*Milwaukee Journal*, August 5, 1973).

31 See Mowbray (1969), Leavitt (1970), Kelley (1971), and Caro (1975) concerning the existence of the highway lobby. The Highway Action Coalition, an antihighway group associated with Environmental Action in Washington, D.C., identified the following organizations participating in the highway lobby: American Movers Conference, American Society for Traffic and Transportation, American Automobile Association, American Petroleum Institute, American Trucking Association, Automobile Manufacturers Association (AMA), Chamber of Commerce of the USA, Council of State Chambers of Commerce, Independent Petroleum Association of America, Motor Commerce Association, National Association of Home Builders of the United States, National Association of Motor Bus Owners, National Automobile Dealers Association, National Limestone Institute, Transportation Association of America, Private Truck Council of America, Outdoor Advertising Association of America, National Tire Dealers and Retreaders Association, National Tank Truck Carriers, National Oil Jobbers Council, National Highway Users Conference, National Defense Transportation Association, Truck Body and Equipment Association, Truck Trailers Manufacturers Association, and Associated Traffic Clubs. This, of course, does not include all the separate petroleum, rubber, automobile, and construction corporations also engaged in lobbying activities.

Both the organizational structure of the highway lobby and the development of its constituency were decentralized. One-sixth of all American businesses, employing one-seventh of all American workers, were (and are) involved in "the production marketing, service, and commercial use of automobiles, trucks, and highways . . . These businesses and workers were spread fairly evenly across every congressional district" (Altschuler, 1980:28). This strategy of decentralizing the location and geographic distribution of highway lobbying organizations and a constituency whose employment was tied to its success was central to Sloan's strategy at GM for developing political support for corporate strategies (Sloan, 1962).

32 See Roy F. Britton, NHUC director, to F. D. Roosevelt, September 30, 1933, GM Files R-89, for further evidence of pressure on transportation policy. Sloan was also active in drafting the 1933 National Transportation Bill and recommended national surveys on motor–rail coordination (*Automotive Daily News*, April 8, 1933; *Detroit News*, April 1, 1934). Alfred H. Swayne, GM vice-president, chaired the Highway Transport Committee of the International Chamber of Commerce. He traveled often with Bureau of Public Roads Chief T. H. MacDonald and representatives of the Automobile Manufacturers Association to inspect highway systems abroad for national highway planning in the United States (AMA news release, September 23, 1936).

33 The National Advisory Committee on a National Highway Program consisted of General Lucius D. Clay, chairman, Continental Can Company; Stephen D. Bechtel, president, Bechtel Corporation; David Beck, president, International Brotherhood of Teamsters; S. Sloan Colt, President, Bankers' Trust Company; and W. A. Roberts, president Allis-Chalmers Manufacturing Company.

34 The federal government financed but did not actually construct the highways, as in Germany. This "pork barrel" nature of the U.S. strategy allowed for state highway departments to dispense with federally contracted monies as a way to curry support for highway spending. This maximized support for and control of highway building and ultimately for planning centralization.

35 For example, when the FBI attempted to investigate complaints of GM monopolization, they gained no cooperation from the ATA. The board of directors decided that "the Association should refuse it [information] to the FBI and should refer it to the Bureau of Public Roads" (Minutes, Board of Director's Meeting, April 8, 1958:7–8). Similarly, the ATA cooperated with GM in constructing its defense; Henry Hogan, chief counsel for GM, wrote: "No doubt the ATA documents submitted by you will be of considerable value to us perhaps in connection with some of the investigative or other proceedings which now or in the near future may be pending against us" (Hogan to Anderson, November 1, 1956). The ATA knew well that by stonewalling the FBI and sending them to the Bureau of Public Roads, they could count on GM friend and owner Francis V. Dupont to stall the release of damaging information.

36 This bureaucratic control of highway planning to dedemocratize it is reflected in numerous policy memoranda (BPR Policy and Procedure Memo, 20-8, August 10, 1956; see also Morehouse, 1965). This is consistent with findings of urban political scholars who have shown the loss of administrative power by large urban populations through organizational changes and control within the govenmental bureaucracies.

37 In most recent court cases, judges have tended to emphasize procedural rather than substantive issues of transit planning. If a community could discover where a particular impact statement had failed to be filed or some hearing procedure overlooked, there was the possibility of halting highway construction. But over the substantive matters of what impact statements should consider or what the power of the community is in hearings, courts have tended to constrain any democratization of transit planning. In highway hearings, cross examination is not required, nor does an accurate courtlike record need to be maintained. The courts have upheld the view that federal highway officials' decisions need not be reviewed (Morningside Lennox Park Association v. State Highway Department); federal

officials have the final say in determining whether procedures and plans were sufficient and proper (D.C. Federation of Civic Associations v. Volpe); planning need not necessarily be intermodal (Citizens for Mass Transit Against Freeways v. Brinegar), and so on.

### 5. Transportation politics: the case of Frankfurt am Main

1 From its early history until today, the physical location of Frankfurt in the middle of Europe has been important to its economic development. From Roman times, paths linked Frankfurt as the main interchange connecting the Rhein-Main areas and north-south German passages.

2 Indeed, there was so much resistance by the ruling elite of Frankfurt to osing that autonomy that they presented major opposition to unification with Prussia (Sterne, 1958:3–5; Hope, 1973).

3 Kohlman was involved in constructing working-class housing develop nents. He provided subsidized transit rates to commuting workers as part of their rent. For examples of other such arrangements of working-class settlements, see Weisser (1975:8–56).

4 Frankfurt's innovations in zoning, land use, housing, transportation, and all other areas of urban planning were significant. Frankfurt was considered exemplary, and the city was often visited by key figures in the developing British and U.S. planning professions and by business leaders (e.g., from the National Civic Federation of the United States), who were attempting to ensure rationalized urban growth. See Müllen (1976–7) for details of municipal measures and exchanges between Frankfurt municipal leaders and other business and planning figures.

5 Adickes's concern was a reflection of a more general corporate liberalism that pervaded German planning, rather than any intense sympathy for the working class. An insight is gained into this emerging planning ideology by examining one of the classic planning texts of the period. Gurlitz (1920:289) notes: "Regulated construction is for a city, particularly for large cities, a goal that can only be achieved with increasing the city's influence upon the outlying area. It [the city] must through administrative–technical measures or through widening its boundaries prevent the intrusion of lowered building standards in its general region. Otherwise, the suburbs will grow with the city, increasing disease and proletarian overpopulation which usually works from the outside to the inside [of a city]. A growth . . . that is generally to be fought." See also Günther (1913) concerning this attitude among managers of municipal enterprises.

6 The price for a 3-kilometer trip for a weekly card for the journey to work was 1.67 pfennig per kilometer and dropped to 1 pfennig per kilometer for distances over 10 kilometers. Such subsidization did much to encourage population dispersion (FSA, 1931/Stadtisches Elektricitats und Bahnamt).

7 Extensions were made from Bockenheim-Perlen Fabrick, Eckenheimer Landstrasse Preunheim and Dornbusch-Ginnheim, 6 December 1911, FSA R 1797/IV Landespolizeiliches Abnahme-Neuerstrassenbahnstrecken. For a full explanation of the Ringbahn extensions accomplished during this period, see Wagner (1889).

8 See speech by City Councilman Hin detailing street and streetcar extensions to Vororte in *Zeitschift für Polizei und Verwaltungs Beamte* (20 November 1909:1–2) and requests for extensions (FSA/R 1743/II, Strassenban und Strassenbahnen Generalia).

9 When the city council withdrew this additional support after the defeat of the

Workers and Soldiers' Council a year later, they were able to do so only under police protection from demonstrators (Lucas, 1969:115). For further details on the 1918–19 revolution and class society in Germany at this time, see Kocka (1973).

10 Ernst May was crucial to the development of the German planning profession and architecture of this period. As Tafuri has pointed out, through highly generalized models May's designs attempted "to make the city assume the aspect of a productive machine" (Tafuri, 1976:116). See also Lane (1968). Another technocratic planning group active during this period was the Frankfurter Polytechnischen Gesellschaft, which supported, with the city's financial aid, the first Institute for Transportation Science (Lerner, 1966:519).

11 See FSA Magistrats Akten, R 1711, Verkehrsamts-Mitglieder Bau und Verkehrsdeputationen.

12 As Schneider (1925:184) notes: "With the laying out of external [commuter] lines, the building of the inner network of street rail lines was placed in the background of general interest."

13 Transportation also became a method for displacing urban problems through such decentralization. In 1931, as unemployment started to rise in Frankfurt, the city administration constructed settlements for the unemployed on the periphery of the city. Special travel subsidization for this "Goldstein settlement" was approved by the city council. Displacing the unemployed was perceived as a way to move the city's problem to the periphery. It was a theme of urban renewal and transportation planning that was to be picked up in the Nazi social policies.

14 Although rail modes tended to dominate transportation during this period, calls for more street construction and the motorization of urban and regional travel were beginning to be heard. These suggestions sometimes accompanied rail expansion proposals to connect the Rhein and Main rivers, thus expanding the regional area of growth (FSA, R1743/II, 11 April 1928).

15 By 1931, decentralization of the workforce was proceeding. Population increases on the city's periphery were consistently more rapid than at the city's center (Gley, 1936:88–9); commuting traffic also increased (Decker, 1929).

16 Abbreviation for Association for Preparing the Hansa Cities–Frankfurt–Basel Autobahn, the main highway lobbying association prior to the Nazi period.

17 Invited to planning meetings for autobahn preparations and for other forms of transportation planning as well were, among others: Eugen Wilhelm, director of the Reichsbank; Avieny, general director of the Nassauischen Landesbank; Dr. Von Schnitzler, director of I. G. Farben; Ernst Hagemeier, general director of the Adlerwerke and head of the Section Automobile Industry; and Karl Luer, president of the Rhein Mainische Industrie und Handelskammer and later director of Adam Opel A. G. (FSA, 15 June 1935, 3416/1).

18 Members of that commission included representatives from the Reich Ministries of Interior and Transportation, the Organization of German Motor Traffic Safety (sponsored largely by the German Automobile Industry), and the German Labor Front (Lingnau, 7 November 1941). Lingnau's participation in this commission and other political activities during the Nazi period provides an interesting insight into the collaboration of many urban administrators. Unlike Niemayer, Lingnau never joined the NSDAP, but maintained his status as a planning technocrat in good standing with the party by his participation in various transportation and social welfare planning bodies, and by his support of the municipality's "Strength through Joy" program under the Nazis (*Frankfurter Volksblatt*, undated FSA clipping, 1937).

19 Discounts were kept, however, for members of Nazi party organizations and the police (27 March 1934, FSA 4117/1).

20 At the direction of the Gemeindetag Commission, Lingnau took particular interest in labor relations. As personnel director of the Frankfurt Transportation System, he received all intelligence reports concerning transport workers and any attempts at labor agitation in the field of public transportation. He saw this as a necessary measure for the maintenance of low wages (see various memoranda, 1935–6, FSA 4111/4 Bd. 1). He sent summaries of all intelligence reports to the Nazi labor organization, the German Labor Front.

21 See Niemayer Papers concerning the Altstadt Sanierungsgesetz (December 1934) and Böhm (1953:4). Two particular areas were targeted for "sanitation" under the renewal plans: (1) densely populated working-class areas and (2) the old Jewish ghetto.

22 Frankfurt nearly became the capital of post–World War II Germany; it was only by a vote of 200–176 that Bonn won. The dominant CDU desired to avoid any connotation of permanence to the division of Germany by letting a major city other than Berlin become the capital. The SPD's proposal was Frankfurt (Iblher, 1970:11).

23 For details on these postwar measures and later urban renewal policy, see Rasehore (1976) and Brede et al. (1975). Concerning changes in postwar Frankfurt's economic structure, see Gunzert (1975) and Lerner (1958).

24 Although the left revived considerably immediately after the war, enabling it to pass such legislation, the effects of cold war politics on the local level in defeating leftist programs gave later, more conservative governments broad legislative powers to restructure the city to corporate ends.

25 See Häuserrat Frankfurt (1974), *Kampf gegen die Fahrpreiserhöhung*, (1974), Roth (1975).

26 Frankfurt has been surpassed only by Munich in its rate of population growth, concentration of employment, growth of service employment, and pro-growth politics of urban renewal and transportation. Munich's situation has been carefully studied in the excellent case analyses Krämer-Badoni et al. (1971:295–320) and Linder, (1975).

27 Frankfurt/Main became notorious throughout the Federal Republic for its traffic congestion during this period. By 1970, 500,000 automobiles were entering the city daily, competing for 30,000 legal parking places. A debate over the role of the automobile in Frankfurt's transportation system developed. The pro-automobile lobby's argument for the freedom of individual travel is contained in the Verband der Automobilindustrie's publication, *Mit dem Auto in die Zukunft*, (1973) and Ehrlich (1973); the argument for public transportation is in Fester (1973), Wünschman (1972), and the FAZ (May 3–4, 1974).

28 The years of SPD municipal government were based essentially on the elements of pro-growth politics. Much work still needs to be done on the deterioration of SPD local politics. Before World War I and during the Weimar period, the SPD viewed local government as an organizational base for mobilizing support for broader reforms (see Göb, 1966). During the post–World War II period, the attempt to ensure rebuilding of cities and economic growth often vitiated progressive aspects of the SPD program. There is no systematic study of SPD local politics. However, insight into the growth orientation of local SPD officials was gained in a special interview with Mayor Rudi Arndt (*Der Spiegel*, March 4, 1974). A criticism of SPD local politics is found in Hauserrat (1974:12–23, 47–51), Wenzel et al. (1974:16–22), and Roth (1975).

### 6. Transportation politics: the case of Chicago

1 Chicago is perhaps one of the most thoroughly studied cities in the world. It served as a research laboratory for whole schools of sociology, geography, and urban history. The present analysis has drawn heavily upon the following studies: Meyerson and Banfield (1955), Mayer and Wade (1969), Short (ed., 1971), and Berry et al. (1976).
2 There are numerous other cases in the records of the Chicago Historical Society concerning the manipulation of streetcar extensions. For example, the Wabash Avenue Property Owners Association was involved in such demands (1894). Information concerning extensions was regularly exchanged between members of Chicago's wealthy for their mutual benefit. J. Russell Jones and Marshall Field financed an extension of the Chicago and Alton Railway. Philip H. Sheridan wrote Jones: "Thanks for the information given in your letter to me of the extension of the Van Buren St. Roads. It will help that portion of the city greatly and, of course, my lots and I hope will amply repay the railroad" (Sheridan to Jones, January 24, 1886, Sheridan Papers, CHS).
3 Frederick Engels first noted this relationship between capital accumulation in land and housing speculation and the spatial ordering of classes to minimize conflicts (Engels, 1945, 1972; Marcus, 1975). Engels discusses how transportation corridors are planned to create wide breaches in working-class areas.
4 Yerkes's life and times were well captured in Theodore Dreiser's *The Titan*.
5 Weber's dissertation provides a complete discussion of the development of franchises in nineteenth-century Chicago (Weber, 1971). See also Deuther (1924:37–40).
6 Other examples about such movements and how they supported socialist and populist mayors in many cities during this period are contained in Stave (1972).
7 It should be recalled that the Civic Federation of Chicago was the organization that later founded the National Civic Federation, a central element in U.S. corporate liberalism of the pre–World War I era (see Jensen, 1956).
8 It is interesting to note how this perspective, which was dominant among reformers and corporate liberals of the time, was uncritically adopted by early Chicago School sociologists, inhibiting perceptions and prohibiting an explanation of the persistence of ethnic class divisions and their function in emerging class structure. Consider this description by Cressey: "The pattern of distribution represents the ecological setting within which the assimilation of the foreign population takes place. And . . . congested areas of first settlement are characterized by the perpetuation of many European cultural traits. After some years of residence in such an area, the group, as it improves its economic and social standing, moves outward to some more desirable residential district creating an area of second settlement . . . This diffusion marks the disintegration of the group and the absorption of the individuals into the general American population" (Cressey, 1939:59–60). Theoretically and empirically, this analysis of the early ecologists was flawed. By assuming that this spatial evolution was a natural process, they ignored economic patterns, political power, and the changing requirements of urban space that affected the continuing division between workplace and residence, and the dissolution of communities as a sometimes conscious, sometimes unintended strategy to organize the city spatially in a way that would avoid social conflict. Also, as Berry et al. (1976:52–71) have demonstrated in their reanalysis of Burgess and Park's classic study, the pattern of spatial development was not toward absorption and integration but towards "resegregation."

253

**9** For example, A. J. Roewade was one of the main architects for the Chicago Association of Commerce and other Chicago business concerns. He was one of the main designers of the city's elevated system (A. J. Roewade to Alderman Francis D. Connery, January 9, 1902, Roewade Papers, CHS). Roewade saw assimilation as crucial for immigrants, whom he considered "a pernicious element in our political life, a corrupting element that makes us all defenseless." He went on: "The immigrant who becomes a citizen is not here to promote the old country's welfare, to conspire against its rulers or to support–consciously or unconsciously–corrupt politics; but to be assimilated and ultimately absorbed in the American nationality" (A. J. Roewade to Senator W. P. Dillingham, August 10, 1911, Roewade Papers, CHS).

**10** Recent historians have noted this transformation occurring in urban politics. See, for example, Hays (1964).

**11** Arnold became one of the founders of traffic engineering in the United States, serving as a transportation consultant for most major cities. He later became head of Chicago Traction's Board of Supervising Engineers. Arnold's plans did much to centralize traffic in the Loop area. Fisher was a key legal technocrat who served reform business organizations over the next three decades.

**12** A detailed history of the Chicago Real Estate Board is found in Hughes (1931). Its involvement in transit and housing issues is related there.

**13** Without the Mueller Certificates for financing, money for municipal ownership could come only from transit revenues in the Traction Fund, which would take decades to accumulate. Even this possibility was eliminated by a later corporate desire, to build a subway with those funds, as will be discussed below. The taxes paid by the transit lines under the ordinances were often used for street improvements benefiting motorists.

**14** Delano and Norton were later involved in the planning of New York City. Delano became head of the National Resources Planning Board under his nephew, President Franklin Roosevelt.

**15** Class was a major factor in the transit company's planning of routes. Deuther (1926:8–9), as a community organizer representing small businessmen and workers in the Northwest side, often stated this to the press and transit authorities. In explaining why routes could not be altered to better serve his neighborhood, Deuther was once told by an traction businessman in an oft-quoted exchange, "You can't mix shovels with silk stockings" (Barrett, 1975:479).

**16** Insull's extensions usually benefited his own real estate investments, first in Wilson, Irving, and Rogers Park and later in more outlying areas such as Niles Center and Westchester. His requests for rate hikes from the Illinois Commerce Commission enabled him to raise the elevated fare by 10 percent thus making $20 million to finance extensions from fare receipts (Insull, 1929:11; Liberal Club of Chicago, 1930: 2–7).

**17** In 1939, one long-time transit observer, S. N. Tideman, discussed the effect of transit extensions in supporting peripheral land speculation: "Our traffic problem is greatly influenced by the development of tremendous dead areas around the center of the city. People are forced to live increasingly greater distances from their work and other activities. Travel by street car through these areas is depressing and avoided" Tideman added: "If we do not get some new wealth within the corporate limits of Chicago to share the tax burden, existing property will be taxed out of existence" (S. N. Tideman, to Paul Douglas, May 16, 1939, Douglas Collection, CHS).

18 Ritchie and his cooperation with GM while building Fifth Avenue Coach in New York is discussed in Chapter 5.

19 Insull's control over local policy decisions during the Thompson administration was extensive. See Richberg to Rathbone (December 10, 1926); Jaruset to Richberg (June 16, 1930); Richberg-Fisher Debate over Traction Ordinance at City Club of Chicago, June 24, 1930; *St. Louis Post Dispatch,* June 19, 1930, in Donald R. Richberg Collection, CHS.

20 Aside from Insull, Thompson received support for his efforts at transit unification from the Chicago Association of Commerce (CAC). The CAC set up numerous campaign groups (e.g., in 1907). The Allied Better Service Committee, the All-Chicago Council, and the Citizens' Committee were all funded by the CAC to support Thompson's efforts (*Chicago Tribune,* November 3, 1918; Deuther, 1926:25).

21 The involvement of various banks in the traction properties is discussed in extensive comments written by Edwin Lyman Lobdell, whose investment house was long involved in traction properties (Edwin Lyman Lobdell Collection, CHS).

22 One final attempt was made in 1925 to achieve municipal ownership by Mayor William Dever, who had opposed the 1907 ordinances. Dever's attempt failed after city bankers refused to renegotiate the purchase price, which would have revised the accounting of the traction properties' capitalization (Albert W. Harris, Harris Trust and Savings; F. O. Wetmore, First National Bank; John J. Mitchell, Illinois Merchant Trust Company to Francis X. Busch, corporation counsel of the City of Chicago, September 6, 1924). The bankers' decision forced Dever to seek the financing of municipal ownership through higher transit fares, a proposition rejected by the electorate on April 7, 1925 (Busch, 1925).

23 On October 14, 1929, Insull established a Banker's Committee to aid in drafting an ordinance consolidating traction properties and building a subway. The members were H. L. Stuart, Halsey, Stuart and Company; Arthur Reynolds, Continental Illinois Bank and Trust; A. W. Harris, Harris Trust; and F. O. Wetmore, First National Bank. As Lobdell noted: "The banks headed by these men have on deposit a large part of the reserves and surplus funds of the Traction Companies" (Lobdell Papers, CHS). The Municipal Committee, appointed by Mayor Thompson, consisted of James Simpson, president of Marshall Field, two bankers, and Col. A. A. Sprague (Douglas, 1929:670).

24 Information concerning the 1930 ordinance is drawn heavily from the newspaper accounts of the time, and from the papers of Donald R. Richberg (Box 9, CHS) and Paul H. Douglas (1930–9, CHS). Richberg, as a labor and utilities lawyer, and Douglas, as alderman, led the fight against Insull by progressive elements in the city. See also Douglas (1929).

25 The resemblance in name and participation of this "Non-Partisan" traction committee to the one established in 1907 is striking. See Fisher (1930); *Chicago Tribune,* June 16, 1930; C. D. Thompson to D. Richberg, June 17, 1930, Richberg Papers, Box 9, CHS; and pamphlets of the Traction Ordinance Committee, Non-Partisan, CHS.

26 Documents relating to the formation of this coalition against the ordinances are found in the D. R. Richberg Papers, CHS. See particularly D. C. Thompson to D. R. Richberg, May 16, 1930; D. R. Richbert to H. L. Ickes, August 29, 1939. See People's Streetcar Ownership League (1928); also Thompson (1930); Farnham-Kuhn Company (1930); Liberal Club of Chicago (1930).

27 In arguing against the extension of the ordinance, Douglas said: "This ordinance was passed by the public as a result of a powerful alliance of utility and financial

interests supported by newspapers and the political machines of both parties . . . At least three members of the City Council Committee on Transportation which had approved the legislation and the ordinance had been permitted to purchase stock at much less than the current market prices . . . Two of the leading Republicans in the Illinois House of Representatives were included in several [investment] pools, one for $310,000 and the other for $75,000. These gentlemen had been in favor of passing the enabling legislation. In addition several prominent members of the local Democratic party . . . were also permitted to buy large amounts of stock at less than the market price" (Douglas, December 29, 1933, City Council Speech, Douglas Aldermanic Papers, CHS).

**28** Organizationally, this conflict was removed from the local public arena and took place simultaneously in the federal court and the Illinois Commerce Commission, which directed negotiations between the municipal and financial authorities. Various committees appointed by the federal court, the Abbott Committee (1936), the Lynch Committee (1937), and the Sidley Committee (1942) all presented reorganization plans, which were rejected by the Illinois Commerce Commission (Chicago Department of Subways and Superhighways, 1947:35–9; Brief in Support of Abbott Plan, Gottlieb and Schwartz, Inc., CHS). (Gottlieb and Schwartz was the law firm handling much traction litigation during the thirties and forties.) Ideologically, this method of policy making justified the absence of public participation. Consider Schwartz's comment (1935:445–6): "After all, the problem is essentially a technical one, difficult of comprehension even by those who have spent years in its study, and it is not reasonable to expect a citizenry . . . to preserve a sound and consistent policy."

**29** For information on service cuts, see *Chicago Daily News* (March 14, 1937) and Sullivan (1940). On equipment declines, see CTA (1965:vii). There was an increasing number of service cuts along CSL routes during this period, which brought about overcrowding and eventually ridership decline. The service that existed worsened with the deterioration of Chicago's rolling stock. The obsolescence of routes continued (83 percent of the passengers had to transfer on each trip). Barrett (1975:477) reports 400 requests for service from "middle class areas" of the city from 1940 to 1970 that went unanswered by the City Council committee on Local Transportation. On efforts to secure better service to the more industrial Southside, there are records of Emily B. Larned (CHS), who, between 1915 and 1923, led community efforts to secure better transit service.

**30** Cook County Traffic Study (1925, N.A. RG30, Box 3469). The development of regional planning was closely associated with automobilization. The Chicago Regional Planning Association (1925:3–5) stated that as far as transportation problems are concerned, "the solution lies in the actual construction of relief measures through the cooperation of the several municipalities with the counties and state of the region . . . to provide for growth in the use of the motor car in the vicinity of Chicago . . . A major activity of the Chicago Regional Planning Association will be to give support and publicity to the work of the highway department of the region."

**31** Aside from extensive highway building, automobilization was also promoted during this period through traffic regulation facilitating automobile traffic at the expense of street congestion and competition with other modes. Very early on, Chicago became a model of pro-automobile traffic regulation. After considerable lobbying by the Chicago Motor Club, the Chicago Association of Commerce commissioned Miller McClintock, a nationally renowned traffic engineer of the period, to study Chicago's street regulatory system. His recommendations were focused upon relieving the congestion resulting from increased commercial and manufacturing activities in the city. He recommended that all traffic regulation become centralized through an appointive authority, the Chicago Traffic Commission, which would act to remove restrictions to automobiles through additional off-street parking, one-way streets, turning rules, and so on (McClintock, 1926:212–13). Auto regulation was actually auto facilitation. Chicago created what was hailed by the auto industry as a "model municipal traffic ordinance" designed to allow the free movement of automobiles (*Automotive Industries*, May 1926:774); (*Motor News*, January 1929:52–3). Engineers and planners working on congestion problems fixed upon the technical issue of freeing obstructions to motor traffic flow rather than its relation to other traffic modes.

32 See McClintock (1932), Massen (1936), Harrington et al. (1937), Chicago Motor Club (1939), and Harrington et al. (1939) for evidence of the growing auto orientation of transportation planning. Alice McCormack Blaine was also very active in securing her family's support for auto planning. She took part in the Chicago Automobile Trade Association and the Chicago Motor Club (Alice McCormack Blaine Papers, Manuscript Division, Wisconsin Historical Society). Her brother, Harold F. McCormack, was active in the Commercial Club's efforts surrounding the Burnham Plan. Unfortunately, his papers at the Wisconsin Historical Society are closed until 1984.

33 This discussion is based upon reports of the Department of Subways and Superhighways, City of Chicago. Aside from the continual building of highways parallel to rail facilities, actions were taken to constrain rail developments, as in requests for rail corridors by the Northwestern Railroad (*Motor News*, June 1926:3) and the Santa Fe, Illinois Central, and Gulf, Mobile, and Ohio Railroads (Department of Subways and Superhighways, 1947:92).

34 The city's failure to promote more consolidated residential development was often blamed upon auto-dominated planning. In 1939, one transportation observer, John A. Lapp (head of the Better Chicago League), wrote to Alderman Douglas (May 16, 1939, Douglas Aldermanic Papers, CHS): "Recent studies of Chicago show that it is growing at only one-half the rate of its suburbs. This is largely attributable to the decadent condition of public transportation and the excessive emphasis placed on the use of the private automobile."

35 The financing of these reorganization schemes was made possible through federal intervention. The Reconstruction Finance Corporation agreed to loan $39 million for the proposed reorganization of a new Chicago Transit Company (*Passenger Transport*, June 21, 1943:6).

36 After gaining what amounted to veto power over the CTA, the Chicago financial community went to great lengths to provide the necessary $84 million. This was not an easy task. When the CTA bonds were issued, Moody's Investor Service reported that "some uncertainty of position characterizes these bonds; hence they cannot be recommended for investment." A. W. Harris, of Harris Trust, who had headed the trustee group of the traction properties over the years, prompted his associate, E. B. Hall (of the Harris-Hall Company) to organize a syndicate to purchase $21 million worth of bonds. Hall organized CTA bond sales throughout the country. Bank of America, First Boston, and Chemical National all invested heavily in these issues (*Mass Transportation*, September 1947:373–4).

37 It should be recalled from Chapter 5 that the NHUC was started by the auto industry under the leadership of GM chairman Alfred Sloan, Jr.

38 Banfield uses the CTA subsidization controversy as a case study of Chicago's

typification of the "mixed decision choice" model in his classic *Political Influence* (1961:91–126). This pluralist interpretation of transportation policy suffers from many of the classic limitations of that perspective. First, Banfield's analysis is limited to the controversy over transit subsidization during a brief period in 1956–7. Reanalysis of the issue in light of the CTA's earlier formation and later subsidy controversies reveals linkages between the supposedly disparate "mixed" parties involved in these decisions. Aside from Banfield's lack of historical treatment, he fails to explore linkages between local pro-highway groups, national corporate capital, and local business groups. This makes the connection between various ruling groups opaque and leads to Banfield's misinterpretation, which has long been uncritically accepted in urban politics.

**39** The Central Area Committee represented Chicago's dominant class which cherished the centrality of the downtown area while mistakenly believing that motorization would best preserve it. Its members were J. L. Block, Inland Steel and Sampson; W. A. Johnson, Illinois Central Railroad; W. V. Kahler, Illinois Bell; D. N. Kennedy, Continental Illinois National Bank; H. J. Livingston, First National of Chicago; H. H. McBain, Marshall Field and Company; C. F. Murphy, Naess and Murphy; W. A. Patterson, United Airlines; J. T. Pirie, Carson, Pirie, and Scott; R. P. Williford, Hilton Hotels; H. D. Pettibone, Chicago Title and Trust Company; K. U. Zwiener, Harris Trust and Savings.

**40** In one interesting case, several different groups related to GM under various circumstances acted separately to convert rail service to buses. The Chicago, North Shore, and Milwaukee Railway served various suburban routes with rail service. The North Shore had been controlled by a syndicate consisting of NCL and Greyhound Lines (both closely related to GM), along with other Chicago and Wisconsin investors. Due to a damaging fraud case, the North Shore went bankrupt, abandoning suburban service, which was converted to buses by the CTA (APTA, 900.01, Chicago, North Shore and Milwaukee; *Passenger Transport*, November 18, 1955).

**41** For details on contracts for modernization and conversion, see *Passenger Transport* (January 23, 1948; March 17, 1950; April 25, 1952; July 11, 1952; November 18, 1955; and February 22, 1957), as well as a talk by W. J. McCarter (October 27, 1950, APTA 900.01 Chicago).

**42** The idea of median service was initiated by the CTA's Ralph Budd; it aided the decentralization of job-commuting traffic during this period. Although decline among median service routes was not as swift as on surface routes, it still occurred. Most CTA and other ridership studies have shown that where riders must switch modes (from a bus feeder line to rail where median service is offered), they are more likely eventually to use their automobile for the journey to work.

**43** Much of the suburban retail development has been sponsored by traditional downtown interests. Taubman Company, Sears Roebuck (through their development subsidiary, Homart Development Corporation), Marshall Field, and J. C. Penney jointly built the largest shopping mall in the world, Woodland Mall. Similarly, new suburban areas in Fox Valley have been financed by Homart and the Urban Investment and Development Corporation (Berry et al., 1976:46).

**44** This was the finding of the Urban System Study of seventy case studies conducted by the DOT in 1976. The Chicago Case Study file interviews showed the dominance of regional and state planners in route selection (Chicago Case Study File, Urban System Study, Federal Highway Administration, Washington, D.C.). I thank Mr. Vincent F. Paparella of the Federal Highway Administration for allowing me to review the Chicago file. Aside from highway planning, the latest action to rationalize city–suburban planning authority came with the formation of the Regional Transportation Authority (RTA), which now coordinates all rail and bus traffic in the Chicago region.

45 An important statement on how this spatial development affected the decline of the pro-growth political coalitions that had encouraged such decentralization is found in Mollenkopf (1975).

46 This brief summary of the complex and lengthy controversy surrounding the Crosstown Expressway is based upon clippings and documents in the Ruth Moore Papers, Box 18, CHS; a file on the Anti-Crosstown Coalition in the records of the Highway Action Coalition, Environmental Action, Washington, D.C.; and Pavlos (1972). Some Daley supporters were later found to have bought land along the Crosstown route; see O'Connor (1976:243–6).

47 The Citizens Action Program was part of a broad community-organizing effort headed by former Students for a Democratic Society (SDS) activist Paul Booth. The Crosstown opposition was part of oppositional efforts against urban renewal (as in Lincoln Park). The greatest community organizing successes were in Spanish and black neighborhoods. Due to residential segregation, interracial coalitions (necessary for successful resistance to urban renewal or highway construction) were difficult to build. See Paul Booth (Personal Papers, University of Illinois, Circle Campus Library, Manuscript Division).

48 Access to transportation services is distributed differentially by class, as can be seen by examining the form of transportation used for the journey to work by income and route use, by various population characteristics (income, education, race) (Chicago Area Transportation Study, 1959). See also Ornati (1968).

## 7. Conclusion: Urban transportation for whom?

1 See Bundesminister für Verkehr (1976), Yago (1980), and Dunn (1981).

2 Suburbanization appears to have been a class-specific process that occurred by successive groups of entrants related to their time of entry (as an immigrant group) into the labor force. The resulting fragmentation of community solidarity in relation to the fragmentation of local government provides an interesting basis for research about the course of urban and class politics in the United States since the nineteenth century. See Warner (1975); Thernstrom and Sennett (1969); Ward (1971); Thernstrom (1973); MacShane (1975); Katznelson (1981).

3 The rise of special governmental transportation units not accountable to any electorate has been steady since the period of urban reform at the turn of the century and was accelerated after World War II (Smith, 1947; Caro, 1975).

4 A recent study of Transit authority board members revealed that 57.6 percent of the respondents were in business, finance, or law. The strong corporate bias of transit board members is reflected in their notions of transportation's function as well (Horn, 1976:15–32). Similarly, governmental authority figures often circulate to other modes of transportation. For example, Arthur D. Lewis, Chairman of the U.S. Railway Association, had been an airline executive. After creating Conrail, he became president of the National Association of Motor Bus Owners (*New York Times*, September 11, 1977).

5 One example of regulation benefiting the corporate strategy of rail destruction was the application of the Holding Company Act of 1934. The Securities and Exchange Commission (SEC) used that act in 1942 to force electric utilities to sell their

holdings in street railways because of the alleged "lack of functional relationship between the electric utility and transportation business" (Federal Utility Regulation, 1951:169). Opponents of this decision argued that the Holding Company Act was never meant to be interpreted this way. The railway properties of United Light and Power (the subject of the 1942 SEC decision) were then acquired by NCL. Shortly after the decision, the SEC staff lawyer, W. C. Gilman, pushing this interpretation of the Holding Company Act, became an independent bus operator and consultant (SEC, 1942:945–72).

6 As recently as July 3, 1979, Representative Bud Shuster, chairman of the National Transportation Policy Study Commission, a multi-million dollar study of U.S. transportation, concluded that in spite of the dangers of the energy crisis and crumbling highways that had to be confronted by massive federal investment "there is no question that America today has the finest transport system in the world." This celebration of U.S. transportation has been echoed by every administration during the last two decades.

7 One particularly popular anti-transit covenant used by transit authorities has been to exclude revenues for use by deficit-producing projects. In recent years, this has eliminated a source of public transit funding for some systems.

8 Due to the growing costs of auto ownership and operation, travel costs have been rising at an increasing rate since 1973 as a percentage of total personal spending (Consumer Price Index, 1976:210; *Capital Times*, November 19, 1979).

9 It has been estimated that maintaining the federal highway system will cost as much as it did to build it. Peter Koltnow, president of the Highway Users Federation for Safety and Mobility (formerly the National Highway Users' Conference, started by GM) and chairman of the Transportation Research Board, stated that highways might become "the Penn Central of the next generation" (*Wall Street Journal*, January 31, 1978).

10 The journey to work is by far the most important. Eighty percent of peak-hour traffic (the indicator used for planning purposes) consists of work trips. Travel time on the journey to work has remained essentially the same on the national aggregate level since 1934 (Liepman, 1944:119–20). It has increased for the largest cities of 1 million or more (Voorhees and Bellomo, 1970:121–35; Guest, 1975:220–5; General Motors, 1979:30). Moreover, work trips vary in length by social position. Minorities travel more hours over longer distances than others, as Greytak (1972:9) notes: "It is the whites in the central city who reap the benefits associated with central location as nonwhite work trips are on the average longer and more time consuming than those of all central city residents, suburbanites or all whites." Travel time also varies by class position, as noted by Guest (1976), Feldman (1977), and Castells (1979). The most recent projections are that by the year 2000, travel time will increase 15–20 percent with continued transportation policies (OTA, 1979:26). The number and quality of highways appear to bear little relationship to traffic congestion. Traffic speed and congestion have not improved, for the most part, with increased highway construction (Taebel and Cornhels, 1977:118). Moreover, congestion is expected to increase rapidly in spite of growing highway construction (OTA, 1979:225).

11 Natural resource depletion is a serious problem created by auto-dependent transportation. The auto industry, for example, consumes 61.8 percent of total synthetic rubber, 74 percent of natural rubber, 46.8 percent of malleable iron, 63 percent of lead, 33.3 percent of zinc, and large amounts of other scarce resources. Taebel and Cornhels (1977:128) note: "Reserves, at present rates of consumption,

are adequate only through the year 2000 in several critical materials. New resources will be available only through costlier extraction of lower grade ores, and
the development of expensive new technologies."

12 To compare the United States with European countries in per capita and total
volume of oil consumption, see Tables 6 and 7 in Crabe and McBride (eds.,
1979:242–3). For further in-depth comparison of fuel consumption in various
areas, including transportation, see the extensive profiles of different countries in
Baile (ed. 1976).

13 See U.S. Bureau of the Census (1978) and Frey (1978). In 1978, highway spending
increased more rapidly than ever before, up 108 percent over the previous year.
Price indexes have averaged an increase of 17 to 20 percent over the past two
years. Both urban and rural highways have participated in this increased construction (*Engineering News Record*, July 27, 1978:8–10; August 3, 1978:55; August 31,
1978:3).

14 After World War I, traffic accidents did not appear in government mortality statistics as a major cause of death. Today, in the fifteen to thirty-four age group, auto
accidents are the leading cause of death. For the population as a whole, it is the
third major cause of death. This means that there are about 48,000 deaths and 4
million injuries annually, with an estimated monetary cost to society of $44 billion.
In spite of increased safety measures, the absolute numbers will continue to rise
(*Historical Statistics of the United States*, Part 1, 1975:58; *Statistical Abstracts of the
United States*, 1978:75–6; OTA, 1979:185–90). Continued downsizing (reduction of
size and weight) with increased vehicle miles traveled can be expected to increase
the death toll, since occupant protection is a function of crash distance and relative
vehicle weights (OTA, 1979:200–10). Also, in the rush to produce downsized
automobiles, manufacturers have been scored for increased safety defects (*New
York Times*, March 12, 1978) and necessary recalls. In 1977, the U.S. automobile
industry recalled more automobiles than it sold. Transportation is also the largest
contributor to U.S. air pollution, accounting for 49 percent of HC emissions, 85
percent of carbon monoxide emissions, and 47 percent of $NO_x$ emissions, and 9
percent of particulate emissions (National Transportation Policy Study Commission, 1979:113). Even with enforcement of current emission control procedures,
the growth in automotive traffic by the end of the century would make it impossible for cities to meet the air quality standards of the 1970 and 1977 Clean Air Acts.
Moreover, virtually every large urban area in the country is currently in violation
of those laws, having failed to implement control standards (OTA, 1979:143–4).
Finally, emission control devices deteriorate at a more rapid rate than expected
and increase HC and $NO_x$ emissions without maintenance. Recent discoveries
have shown public health problems related to auto traffic not previously known
(e.g., nitrosamines, carcinogenic and mutagenic properties of diesel exhaust, etc.).

15 There can be little doubt that highways continue to dominate federal planning.
After some limited success, those opposed to highways have gained little. Indeed,
the diversions from the Highway Trust Fund were seen by the highway lobby as a
measure to preserve federal commitment to highways. T. Randolph Russell, an
official of the American Road Builders Association, noted the interest in keeping
the Highway Trust Fund intact: "There's a lot of concern here about the future of
the Highway Trust fund, so, it's a minor concern if part of it will be diverted to
transit" (*National Journal Reports*, April 26, 1975:614). After the initial 1973 legislation, 1975 and 1976 amendments permitted use of diverted funds for other highways rather than mass transit alone.

**16** Over the years, the concentration of power by highway contractors within the highway lobby has increased due to the impact of government contracting procedures. The McGraw-Hill Construction Survey recently reported that "these federal aid highway construction contracts have favored large roadbuilders. In 1977, for example, DOT reported that the top 6 percent of contracts account for half of the country's total awards, whereas the bottom 54 percent of contracts divided up only 7 percent of the total value" (*Engineering News Record*, July 27, 1978:9).

**17** A recent study of transportation referenda in California shows the shift between 1970 and 1974 over the issue of diversions from the state Highway Trust Fund to mass transit. Whitt (1982) shows the shift of corporate support for a total highway commitment to an emerging business consensus concerning the need for transit after the 1973 oil crisis. Whitt's excellent study details the impact of changing structural conditions upon corporate strategy in public policy.

**18** Earlier, I described the failures of the Highway Trust Fund diversions in promoting mass transit (Yago, 1978). With organizational and procedural arrangements continuing to support highways, little effort has been made to use available transfer monies. Moreover, as noted above, 1975 and 1976 amendments to the 1973 legislation allowing diversions enabled the use of interstate funds for other highways. Classically, in Minneapolis only 13 percent of substitute funds ended up being used for transit purposes (Wascoe, 1979:56). Similarly, Secretary Brock Adams threatened to remove funds from areas that have failed to build missing links in the interstate system (*Wall Street Journal*, January 31, 1978).

**19** DOT carried out a study on the administration of urban highway building in 1976. It found, in a survey of thirty-three "metropolitan planning organizations," that transportation plans were rarely initiated by local officials, but usually by state planners (DOT, 1976).

**20** See *State Government News* (July 1975) and National Research Council (1952).

**21** The DOT proposal to establish a Surface Transportation Administration combining the UMTA and FHWA was a leading priority of the Carter administration. The lack of balance between the two bureaucracies is notable: UMTA has 600 employees, compared to FHWA's 4,900. Outside of Washington, UMTA has 150 staff people compared to FHWA's 3,300. Fears that mass transit concerns will be absorbed by a highway-laden bureaucracy seem reasonable and would leave the DOT without a major internal voice for transit proposals (*Mass Transit*, January–February 1979:92).

**22** See note 13.

**23** The proliferation of anti-rail studies reflects the deficiencies of transportation research. Utilizing hypothetical cost–benefit estimates extrapolated into the future, they have yielded a gloomy forecast for the viability of rail transit. The assumptions of the methods used are seriously flawed. However, in spite of the vigorous criticisms of these reports they have remained the basis of policy research and have been well received by congressional committees.

**24** A recent survey done by Peter D. Hart for DOT on public attitudes concerning transportation indicated that 62 percent of the respondents felt that more tax money should be spent on public transportation (Wiese, 1978:34).

**25** UMTA was encouraged by federal legislation to promote aerospace conversion to transportation. The 1970 UMTA legislation stated: "The Secretary of Transportation shall in all ways (including the provision of technical assistance) encourage industries adversely affected by reductions in Federal Government spending on space, military, and other Federal projects to compete for the contracts provided for under sections 3 and 6 of the Urban Mass Transportation Act of 1964 as amended by this Act" (U.S. DOT, UMTA, 1976:29). In spite of this preferential arrangement, the aerospace/military industry was in no position to compete with traditional transportation producers. Rohr Industries, led during the early seventies by Burt Raynes, is a classic case of weak entry into a monopolized market. Encouraged by successful contracts to build BART cars, Rohr attempted to adapt space-age technology to mass transit needs. When expected massive federal support for transportation did not materialize after the first energy crisis of 1973, Rohr sustained $60 million worth of losses from its rail business. These losses violated loan agreements allowing creditors to obtain control over all of Rohr's properties other than inventories and forced Rayne's ouster (*Wall Street Journal*, June 5, 1976).

26 The highway lobby has gone to considerable trouble through public relations activities to prove that there is no highway lobby. The *Wall Street Journal* detailed the public relations effort mounted by federal highway administrators, gasoline and auto manufacturers, and road builders through TRIP (The Road Information Program), which conducted a widespread advertising campaign to promote highways (*Wall Street Journal*, February 12, 1972). Similarly, the American Road Builders Association, the Association of General Contractors, and the Highway Users Federation spent an additional $500,000 annually advertising the deteriorating conditions of roads (*Business Week*, January 17, 1977:32). As noted above, other members of the traditional highway lobby attempted to promote the image of having general interest in all forms of transportation. Pure Oil, Mobil, Jersey Standard, Atlantic Richfield, and Texaco all became supporters of Trust Fund diversions (*Business Week*, October 21, 1972:18–19). Similarly, every auto manufacturer now has a transportation systems division investigating the public transit market while ignoring rail transit.

27 A consortium of six cities (Long Beach and Oakland, California; Houston, Dallas, and San Antonio, Texas; and Brockton, Massachusetts) was organized by GM's sales division to purchase the first advanced design, RTS-II buses. AM General, a subsidiary of American Motors, contested the contract, which included 80 percent federal subsidization, under the provision of the UMTA law that makes illegal sole source bidding for the 393 buses involved. A temporary freeze on the purchase was lifted by the U.S. District Court (B. R. Stokes to APTA Transit System Members, 21 April 1977, APTA Files; *Mass Transit*, December 1977:52). AM General did not appeal the case beyond the district court. This was surprising since, according to lawyers within the Antitrust Division, AM General appeared to have a fairly solid case under the antitrust and UMTA laws. One possible explanation of this reluctance was given by one AM General official whom I interviewed. He thought that American Motors was not interested in "rocking GM's boat," since they carried a lot of weight in the Defense Department where AM's more profitable public contracts were located.

28 The advisory panels of recent government transportation studies have been heavily weighted with car coalition representatives. On the Automobile Assessment Advisory Panel for the Office of Technology Assessment Study, there were: Dr. William G. Agnew, GM Research Labs; Leo Blatz, Exxon; John J. Byrne, GEICO (auto insurance); Dr. Lamont Eltinge, Eaton Corporation Research Center (auto parts supplier); Kent Joscelyn, Highway Safety Research Institute; and Archie Richardson, Auto Owners Action Council. There were also consumer and academic representatives on this panel. However, as one panel member said to me: "It was the auto industry that narrowed the focus of the study to the future of

their product and rejected research designs and recommendations challenging their concerns." The Public Advisory Panel of the National Transportation Policy Study Commission was even more blatantly weighted toward the highway lobby. Four of the six members were directly tied to that coalition: Gilbert E. Carmichael, National Highway Safety Advisory Committee; William F. Cellini, Illinois Asphalt Pavement Association; Richard L. Herman, Herman Brothers (a trucking company); and James D. Pitcock, Williams Brothers Construction Company (a highway construction firm).

29 The hypothetical cost models upon which all of the pro-bus studies are based are fundamentally flawed and require a methodological criticism that can only be briefly suggested. The basic problems with these studies are that they (1) assume fixed population densities as the basis of projected ridership, thereby ignoring studies showing the impact of transportation development upon land use patterns; (2) extrapolate current ridership loads into the future to show the expense of rail, while ignoring studies showing that rail investment would attract greater ridership; (3) include construction costs for rail rights of ways while ignoring those for buses, making the construction cost comparisons unequal and invalid; (4) ignore benefits of safety, travel time, and environmental and energy costs; and (5) use profit maximization rather than productivity criteria in comparing modes. Finally, the studies suggest and are used to promote anti-rail policy analysis, rather than to pose the more critical question of which mix of transportation modes might lead to the most balanced transportation system. McShane, Bloch, and Ihlo (1981) have looked at specific operating systems to examine different efficiency rates between electricity and liquid fuel sources. They show rail efficiencies considerably higher than those of buses in previous governmental and corporate studies. Boris Pushkarev (1980) of the Regional Plan Association has utilized input–output data to show that indirect consumption in maintenance, wayside, and construction adds about 40 percent to gross fuel used in vehicle operation for buses not considered in earlier studies.

30 New DOT accounting procedures allow for increased transit project starts but fail to guarantee funding to project completion.

31 In spite of similarly low population densities (e.g., Hamburg has a population density similar to Los Angeles), West European cities experience numerous operation and environmental efficiencies due to their extensive transit networks (APTA, 1977:15–17). In terms of energy, the U.S. transportation sector accounts for about 50 percent of all petroleum consumption, whereas in Western Europe it ranges from 25 to 30 percent (Pisarski and De Terra, 1975:308–9).

32 GM's advanced design bus, RTS-II (Reduced Tension Suspension) was fraught with problems during development and production. Now that some of the buses are in use, their initial evaluation by some transit experts has not been overwhelming. Apparently, the suspension system is insufficient for the bus's weight, which has led to a GM directive to transit mechanics requiring additional parts to be added to the suspension system. The brake systems are also defective, requiring replacement every 8,000 miles (*Mass Transit*, November 1979).

33 The decline in U.S. subway production has been precipitous. The lack of standardization and industrial expertise has undermined the whole rail industry and made profits unattainable by those companies involved in subway production (*New York Times*, February 6, 1977).

34 UMTA failed to enforce the standardized specifications for light rail vehicles in 1978, shortly after specifications were approved. Consequently, a $31 million

Cleveland rail contract was given to an Italian firm, Breda Construzioni, over the U.S. firms that had bid. Pullman Standard and Boeing both threatened lawsuits, but retired from rail production before legal action could be pursued (*Mass Transit*, November 1978:11; May 1979:26).

35 Technological devolution has not been limited to the rail industry. U.S. firms spend less per capita on research and development than their European or Japanese counterparts. Few of the most important recent industrial innovations have come from the United States. Technological decline is often discussed as a major cause for the decline of U.S. productivity. For the most part, foreign industries have benefited from U.S. multinational investment abroad, while local industries have stagnated. (For more discussion, see *Business Week*, March 8, 1976:20; February 16, 1976:56–60; *Science Digest*, May 1976; *Dunn and Bradstreet Review*, July 1976.)

36 Several experiments at community control over transportation planning have suggested possible success in increasing ridership through more responsive route patterns. See the experience of the Citizens' Advisory Committee in New York City (NYT, November 27, 1977); in Italy, the neighborhood councils (Jaeggi, 1977:61–76); and the United States (DOT, 1976).

37 Much has been written in recent years about market saturation in the automobile industry (Rothchild, 1973). The prospects of a shrinking auto market over the next decades have focused interest upon the international market, where the business press predicts future "car wars." According to a recent OECD study (1978) of the world automobile industry, auto production is to continue a pattern of slow growth until 1990, after which a rapid decline is projected. It is towards this pattern of stagnation that current energy and transportation policy by corporations is directed.

38 I have been able to mention only in passing the distributional consequences of transit decline. The main benefit of transportation is the expansion of information, goods, services, educational and employment opportunities, land, recreation, and so forth available to those with access to transportation. Since the McCone Commission first investigated the impact of rail transit abandonments upon the Watts riot in Los Angeles, the distribution of transportation services has been periodically considered and is suggestive of the impact of physical mobility upon social mobility. Earlier, I presented data on the inequities in the compulsory time spent in work-related travel. The deficiencies in mass transit that have created distance barriers for the working poor who live far from job opportunities have been documented (Davies and Albaum, 1972). Low levels of transit service and auto ownership also function to prevent women's labor force participation and occupational mobility (Lopata, 1980:161–9). The impacts of increased travel time upon familial and community organization, as well as individual health, are beginning to be researched and are discussed in a recent review of social psychological research in this area (Yago, 1983).

# References

Abraham, David. 1981. *The Collapse of the Weimar Republic.* Princeton, N.J.: Princeton University Press.

Abrahamson, Mark and M. A. DuBick. 1977. "Patterns of Urban Dominance: The U.S. in 1890" *American Sociological Review,* 42 (October):756–68.

Achterberg, Erich. 1956. *Frankfurter Bankherren.* Frankfurt/Main: Knapp.

Adams, J. 1981. *Transit Planning: Vision and Practice.* London: Routledge and Kegan Paul.

Adams, T. 1935. *Outline of Town and City Planning: A Review of Past Efforts and Modern Aims.* New York: Russell Sage.

Adickes, Franz. 1980. "Die Förderung des Arbeiterwohnungswesens," Bericht über die erste Versammlung des Vereins für Förderung des Arbeiterwohnungswesens 23 April 1900 zu Frankfurt/Main.

Adler, Franz. 1904. *Wohnungsverhältnisse und Wohnungspolitik der Stadt Frankfurt am Main zu Beginn des 20, Jahrhunderts.* Frankfurt/Main: Schnapper.

Adler, Seymour. 1980. Redundancy in Public Transit: The Political Economy of Public Transit in the San Francisco Bay Area, 1945–63. University of California, Berkeley: Institute of Urban and Regional Development.

Aglietta, Michel. 1979. *A Theory of Capitalist Regulation.* New York: Schocken Books.

Aiken, Michael and Samuel B. Bachrach. 1976. Politics, the Urban System, and Bureaucratic Structure: A Comparative Analysis of 44 Local Governments in Belgium. Department of Sociology, University of Wisconsin-Madison, Mimeo.

Aiken, Michael and Guido Martinotti. 1981. "The Turn to the Left Among Italian Cities and Urban Public Policy." Delivered at the meeting of the Research Committee on Regional and Urban Development, 10th World Congress of Sociology, Mexico City, August.

Aiken, Michael and Paul Mott (eds.). 1970. *The Distribution of Community Power.* New York: Random House.

Alonso, William and Elliot Meridich. 1970. Spontaneous Growth Centers in Twentieth Century American Urbanization, Working Paper #13. Center for Planning and Development Research. Cambridge, Mass., Mass.

Alford, R. 1975. *Health Care Politics.* Chicago: University of Chicago Press.

Altschuler, Alan. 1980. *Urban Transportation Policy.* Cambridge, Mass. MIT Press.

Altvater, Elmar et al. 1974. "Zur Entwicklung des Kapitalismus in Westdeutschland," in Volkhard Brandes (ed.), *Pespektiven des Kapitalismus.* Frankfurt/Main: EVA.

Alwin, Duane F. and Rober M. Hauser. 1975. "The Decomposition of Effects in Path Analysis," *American Sociological Review,* 40 (February):37–47.

American Public Transit Association. 1974. Demand-responsive transportation systems and services. Washington, D.C.: Transportation Research Board, National Research Council.

American Public Transit Association. 1977. *The Case for Rail Transit.* Washington, D.C.

American Public Transit Association. 1981. UMTA/APTA Research and Development Priorities Conference, Proceedings.

# References

American Public Transit Association. 1982. *Transit Fact Book*. Washington, D.C.

American Transit Association. 1971. 1970 Transit Operating Report, Statistical Department. Washington, D.C.

Andic, Suphan and Jindrich Veverka. 1964. "The Growth of Government Expenditure in Germany since the Unification," *Finanzarchiv*, 23:169–277.

Andrews, Wayne. 1946. *Battle for Chicago*. New York: Harcourt Brace Jovanovich

Arnold, Bion J. 1905. *Report on the Chicago Transportation Problem*. New York: McGraw-Hill.

Averitt, Robert. 1968. *The Dual Economy: The Dynamics of American Industry Structure*. New York: Norton.

Bach, Ira J. 1973. "A Reconsideration of the 1909 'Plan of Chicago'," *Chicago History*, 2 (3) (Spring):132–40.

Badstübner, Rolf. 1965. *Restauration in West-Deutschland, 1945–1949*. Berlin: Dietz.

Banfield, Edward C. 1961. *Political Influence*. New York: Free Press.

Bangert, Wolfgang. 1937. *Baupolitik und Stadtgestaltung in Frankfurt/Main*. Würzburg: Triltsch.

Barrett, Paul F. 1975. "Public Policy and Private Choices: Mass Transit, the Auto, and Public Policy in Chicago between the Wars," *Business History Review*, (49):473–97.

Barrett, Paul F. 1976. Mass Transit, the Automobile, and Public Policy in Chicago, 1900–1930. Unpublished Ph.D. dissertation. Department of History, University of Illinois.

Barton, George. 1948. *Street Transportation in Chicago: An Analysis of Administrative Organization and Procedure*. Evanston, Ill: Associated Consultants.

Basile, Paul S. (ed.). 1976. *Energy Demand Studies: Major Consuming Countries*. Cambridge, Mass.: MIT Press.

Bean, W. 1968. *Boss Ruef's San Francisco*. Berkeley: University of California Press.

Berry, Brian J. L. et al. 1976. *Chicago: Transformations of an Urban System*. Philadelphia: Lippincott.

Berry, Brian J. L. 1978. "Latent Structure of Urban Systems: Research Methods and Findings," in L. S. Bourne and J. W. Simmons (eds.), *Systems of Cities*, New York: Oxford University Press.

Berry, Brian J. L. and W. L. Garrison. 1958. "The Functional Bases of the Central-Place Hierarchy," *Economic Geography*, 34 (April):145–54.

Berry, Brian J. L. and F. E. Horton. 1970. *Geographic Perspectives on Urban Systems*. Englewood Cliffs, N.J.: Prentice-Hall.

Berry, Brian J. L. and Elaine Neils. 1969. "Location, Size, and Shape of Cities as Influenced by Environmental Factors: The Urban Environment Writ Large," in H. S. Perloff (ed.), *The Quality of the Urban Environment*. Baltimore: Johns Hopkins University Press.

Beusster, Fritz. 1916. *Städtiche Siedlungspolitik nach dem Kriege*. Berlin: Karl Hermanns.

Biel, Friedrich. 1922. *Das Linksmainische Vorortgebiet von Frankfurt/Main und Offenbach*. Frankfurt/Main: Magistrat.

Bielby, William T. and Robert M. Hauser. 1977. "Structural Equation Models," *Annual Review of Sociology*, 3:137–61.

Blaum, Kurt. 1946. *Wiederaufbau zerstörter Städte: Grund und Vorfragen dargestelt an den Problemen der Stadt Frankfurt/Main*. Frankfurt/Main: Cobet.

Board of Supervising Engineers. 1927 *Chicago Traction: 20th Annual Report*. Chicago.

Böhm, Herbert. 1953. "Städtebauliche Grundlegung für ein neues Frankfurt," in Max Kurz (ed.), *Frankfurt baut auf*. Frankfurt/Main: Kurz.

Bohme, Helmut. 1968. *Frankfurt und Hamburg*. Frankfurt/Main: Europäische Verlagsanstalt.

# References

Bonnell, Victoria. 1980. "The Uses of Theory, Concepts and Comparison in Historical Sociology," *Comparative Studies in Society and History*, 2(2) (April):162–173.

Bothe, Friedrich. 1906. *Beiträge zur Wirtschafts- und Sozialgeschichte der Reichsstädte Frankfurt und Leipzig*. Berlin: Duncker & Humblot.

Brady, R. A. 1974. *The Rationalization Movement in German Industry*. New York: Howard Fertig.

Brauns, Hans-Jochen and David Kramer. 1976. "Political Repression in West Germany: 'Berufsverbote' in Modern German History," *New German Critique*, 7 Winter):105–21.

Braunthal, Gerald. 1972. *The West German Legislative Process: A Case Study of Two Transportation Bills*. Ithaca, N.Y.: Cornell University Press.

Brede, H. et al. 1975. *Ökonomische und politische Determinanten der Wohnungsversorgung*. Frankfurt/Main: Edition Suhrkamp.

Budd, Ralph. 1952. "What Price Local Transit's Future?" *Public Utilities Fortnightly* (September 25):3–10.

Bundesminister für Verkehr. 1976. *Verkehrspolitik '76: Grundsatzprobleme und Schwerpunkte*, Bonn: Bundesverkehrsministerium.

Bunting, D. 1972. Rise of Large American Corporations, 1896–1905. Ph.D. Thesis, Department of Economics, University of Oregon, Eugene.

Burgess, Ernest W. (ed.). 1926. *The Urban Community*. Chicago: University of Chicago.

Burnham, Daniel H. and Edward H. Bennett. 1909. *Plan of Chicago*. Chicago: Commercial Club.

Burnham, Daniel H., Jr. and Robert Kingery. 1956. *Planning the Region of Chicago*. Chicago: Chicago Regional Planning Association.

Burnham, J. C. 1961. "The Gasoline Tax and the Automobile Revolution," *Mississippi Valley Historical Review*, 48:435–59.

Burton, Ralph. 1939. Mass Transportation in the Chicago Region. Unpublished Ph.D. dissertation. Department of Political Science, University of Chicago.

Busch, Francis X. 1925. Outstanding Features and Salient Provisions of an Ordinance Providing for a Comprehensive Municipal Local Transportation System. Chicago: City Council.

Busch, Klaus. 1966. *Strukturwandlungen der Westdeutschen Autoindustrie*. Berlin: Drucker.

Caro, Robert. 1975. *The Power Broker*. New York: Vintage Books.

Castells, Manuel. 1979. *The Urban Question*. Cambridge, Mass: MIT Press.

Cavin, Ruth. 1976. *Trolleys*. New York: Hawthorn Books.

Chandler, Alfred D., Jr. 1968. *Strategy and Structure*. Garden City, N.Y.: Doubleday.

Chandler, Alfred D., Jr. and H. Daems. 1974. "The Rise of Managerial Capitalism and Its Impact of Investment Strategy in the Western World and Japan," in H. Daems and H. van der Wee (eds.), Hague: Den Haag.

Charles River Associates. 1972. Measurement of the Effects of Transportation Changes. Report Submitted to Urban Mass Transit Administration, July.

Cheape, C. W. 1980. *Moving the Masses: Urban Public Transit in New York, Boston, and Philadelphia 1880–1912*. Cambridge, Mass.: Harvard University Press.

Cheslow, Melvyn D. and Mary Lou Olsson. 1975. *Transportation and Metropolitan Development*. Washington, D.C.: Urban Institute.

Chicago Area Transportation Study: Final Report. 1959. Study conducted under the sponsorship of the State of Illinois, Department of Public Works, Cook County, Board of Commissioners, and City of Chicago Mayor, in cooperation with the U.S. Department of Commerce, Bureau of Public Works.

# References

Chicago Association of Commerce. 1930. Approval of the Traction Ordinance, June.

Chicago City Council Committee on Local Transportation. 1952. Annual Report.

Chicago Department of Subway and Superhighways Annual Report. 1947.

Chicago Historical Society. 1929. Proceedings.

Chicago Historical Society. 1934. Amended Reorganization Plan and Amended Reorganization Agreement of Chicago Local Transportation Company, mimeo.

Chicago Motor Club. 1939. Factors suggested for Investigation Dealing with Superhighway Construction. Chicago: Committee on Traffic and Public Safety, City Council.

Chicago Plan Commission. 1929. The Outer Drive. Chicago: Chicago Plan Commission.

Chicago Plan Commission. 1943. Planning New Neighborhoods, Subdivision Design and Standards.

Chicago Plan Commission. 1945. Chicago Industrial Development.

Chicago Regional Planning Association. 1925. Highways in the Region of Chicago.

Chicago Traction and Subway Commission. 1916. Report.

Chicago Transit Authority. 1952. "Local Transit in Chicago," *Traffic Engineering*, (September):457–63.

Chicago Transit Authority. 1965. Historical Information.

Christaller, Walter (trans. by C. W. Baskin). 1966. *Central Places in Southern Germany*. Chapel Hill: University of North Carolina Press.

Christiansen, Harry. 1975. *Trolley Trails through Greater Cleveland and Western Ohio*. Cleveland: Western Reserve Historical Society.

City Club of Chicago, Committee on Passenger Traffic. 1914. Comprehensive Subway Question.

City Club of Chicago. 1936. Local Transportation: The Chicago Area.

City Council of Chicago, Committee on Local Transportation. 1962. Annual Report.

Cochran, Thomas C. 1957. *The American Business System: A Historical Perspective, 1900–1950*. Cambridge, Mass.: Harvard University Press.

Committee for Economic Development. 1965. *Developing Metropolitan Policies*. New York.

Cohen, Jacob and Patricia Cohen. 1975. *Applied Multiple Regression/Correlation Analysis for the Behavioral Sciences*. New York: Wiley.

Commoner, Barry. 1973. "A Special Analysis of American Railroads," *Harpers* (December):24–32.

Commoner, Barry. 1975. "Testimony Before U.S. Senate Subcommittee on Transportation," Hearings on the Future of the Highway Program. Saint Louis: Center for the Biology of Natural Systems, Washington University, Mimeo.

Comptroller General of the United States. 1977. Why Urban System Funds Were Seldom Used for Mass Transit. Washington, D.C.: General Accounting Office, March.

Condit, C. W. 1973. *Chicago, 1910–1929*. Chicago: University of Chicago Press.

Congressional Budget Office. 1977. Urban Transportation and Energy: The Potential Savings of Different Modes. Committee on Environment and Public Works, U.S. Senate. Washington, D.C.: U.S. Government Printing Office.

Cooks, James B. 1968. *Politics and Progress: The Rise of Urban Progressivism in Baltimore, 1895–1911*. Baton Rouge: Louisiana State University Press.

Council on Municipal Performance. 1975. "City Performance," Municipal Performance Report 1/6: 11–17.

Cowan, Robert G. 1971. *On the Rails of Los Angeles*. Los Angeles: Historical Society of Southern California.

# References

Crabe, David and Richard McBride (eds.). 1979. *The World Energy Book*. Cambridge, Mass.: MIT Press.

Cramer, Robert E. 1952. Manufacturing Structure of the Cicero District, Metropolitan Chicago. Chicago: Department of Geography, University of Chicago.

Crane, Galen. 1971. Models for Park Usage: Ideology and the Development of Chicago's Public Parks. Unpublished Ph.d. dissertation. Chicago: Division of Social Sciences, University of Chicago.

Crenson, Matthew. 1971. *The Un-Politics of Pollution*. Baltimore: Johns Hopkins University Press.

Cressey, Paul F. 1938. "Population Succession in Chicago: 1898–1930," *American Journal of Sociology*, 44/(1) (July):59–69.

Croon, Helmuth et al. (ed.). 1977. *Kommunale Selbstverwaltung im Zeitalter der Industrialisierung*. Stuttgart: W. Kohlhammer.

Cutler, Irving (ed.). 1970. *The Chicago Metropolitan Area: Selected Geographic Readings*. New York: Simon & Schuster.

Dahlheimer, Harry. 1951. *Public Transportation in Detroit*. Detroit: Wayne State University Press.

Daniels, P. W. 1972. "Transport Changes Generated by Decentralized Offices," *Regional Studies*, 6:273–89.

Davies, Christopher S. and Melvin Albaum. 1972. "The Mobility Problems of the Poor in Indianapolis," *Antipode*, 1:67–87.

Davis, James L. 1965. *The Elevated System and the Growth of Northern Chicago*. Studies in Geography. Evanston, Ill.: Northwestern University.

Davis, M. 1978. "Fordism in Crisis: A Review of Michel Aglietta's *Regulation of Crisis*," *Annals*, 2/2:207–69.

Decker, Walter. 1929. Die Tagespendelwanderung der Berufstätigen nach Frankfurt/Main, dissertation Johann-Wolfgang Goethe Universität, Frankfurt/Main.

Demkovich, Linda E. 1975. "Transportation Report: Highways Continue to Dominate Federal Planning," *National Journal Reports* (April 26):612–17.

Department of Subways and Superhighways. 1947. Annual Report, Chicago.

Desai, A. V. 1969. *Real Wages in Germany, 1871–1913*. Oxford: Oxford University Press (Clarendon Press).

Despicht, Nigel S. 1969. *The Transport Policy of the European Communities*. London: Chatham.

Deuther, Tomaz. 1926. *Civic Questions Concerning Chicago Traction*. Chicago: Northwest Commercial Association.

Deutscher Industrie und Handelstag. 1968. *Verkehrspolitik für eine wachsende Wirtschaft*. Bonn: Deutscher Industrie-und Handelstag.

Dewees, Donald. 1970. "The Decline of American Street Railways," *Traffic Quarterly*, 24 (September):563–82.

Dickinson, Robert E. 1961. *The Western European City*. London: Routledge & Kegan Paul.

Douglas, Paul H. 1929. "Chicago's Persistent Traction Problem," *National Municipal Review*, 18/11 (November):669–75.

Duncan, Beverly and Stanley Lieberson. 1970. *Metropolis and Region in Transition*. Beverly Hills, Calif.: Sage.

Duncan, O. D. et al. 1960. *Metropolis and Region*. Baltimore: Johns Hopkins University Press.

Dunn, James A. 1978. "Urban Transportation Policy in West Germany and the United States: The Limits of Subsidy," paper presented before the American Political Science Association, New York.

# References

Dunn, James A. 1981. *Miles to Go*. Cambridge, Mass.: MIT Press.

Edwards, C. D. 1966. *Dynamics of the U.S. Automobile Industry*. Columbia, S.C.: University of South Carolina Press.

Ehrlich, Eckhard. 1973. *Demographische Determinanten des städtischen Personenverkehrs*. Braunsnweig: Vulkan.

Eliott, James M. 1970. Testimony before the Committee on Banking and Currency, House of Representatives, 91st Congress, Washington, D.C.

Emrich, Allen. 1974. Comparative Urban Growth in 19th Century Frankfurt/Main, San Francisco, and Rotterdam. Unpublished Ph.D. dissertation. Department of History, University of Chicago.

Engels, Friedrich. 1945, (1872). *Die Lage der arbeitenden Klasse in England*, in Marx-Engels Gesamtausgabe, Bd. 11. Berlin: Dietz.

*Die Wohnungsfrage*, in Marx-Engels Gesamtausgabe, Bd. 14. Berlin: Dietz.

Evans, A. 1972. "The Pure Theory of City Size in an Industrial Economy," *Urban Studies*, 9:(49–77).

Farnhan-Kuhn Company. 1930. Pamphlet on the Chicago Traction Question. Chicago: Farnhan-Kuhn Realtors.

Farrell, Michael R. 1973. *Who Made All Our Streetcars Go? The Story of Rail Transit in Baltimore*. Baltimore: National Railway Historical Society.

Federal Electric Railways Commission. 1920. Proceedings. Washington, D.C.: Government Printing Office.

Federal Utility Regulation. 1951. Annotated Supplement A. Washington, D.C.: Public Utilities Reports, Inc.

Feldman, Gerald D. and Ulrich Nocken. 1975. "Trade Associations and Economic Power: Interest Group Development in the German Iron and Steel and Machine Building Industries," *Business History Review*, 49/4 (Winter):413–45.

Feldman, Marshall M. A. 1977. "A Contribution to the Critique of Urban Political Economy: The Journey to Work," *Antipode*, 9/2 (September):30–41.

Fester, Joachim. 1973. "Verkehrsplanung in der Innenstadt," *Die neue Stadt*, 4:(66–8).

Fischer, Claude. 1976. *The Urban Experience*. New York: Harcourt Brace Jovanovich.

Fischer, Walter L. 1907. *The Traction Ordinance*. Chicago: City Club.

Fisher, Walter L. 1930. *Analysis of the Traction Ordinance*. Chicago: Non-partisan Traction Ordinance Committee.

Flink, J. 1975. *The Car Culture*. Cambridge, Mass.: MIT Press.

Flynn, John J. and John E. Wilkie. 1887. *History of the Chicago Police*. Chicago: Chicago Police Book Fund.

Fogelsong, Richard. 1976. "Toward a Political Economy of Urban Planning: An Exploratory Inquiry," paper delivered to the American Political Science Association, September, 2–5, Chicago.

Forbes, Howard. 1905. *Public Safety and the Interurban Road vs. the Railroad Monopoly in Massachusetts*. Cambridge, Mass.: Harvard University Press.

*Fortune*. 1971. "The 500 Largest Industrial Corporations," (May):172–88.

Frey, William H. 1978. "Population Movement and City–Suburb Redistribution: An Analytic Framework," *Demography*, (15):571–88.

Friedland, Roger. 1981. "Central City Fiscal Strains: The Public Costs of Private Growth," *International Journal of Urban and Regional Research*, 5 (September):356–76.

Friedland, Roger, 1982. *Power and Crisis in the Central City*. London: MacMillan.

Fuller, J. W. 1981. "Inflationary Effects of Transportation," *Annals of the American Academy of Political and Social Science*, 456 (July):112–22.

# References

General Motors Corporation. 1979. *The Real World of Public Transit*. Warren, Mich. GM Transportation Systems.

Gideon, Siegfried. 1948. *Mechanization Takes Command*. New York: Norton.

Gilbert, Paul and Charles L. Bryson. 1929. *Chicago and Its Makers*. Chicago: Mendelsohn.

Gley, Werner. 1936. "Stadtgeographische und statistische Untersuchung," in W. Hartke (ed.), *Festschrift zur Jahrhundertfeier des Vereins für Geographie und Statistik zu Frankfurt/Main*. Frankfurt/Main: Ravenstein.

Göb, Josef. 1966. *50 Jahre Deutsche Kommunalpolitik*. Stuttgart: Kohlhammer.

Goodwyn, Lawrence. 1976. *Democratic Promise: The Populist Movement in America*. New York: Oxford University Press.

Gordon, William R. 1970. *90 Years of Buffalo Railways: 1860–1950*, Buffalo: Gordon.

Gordon, William R. 1975. *94 Years of Rochester Railways*. Albon, N.Y.: Eddy Print Corp.

Gottlieb, Manuel. 1976. *Long Swings in Urban Development*, New York: National Bureau of Economic Research.

Green, Mark. 1976. "The Corporation and the Community," in R. Nader and R. Green (eds.), *Corporate Power in America*. New York: Viking.

Greer, Edward. 1979. *Big Steel*. New York: Monthly Review Press.

Griffith, Ernest S. 1974. *A History of American City Government: The Progressive Years and Their Aftermath, 1900–1920*. New York: Praeger.

Grottkopp, Wilhelm. 1954. *Die Grosse Krise*. Dusseldorf: Econ-Verlag.

Grunfeld, Y. 1961. "The Interpretation of Cross Section Estimates in a Dynamic Model," *Econometrica*, 35:397–404.

Greytak, David. 1972. *Residential Segregation, Metropolitan Decentralization, and the Journey to Work*. Arlington, Va.: National Technical Information Center.

Guest, Avery M. 1973. "Urban Growth and Population Densities," *Demography*, 10/1 (February):53–69.

Guest, Avery M. 1975. "The Journey to Work: 1960–70," *Social Forces*, 54:220–5.

Guest, Avery and Christopher Cluett. 1976. "Analysis of Mass Transit Ridership Using 1970 Census Data," *Traffic Quarterly*, (January):143–61.

Guhl, Detlef. 1975. *Schnellverkehr im Ballungsraum*. Düsseldorf: Alba.

Gunzert, W. 1975. *Die Verkehrsmisere in unseren Städten-Beispiel Frankfurt/Main*. Frankfurt: Rundschau Verlag.

Gurlitz, Cornelius. 1920. *Handbuch des Städtebaues*. Berlin: Müller.

Günther, Arthur. 1913. *Die Kommunalen Strassenbahnen Deutschlands*. Jena: Fischer.

Hackney, David. 1978. "The Trolley Is Back," *Mass Transit*, 5/11 (November):6–11, 24.

Halaby, Charles N. 1980. "Dynamic Models and Attainment in the Workplace," *Social Science Research*. New York: Academic Press.

Hansen, Walter G. 1959. "How Accessibility Shapes Land Use," *Journal of the American Institute of Planners*, (May):73–76.

Hardach, Gerd. 1977. "Klassen und Schichten in Deutschland 1848–1970: Probleme einer historischen Sozialstrukturanalyse," *Geschichte und Gesellschaft*, 3/4:503–24.

Harrington, Philip et al. 1937. *A Comprehensive Local Transportation Plan for Chicago*. Chicago: City Council.

Harrington, Philip et al. 1939. *A Comprehensive Superhighway Plan for the City of Chicago*. Chicago: City Council.

Harrison, Carter. 1935. *Stormy Years*. Indianapolis: Bobbs-Merrill.

Hartenstein, W. and K. Liepelt. 1961. *Mann auf der Strasse*. Frankfurt/Main: EVA.

# References

Hartog, Rudolf. 1965. "Stadtplanung und Stadterweiterung im 19. Jahrhundert," in *Raumordnungs 19 Jahrhundert:* 46–64, Hannover: Jänecke.

Hartwich, Hans. 1967. *Arbeitsmarkt, Verbände und Staat 1918–1933.* Berlin: de Gruyted.

Harvey, David. 1973. *Social Justice and the City.* Baltimore: Johns Hopkins University Press.

Harvey, David. 1974. "Class-Monopoly Rent, Finance Capital, and the Urban Revolution," *Regional Studies,* 8:320–33.

Harvey, David. 1974. "The Urban Process Under Capitalism – A Framework for Analysis," *International Journal of Urban and Regional Research,* 2:101–3.

Häuserrat Frankfurt. 1974. *Wohnungskampf in Frankfurt.* Munich: Trikont-Verlag.

Hawley, Amos. 1950. *Human Ecology.* New York: Ronald Press.

Hawley, Amos. 1970. *Urban Society.* New York: Ronald Press.

Hays, Samuel P. 1964. "The Politics of Reform in Municipal Government in the Progressive Era," *Pacific Northwest Quarterly,* (October):157–69.

Heidenheimer, Arnold J. 1967. *The Governments of Germany,* New York: Crowell.

Heyn, Udo E. G. 1972. Private Banking and Industrialization: The Case of Frankfurt/ Main. Unpublished Ph.d. dissertation. Department of Economics, University of Wisconsin-Madison.

Hilferding, Rudolf. 1947 (1910). *Das Finanzkapital.* Berlin: Dietz.

Hilton, George and J. F. Due. 1960. *The Electric Interurban Railways in America.* Stanford, Calif.: Stanford University Press.

Hirst, E. 1973. "Energy Intensiveness of Passenger and Freight Transport Modes." Oak Ridge, Tenn.: Oak Ridge National Laboratory, April.

Hoffman, Walther G. 1965. *Das Wachstum der Deutschen Wirtschaft seit der Mitte des 19. Jahrhunderts.* Berlin: Springer.

Hoffman, Wolfgang. 1974. *Zwischen Rathaus und Reichskanzlei: Die OBM in der Kommunal und Staatspolitik des deutschen Reiches von 1890–1933.* Stuttgart: Kohlhammer.

Holli, M. 1969. *Reform to Detroit: Hazen Pingree and Urban Politics.* New York: Oxford University Press.

Holmes, E. H. 1973. "The State of the Art in Urban Transportation Planning," *Transportation,* 4:379–402.

Holt, Glenn. 1972. "The Changing Perception of Urban Pathology: An Essay on the Development of Mass Transportation in the United States," in K. T. Jackson and S. K. Schultz (eds.), *Cities in American History.* New York: Oxford University Press.

Holtzner, Lutz. 1978. "Urbanism in West Germany: An Alternative Case of Modernization," *Urbanism Past and Present,* 6(Summer):22–8.

Hooker, George E. 1914. *Through Routes for Chicago's Steam Railroads.* Chicago: City Club.

Hope, Richard. 1973. *Urban Railways and Rapid Transit.* London: IPC Transport Press, Ltd.

Hopfinger, K. B. 1956. *Beyond Expectation: The Volkswagen Story.* London: G. T. Foules.

Horn, Keven H. 1976. "Transit Board Members: Who Are They and What Do They Do?" *Transit Journal,* 2/4 (November):15–32.

Horst, Michelke and Claude Jean-Maire. 1972. *Hundert Jahre Frankfurter Strassenbahnen, 1872–1972.* Villingen: Verlag Eisenbahn.

Hoyt, Homer. 1933. *One Hundred Years of Land Values in Chicago.* Chicago: University of Chicago Press.

Huffschmid, Jörg. 1969. *Die Politik des Kapitals: Konzentration und Wirtschaft in der BRD.* Frankfurt/Main: Edition Suhrkamp.

# References

Hüfner, Willi. 1936. *Die Neurodnung der deutschen Verkehrswirtschaft unter dem Einfluss der Arbeitsbeschaffungsmassnahmen.* Berlin: Junker und Dünnhaupt.

Hughes, Everett C. 1931. *The Growth of an Institution: The Chicago Real Estate Board.* Chicago: Society for Social Research of the University of Chicago.

Iblher, Peter. 1970. *Hauptstadt oder Hauptstädte? Die Machtverteilung zwischen den Grossstädten der BRD,* Opladen: Leske.

Independent Anti-Boodle League (IABL). 1899. *Listen to the Voice of the People.* Chicago: Independent Anti-Boodle League.

Insull, Samuel. 1929. *The Traction Lame Duck.* Chicago.

Interurban Roadways Committee of the Commercial Club of Chicago. 1908. *Interurban Roadways about Chicago.*

Isard, Walter F. (ed.). 1960. *Methods of Regional Analysis: An Introduction to Regional Science.* Cambridge, Mass.: MIT Press.

Isard, Walter F. 1962. *Location and Space-Economy.* Cambridge, Mass.: MIT Press.

Isbarg, Gerhard. 1967. *Central Places and Local Service Areas.* Bad Godesberg: Bundesministerium für Landeskunde und Raumordnung.

Jackson, J. J. 1969. *New Orleans in the Gilded Age: Politics and Urban Progressivism 1880–1896.* Baton Rouge: Louisiana State University Press.

Jaeger, H. 1974. "Business History in Germany: A Survey of Recent Developments," *Business History Review,* 48:18–48.

Jäggi, M. et al. 1977. *Red Bologna.* London: Writers and Readers.

Jäggi, Urs. 1973. *Kapital und Arbeit in der Bundesrepublik.* Frankfurt/Main: Fischer.

James, F. Cyril. 1938. *The Growth of Chicago Banks: The Modern Age,* Vol. II. New York: Harper.

Jensen, Gordon. 1956. The National Civic Federation: American Business in an Age of Social Change and Reform, 1900–1910. Princeton, N.J.: Ph.D. dissertation. Department of History, Princeton University.

John, Gunther. 1966. *Die Verkehrsinvestitionen in der BRD und ihr Einfluss auf die Wirtschaftsentwicklung.* Berlin: Duncker und Humblot.

Joint Committee on Federal Aid in Construction of Post Roads. 1913. *Good Roads Hearing.* Washington: U.S. Government Printing Office.

Jürgensen, Harald. 1968. *Konzentration und Wettbewerb im gemeinsamen Markt: das Beispiel der Automobilindustrie.* Göttingen: Vandenhoeck and Ruprecht.

Kaftan, Kurt G. 1956. *Der Kampf um die Autobahnen.* Berlin: Wignakow.

Kain, John F. 1967. "Urban Travel Behavior," in L. Schnore and Henry Fagin (ed.), *Urban Research and Policy Planning.* Beverly Hills, Calif.: Sage.

Kain, John F. and M. E. Beesley. 1965. "Forecasting Car Ownership and Use," *Urban Studies,* 2 (November):163–85.

Kalecki, Michael. 1972. *The Last Phase in the Transformation of Capitalism.* New York: Monthly Review Press.

Kampf gegen die Fahrpreiserhöhung. 1974. Frankfurt/Main: KBW.

Kampfsmeyer, Hans. 1957. "Praxis und Pläne in: Flüssiges Frankfurt," *Frankfurter Rundschau,* (May):22.

Kasperson, Roger E. 1971. "Toward a Geography of Urban Politics: Chicago, A Case Study," in L. S. Bourne (ed.), *Internal Structure of the City.* New York: Oxford University Press.

Katznelson, Ira. 1976. "The Patterning of Class in the U.S.," paper delivered at Annual Meeting of the American Political Science Association, Chicago.

Katznelson, Ira. 1979. "Community, Capitalist Development, and the Emergence of Class," *Politics and Society,* 9/2:203–37.

# References

Katznelson, Ira. 1981. *City Trenches: Urban Politics and the Patterning of Class in the United States.* New York: Pantheon.

Kefauver, Estes. 1962. *In a Few Hands: Monopoly Power in America.* New York: Penguin Books.

Kelley, Ben. 1971. *The Pavers and the Paved.* New York: Donald W. Brown.

Kelley, Edward J. et al. 1937. *A Comprehensive Local Transportation Plan.* Chicago: City of Chicago.

Kennedy, Edward D. 1941. *The Automobile Industry.* New York: Reynal & Hitchkock.

Kieffer, Stephen A. 1958. *Transit and the Twins,* Minneapolis: Twin City Rapid Transit Co.

Kilger, Wolfgang. 1960. "*Industrie und Konzentration,*" in Helmut Arndt (ed.), *Die Konzentration in der Wirtschaft.* Berlin: Duncker and Humblot.

Kindelberger, C. P. 1967. *Europe's Postwar Growth: The Role of Labor Supply,* Cambridge, Mass.: Harvard University Press.

King, Alan L. 1975. "Identifying Community Transportation Concerns," *Traffic Quarterly,* 29/3 (July):317–31.

Kittel, Theodor. 1935. "Autostrassen im Neuen Staat," *Nationalsozialismus in Staat, Gemeinde und Wirtschaft.* Essen: National-Zeitungs-Verlag.

Klapper, Edmund. 1910. *Die Entwicklung der deutschen Automobilindustrie.* Berlin: Boll und Pickardt.

Klemmer, Paul. 1971. *Der Metropolisierungsgrad der Stadtregionen.* Hannover: Jaenecke.

Kim, Jae-On. 1978. *Factor Analysis.* Beverly Hills, Calif.: Sage.

Kocka, Jürgen. 1975. *Unternehmen in der deutschen Industrialisierung,* Göttingen: Vandenhoeck & Ruprecht.

Kocka, Jürgen. 1973. *Klassengesellschaft im Krieg.* Göttingen: Vandenhoeck und Ruprecht.

Kocka, Jürgen and Hannes Siegrist. 1978. *Die grössten deutschen Industrieunternehmen im späten 19. und frühen 20.* Jahrhundert, Interdisciplinarisches Institut, Universität Bielefeld, Mimeo.

Köhne, Hermann. 1931. Untersuchungen über die Automobilisierung des deutschen Verkehrswesen. Munich: Technische Hochschule.

Kölmann, Wolfgang. 1976. "The Process of Urbanization in Germany at the Height of the Industrialization Period," in A. Lees and L. Lees (eds.), *The Urbanization of European Society in the Nineteenth Century.* Lexington, Mass.: Heath.

König, Heinz. 1960. "Kartelle und Konzentrationen," in H. Arndt (ed.), *Die Konzentration in der Wirtschaft.* Berlin: Duncker and Humblot.

Krämer-Badoni, Thomas et al. 1971. *Zur sozio-ökonomischen Bedeutung des Automobils.* Frankfurt/Main: Suhrkamp.

Kuhn, Alfred. 1952. *Arbitration in Transit.* Philadelphia: University of Pennsylvania Press.

Kurt, Alfred. 1956. Zur Geschichte von Strassen und Verkehr im Land zwischen Rhein und Main, Unpublished Ph.D. thesis, Philosophische Fakultät, Johann-Wolfgang-Goethe Universität, Frankfurt/Main.

Landes, David. 1969. *The Unbound Prometheus.* Cambridge: Cambridge University Press.

Lane, Barbara M. 1968. *Architecture and Politics in Germany, 1918–45.* Cambridge, Mass.: Harvard University Press.

Lansing, J. B. and G. Hendricks. 1967. *Automobile Ownership and Residential Density.* Ann Arbor: University of Michigan Press.

Lansing, J. B. et al. 1964. *Residential Location and Urban Mobility.* Ann Arbor: University of Michigan Press.

275

# References

Lärmer, Karl. 1975. *Autobahnen in Deutschland, 1933–1945*. Berlin: Akademie Verlag.

Lauck, Fritz. 1926. Eingemeindungsfragen und die Eingemeindungspolitik. Inaugaral-Dissertation. Frankfurt/Main: Johann-Wolfgang-Goethe Universität.

Leach, Paul R. 1925. *Chicago's Traction Problem*. Chicago: Chicago Daily News Reprints.

Leavitt, Helen. 1970. *Superhighway-Superhoax*. Garden City, N.Y.: Doubleday.

Lee, David A. 1978. "The Recent Public Record of Transit Votes," in General Motors Corporation Proceedings, Making Public Transit Happen Symposium, GM Transportation System, April.

Leech, Harper and John Carroll. 1938. *Armour and Its Times*. New York: Appleton-Century-Crofts.

Legitt, David. 1974. The Politics of Mass Transportation: State and City Policy Making in the Federal System. Unpublished Ph.D. dissertation. Department of Political Science, University of Wisconsin-Madison.

Lenin, Vladimir I. 1968. *Imperialism*. Moscow: Progress Publishers.

Lerner, Franz. 1958. *Frankfurt-am-Main und seine Wirtschaft seit 1945*. Frankfurt/Main: Ammelburg.

Lerner, Franz. 1966. *Bürgersinn und Bürgertat, Geschichte der Frankfurter Polytechnischen Gessellschaft, 1816–1966*. Frankfurt/Main: Waldemar Kramer.

Levy, Hermann. 1966. *Industrial Germany: A Study of Its Monopoly Organizations and their Control by the State*. New York: Kelley.

Liberal Club of Chicago. 1930. *Chicago's Traction Situation: A Factual Analysis*.

Liepman, Kate. 1944. *The Journey-to-Work: Its Significance for Industrial and Community Life*. London: Routledge & Kegan Paul.

Lincoln, James. 1972. The Structure of Metropolitan Dominance. Unpublished Ph.D. dissertation. Department of Sociology, University of Wisconsin-Madison.

Lind, A. R. 1975. *Chicago Surface Lines*. Park Forest, Ill.: Transport History Press.

Linder, Wolf. 1973. *Der Fall Massenverkehr: Verwaltungsplanung und städtische Lebensbedingungen*. Frankfurt/Main: EVA.

Linder, Wolf. 1975. *Erzwungene Mobilität*. Frankfurt/Main: EVA.

Link, Werner. 1970. *Die amerikanische Stabilisierungspolitik in Deutschland, 1921–32*. Düsseldorf: Droste.

Lloyd, Henry D. 1903. *The Chicago Traction Question*. Chicago: Western Newspaper Union.

Logan, Thomas. 1972. The Invention of Zoning in the Emerging Planning Profession of Late 19th Century Germany. Unpublished Ph.D. dissertation. Chapel Hill: Department of City and Regional Planning, University of North Carolina.

Lopata, Helen Z. 1980. "The Chicago Woman: A Study of Patterns of Mobility and Transportation," *Signs*, 5 (Spring):161–9.

Lösch, August. 1952. *The Economics of Location*, trans, by W. H. Woglom and W. F. Stolper. New Haven, Conn.: Yale University Press.

Lucas, Erhard. 1969. *Frankfurt unter der Herrschaft des Arbeiter- und Soldatenrats, 1918–19*. Frankfurt/Main: Verlag Neue Kritik.

Ludwig, Heinrich. 1940. *Geschichte des Dorfes und der Stadt Bockenheim*. Frankfurt/Main: Waldemar Kramer.

MacMurray, G. T. 1945. "Chicago Weights Public Ownership," *Bus Transportation* (May):28–32.

MacShane, Clay. 1974. *Technology and Reform: Street Railways and the Growth of Milwaukee, 1887–1900*. Madison: State Historical Society of Wisconsin for the Department of History, University of Wisconsin.

# References

MacShane, Clay. 1975. American Cities and the Coming of the Automobile in the Nineteenth Century. Unpublished Ph.D. dissertation. Department of History, University of Wisconsin-Madison.

McClintock, Miller. 1926. Report and Recommendations of the Metropolitan Street Traffic Survey. Chicago: Chicago Association of Commerce.

McClintock, Miller. 1932. *The Greater Chicago Traffic Area: A Report of Major Traffic Facts of the City of Chicago and Surrounding Region*, 3 vols. Prepared for the Illinois Commission on Future Roads Program and Committee on Traffic and Public Safety. Chicago: City Council.

McDonald, Forest. 1958. "Samuel Insull and the Movement for State Regulatory Commissions," *Business History Review*, 23/36 (August):248–53.

McDonald, Forest. 1962. *Insull*. Chicago: Illinois.

McKay, John. 1976. *Tramways and Trolleys: The Rise of Urban Mass Transport*. Princeton, N.J.: Princeton University Press.

McKenzie, Roderick D. 1968. *Human Ecology*, edited and with an introduction by A. H. Hawley. Chicago: University of Chicago.

McShane, W., A. Bloch, and W. Ihlo. 1981. *The Energy Advantages of Public Transportation*. Washington, D.C.: Urban Mass Transportation Administration.

Madala, G. S. 1977. *Econometrics*. New York: McGraw-Hill.

Magistrat des Frankfurter Siedlungsamtes. 1927. *Frankfurter Verkehrsfragen*. Frankfurt/Main.

Magistrat: Stadt Frankfurt/Main. 1961. *Gesamtverkehrsplanung der Stadt. Frankfurt/Main*.

Magistrat: Stadt Frankfurt/Main. 1973. *Gesamtverkehrsplanung Frankfurt/Main*. Grundnetzprogramm U-Bahn und S-Bahn, 1973–85, Magistratsverlag.

Magistrat: Stadt Frankfurt/Main. 1973. *Mittelfristiges Verkehrsprogramm*.

Magistrat: Städtisches Verkehrsamt. 1925. *Frankfurter Verkehrsprobleme und Beiträge zu ihrer Lösung*. Frankfurt/Main.

Maier, Charles. 1970. "Between Taylorism and Technocracy: European Ideologies and the Vision of Industrial Productivity in the 1920's," *Journal of Contemporary History*, 5/1 (April):17–61.

Maier, Charles. 1975. *Rebuilding Bourgeois Europe*. Princeton, N.J.: Princeton University Press.

Maltbie, Milo R. 1901. The Street Railways of Chicago. Report of the Civic Federation of Chicago. Chicago: Reform Club Committee on Civic Affairs.

Mamon, Joyce A. and Harvey Marshall. 1977. "The Use of Public Transportation in Urban Areas: Toward a Causal Model," *Demography*, 14/1 (February): 19–31.

Mantel, E. H. 1971. "Economic Biases in Urban Transportation Planning and Implementation," *Traffic Quarterly*, 25:117–30.

Marcus, Steven. 1975. *Engels, Manchester and the Working Class*. New York: Vintage.

Maschke, E. 1970. "Outline of the History of German Cartels from 1873–1914," in M. Crouzet et al. (eds.), *Essays in European Economic History*. London: E. Arnold.

Massen, John A. 1936. Some Aspects of Chicago's Local Transportation Problem. Chicago: Committee on Traffic and Public Safety, City Council.

Mather, Neil W. 1976. An Empirical Study of Public and Private Supply of Electricity. Unpublished Ph.D. dissertation. Department of Economics, University of Wisconsin-Madison.

Mauer, Hermann. 1936. *Das Zusammenschlussproblem in der deutschen Automobilindustrie*. Schaffhausen: Meier.

# References

Mauersberg, Hans. 1960. *Wirschafts und Sozialgeschichte Zentraleuropäischer Städt in neuer Zeit.* Göttingen: Vandenhoeck and Ruprecht.

May, Ernst. 1928. "Grundlagen der Frankfurter Wohnungsbaupolitik," *Das Neue Frankfurt*, (7/8):113–57.

May, Ernst. 1930. "5 Jahre Wohnungsbautätigkeit," *Das Neue Frankfurt*, 10:21–35.

Mayer, Harold M. and Richard C. Wade. 1969. *Chicago: Growth of a Metropolis.* Chicago: University of Chicago Press.

Mazerath, Horst. 1970. *Nationalsozialismus und kommunale Selbstverwaltung.* Stuttgart: Kohlhammer.

Mazza, Frank and Sheila McCarthy. 1975. "Referendums Around the Nation," *Mass Transit*, (January):18, 26, 28.

Menke, Rudolf. 1975. *Stadtverkehrsplanung.* Stuttgart: Kohlhammer.

Menne, P. 1964. *Die Stadt: Frankfurt am Main und ihr Raum.* Frankfurt Stadt Archiv, Mimeo.

Merriam, C. E. (1929) 1970. *Chicago: A More Intimate View of Urban Politics.* New York: Arno.

Mertens, Dieter. 1962. "Veränderungen der Industriellen Branchenstruktur in der BRD, 1950–1960," in H. Koenig (ed.), *Wandlungen der Wirtschaftsstruktur in der BRD.* Berlin: Duncker and Humblot.

Meyer, John R., John F. Kain and Martin Wohl. 1972. *The Urban Transportation Problem.* Cambridge, Mass.: Harvard University Press.

Meyerson, Martin and Edward C. Banfield. 1955. *Politics, Planning, and the Public Interest.* New York: Free Press.

Miller, Zane L. 1968. *Boss Cox's Cincinnati,* New York: Oxford.

Mills, C. Wright. 1946. Small Business and Civic Welfare. Report of the Smaller War Plants Corp. to the Special Committee to Study Problems of American Small Business, U.S. Senate, 79th Congress, 2nd Session Senate Document #206, Washington, D.C.

Miquel, Johannes von. 1886. "Die Wohnungsnot der ärmeren Klassen in deutschen Grossstädten," *Schriften des Vereins für Sozialpolitik*, 30:10–20.

Mohler, Charles K. 1912. Report on Passenger Subway and Elevated Railroad Development. Committee on Traffic and Transportation, City Club of Chicago, April.

Mohler, Charles K. 1919. "The Fate of the Five Cent Fare," *National Municipal Review*, 8/7 (September):481–93.

Mohler, Charles K. 1923. "Chicago's Vicissitudes Under State Regulation of Street Railways," *National Municipal Review*, 7(4) (April):1–7.

Mollenkopf, J. H. 1975. "The Post-War Politics of Urban Development," *Politics and Society*, 5/3 (Fall):245–295.

Mooney, James. 1931. "The Line and Staff Principle in Industry," *The Military Engineer*, (January–February):3–9.

Mooney, James. 1933. *Reviving Business through Lower Automotive Taxation.* Berlin: International Motor Transport Congress.

Morehouse, Thomas A. 1965. The Determinants of Federal Policy for Urban Transportation Planning under the Federal Aid Highway Act of 1962. Unpublished Ph.D. dissertation. Department of Political Science, University of Minnesota.

Mowbray, R. 1969. *Road to Ruin.* Philadelphia: Lippincott.

Mullen, John Robert. 1976–7. "American Perceptions of German City Planning at the Turn of the Century," *Urbanism Past and Present*, 3 (Winter):5–15.

Müller, A. 1936. *Hitler's Motorisierte Stossarmee.* Paris: Editions du Carrefour.

# References

Müller-Raemisch, H. R. 1967. *Frankfurt: Stadt in der Entwicklung*. Berlin: Länderdienst-Verlag.

Murphy, Quinn W. 1955. "The Great Lakes Greyhound Story," *Motor Coach Age*, (November):3–10.

Muth, Richard. 1969. *Cities and Housing*. Chicago: University of Chicago Press.

National Research Council. 1952. *State Highway Administrative Bodies*. Washington, D.C.: Highway Research Board.

National Transportation Policy Study Commission. 1979. *National Transportation Policies through the Year 2000*. Washington, D.C.: U.S. Government Printing Office.

Navin, Thomas R. 1970. "The 500 Largest American Industries in 1917," *Business History Review*, 44/3 (Autumn):360–86.

Nelson, Walter. 1965. *Small Wonder: The Amazing Story of the Volkswagen*. Boston: Little, Brown.

Neumann, Franz. 1942. *Behemoth: The Structure and Practice of National Socialism*. London: Gollancz.

Newton, Ken. 1979. "Central Place Theory and Local Public Expenditure in Great Britain," presented at the International Political Science Association Congress, Moscow, Mimeo.

New York Committee on Municipal Ownership of Street Railways. 1896. Summary Report.

Niemayer, Rudolf. 1931. "Raumordnung im Rhein/Main-Gebiet," *Das Neue Frankfurt*, 8 :35–41.

Norton, Robert. 1979. *City Life Cycles and American Urban Policy*. New York: Academic Press.

O'Connor, Len. 1976. *Clout*. New York: Avon Books.

Office of Technology Assessment. 1975. *Energy, the Economy, and Mass Transit*. Washington, D.C.: Goverment Printing Office.

Office of Technology Assessment. 1979. *Changes in the Future Use and Characteristics of the Automobile Transportation System*. Washington, D.C.: Government Printing Office.

Organization for Economic Cooperation and Development. 1978. *The Future of the Automobile Industry*. Paris.

Ornati, Oscar. 1968. *Transportation and the Poor*. New York: Praeger.

Overton, Richard C. 1955. "Ralph Budd: Railroad Entrepreneur," *The Palimpset: Journal of the State Historical Society of Iowa*, 36/11 (November):421–80.

Owen, Wilfred. 1965. *The Metropolitan Transportation Problem*. Washington, D.C.: Brookings Institution.

Park, R. E. and E. W. Burgess. 1925. *The City*. Chicago: University of Chicago Press.

Park, Robert E. 1952. *Human Communities*. New York: Free Press.

Passer, H. C. 1953. *The Electrical Manufacturers: 1875–1900*, Cambridge, Mass.: Harvard University Press.

Pavlos, E. A. 1972. "Chicago's Crosstown: A Case Study in Urban Expressways," in D. Miller (ed.), *Urban Transportation Policy*. Lexington, Mass.: Lexington Books.

Peat, Marwick, Livingston, and Company. 1969. Evaluation of a Bus Transit System in a Selected Urban Area. Prepared for the Bureau of Public Roads, Federal Highway Administration, Washington, D.C.

Peat, Marwick, Mitchell, and Company. 1975. An Econometric Analysis of Public Transportation Planning Norms. Technical Memorandum Prepared for the Office of the Secretary, Department of Transportation, Washington, D.C.

People's Streetcar Ownership League. 1928. *Chicago's Local Transportation Problem*. Chicago.

279

# References

Pflug, Friedrich. 1929. "Der Kraftfahrzeugverkehr," in B. Harms (ed.), *Strukturwandlungen der Deutschen Volkswirtschaft*. Berlin: Hobbing.

Pisarski, Alan E. and Neils DeTerra. 1975. "American and European Transportation Responses to the 1973–74 Oil Embargo," *Transportation*, 4 :291–312.

Pred, Alan R. 1976. *The Spatial Dynamics of the U.S. Urban-Industrial Growth, 1800–1914*. Cambridge, Mass.: MIT Press.

Pred, Alan R. 1974. *Major Job-Providing Organizations and Systems of Cities*. Washington, D.C.: Association of American Geographers.

Prentiss, William. 1903. Street Car Strike/Municipal Ownership. Chicago, Pamphlet.

Preston, Richard E. 1978. "The Structure of Central Place Systems," in L. S. Bourne and J. W. Simmons (eds.), *Systems of Cities*. New York: Oxford University Press.

Pushkarv, Boris. 1980. Operating Energy Efficiencies. New York: Regional Planning Association, Mimeo.

Putman, Stephen H. 1975. "Urban Land Use and Transportation Models: A State-of-the Art Review," *Transportation Research*, (July):187–202.

Quaife, Milo, M. 1923. *Chicago's Highways Old and New*. Chicago: D. F. Keller and Company.

Rae, John B. 1965. *The American Automobile: A Brief History*. Chicago: University of Chicago Press.

Rasehorn, T. 1976. *Wohnen in der Demokratie: Soziales Mietrecht der BRD*. Darmstadt: Luchterhand.

Rebentisch, Dieter. 1975. *Ludwig Landman*. Wiesbaden: Steiner.

Reifschneider, Felix E. 1949. *Interurbans of the Empire State*. Orlando, Fla.

Richardson, Harry W. 1972. *Urban Economics*. Baltimore: Penguin Books.

Ridder, Klaus. 1969. *Vertikale Konzentration, Diversifikation und freier Wettbewerb im Verkehr*. Gottingen: Vandenhoeck and Ruprecht.

Riesser, Jacob. 1911. *The German Great Banks and Their Concentrations in Connection with the Economic Development of Germany*. Washington, D.C.: Natinal Monetary Commission.

Roth, Jürgen. 1975. *Z. B. Frankfurt: Die Zerstörung einer Stadt*. Frankfurt/Main: C. Bertelsmann.

Roth, Karl-Heinz. 1975. *Die "andere" Arbeiterbewegung*. Munich: Trikont.

Rothchild, Emma. 1973. *Paradise Lost: The Decline of the Auto-Industrial Society*. New York: Random House.

Rowe, L. S. 1906. "Municipal Ownership and Operation of Street Railways in Germany," *Annals of the American Academy of Science*, 27/1:3–12.

Rüleke, Jürgen. 1977. "Population Growth and Urbanization in Germany in the 19th Century," *Urbanism Past and Present*, (Summer):21–32.

St. Clair, D. J. 1981. "The Motorization and Decline of Urban Public Transit 1935–50," *Journal of Economic History*, 41 (September):579–600.

Sandhäger, Heinz. 1967. *Verkehrswege-Investitionen als Stabilisierungspolitisches Instrument*. Gottingen: Vandenhoeck and Ruprecht.

Saunder, Dan E. 1971. *Wheelin' and Dealin'*. North Newton, Kan.: Mennonite Press.

Schächterle, K. and G. Holdschür. 1965. *Gesamtverkehrsplanung Frankfurt am Main, Planungsfall*. Ulm: Neu Ulm.

Schilderberger, Friedrich. 1976. *Gottlieb Daimler and Karl Benz: Pioniere der Automobilindustrie*. Zurich: Musterschmidt.

Schippert, Carl. 1933. *The Antagonistic Attitude of the Railways towards Motor Transport and Its Economic and Social Consequences in Germany*. Berlin: International Motor Transport Congress.

# References

Schmacke, Ernst and W. Grottkopp. 1977. *Die Grossen 500: Deutschlands führende Unternehmen und ihr Management*. Dusseldorf: Droste.

Schmidt, E.P. 1935. The Development of the Street Railway Industry. Unpublished Ph.D. dissertation. University of Wisconsin-Madison.

Schmidt, K.A. 1958. *Studie über die Verkehrsverhältnisse in Frankfurt/Main*. Frankfurt/Main: Stadt Frankfurt Main.

Schneider, Ellen. 1962. "Die Stadt 'Offenbach' am Main im Frankfurter Raum." Inaugural Dissertation zur Erlangung des Doktorgrades Phil. Fakultät der Johann-Wolfgang-Goethe Universität, Frankfurt/Main.

Schneider, Wilhem. 1925. Siedlung und Verkehr in Gross-Frankfurt. Inaugural-Dissertation zur Erlangung des Doktorgrades der Phil. Fakultät der Johann-Wolfgang-Goethe Universität Frankfurt/Main.

Schnore, Louis. 1968. *The Urban Scene*. New York: Free Press.

Schott, Siegmund. 1912. *Die grossstädtischen Agglomerationen des Deutschen Reichs, 1871–1910*. Breslau: Korn.

Schultze, Joachim Heinrich. 1929. "Die Berufsstruktur der rheinmainischen Bevölkerung," *Rhein-Mainische Forschungen*, 2:3–5.

Schwartz, Ulysses S. 1935. "The Chicago Traction Problem." Speech before the City Club of Chicago, November 18. Chicago: City Club.

Scott, Mel. 1969. *American City Planning Since 1890*. Berkeley: University of California Press.

Securities and Exchange Commission (SEC). 1942. *Decisions and Reports*, Vol. 10. Washington, D.C.: Government Printing Office.

Seltzer, L. H. 1928. *A Financial History of the American Automobile Industry*. Boston: Houghton-Mifflin.

Short, James F., Jr. (ed.). 1971. *The Social Fabric of the Metropolis: Contributions of the Chicago School of Urban Sociology*. Chicago: University of Chicago Press.

Siebertz, Paul. 1943. *Karl Benz: Ein Pionier der Verkehrsmotorisierung*. Berlin: Lehmann.

Simpson and Curtis, Transportation Engineers. 1969. "Public Attitudes towards Transit," Interim Report, No. 4. Philadelphia.

Skocpol, Theda and Margaret Sommers. 1980. "The Uses of Comparative History in Macrosocial Inquiry," *Comparative Studies in Society and History*, 22/2 (April):174–97.

Sloan, Alfred. 1962. *My Years at General Motors*. Garden City, N.Y.: Doubleday.

Smerk, George. 1975. *Urban Transportation Policy*. Bloomington: University of Indiana Press.

Smith, R. 1974. *Ad Hoc Governments*. Beverly Hills, Calif.: Sage.

Snell, Bradford C. 1974. *American Ground Transport*. Washington, D.C.: Subcommittee on Antitrust and Monopoly of the Judiciary Committee, U.S. Senate.

Sombart, Werner. 1954. *Die deutsche Volkswirtschaft im 19. Jahrhundert und am Anfang des 20 Jahrhunderts*. Stuttgart: Kohlhammer.

Soot, Siim, et al. 1976. "The Chicago Area Regional Transportation Authority Referendum," *Traffic Quarterly*, (July):329–46.

Sorenson, Aage B. 1974. "A Model for Occupational Careers," *American Journal of Sociology*, 80():44–57.

Stadt Frankfurt/Main. 1969. *Stadtentwicklungsplanung und Gesamtverkehrsplan*, Frankfurt/Main: EVA.

Statistisches Amt und Wahlamt Frankfurt. 1907. *Statistisches Handbuch der Stadt Frankfurt/Main*.

Statistisches Amt und Wahlamt Frankfurt. 1927. *Statistisches Handbuch der Stadt Frankfurt/Main*.

# References

Statistisches Amt und Wahlamt Frankfurt. 1952–1972. *Statistisches Jahrbuch Frankfurt/ Main.*

Statistisches Amt und Wahlamt Frankfurt. 1975. *Frankfurter Verkehrsprobleme im inter- kommunalen Vergleich.* Frankfurter Statistische Berichte, Sonderheft 30.

*Statistisches Jahrbuch deutscher Städte,* M. Neefe (ed.) 1902/3. Jena: G. Fischer.

*Statistisches Jahrbuch deutscher Gemeinden.* 1972/73. Stuttgart: Kohlhammer.

Statistisches Reichsamt Abteilung Für Arbeiter-Statistik. 1910. *Wohnungsfürsorge in deutschen Städten.* Berlin: Carl Hermanns.

Statistisches Reichsamt (ed.) 1938. *Die Kraftverkehrswirtschaft im Jahre, 1937.* Berlin: Schmidt.

Stave, Bruce. 1972. *Socialism and the Cities,* Port Washington, N.Y.: Kennikat Press Corp.

Stedman, Seymour. 1914. "To Straphangers Who Vote," in *Issues of 1914.* Chicago: Cook County Socialist Party.

Stipak, Brian. 1973. "An Analysis of the 1968 Rapid Transit Vote in Los Angeles," *Transportation,* 2:71–86.

Stöber, Gerhard. 1964. *Struktur und Funktion der Frankfurter City.* Frankfurt/Main: EVA.

Stokes, Burton R. 1977. Testimony Before the Subcommittee on Transportation, U.S. Senate Committee on Environment and Public Works, Washington, D.C., October, Mimeo.

Sullivan, J. W. 1940. *Historical Data – Chicago Transportation.* Chicago: Chicago Surface Lines.

Swatek, Dieter. 1972. *Unternehmenskonzentration als Ergebnis und Mittel der National- Sozialistischen Wirtschaftpolitik.* Berlin: Duncker & Humbolt.

Swayne, Alfred E. 1934. *The Highway Users' Problem,* New York: Auto Manufacturers Association.

Taebel, Delbert A. and James V. Cornhels. 1977. *The Political Economy of Urban Trans- portation,* Port Washington, N.Y.: Kennikat Press Corp.

Tafuri, Manfredo. 1976. *Architecture and Utopia: Design and Capital Development.* Cam- bridge, Mass.: MIT Press.

Tarr, Joel. 1973. "From City to Suburb: The 'Moral' Influence of Transportation Tech- nology," in B. Callow (ed.), *Urban History.* New York: Oxford University Press.

Taylor, Eugene S. 1929. "Chicago's Superhighway Plan," *National Municipal Review,* 18/6 (June):371–6.

Thernstrom, Stephan. 1973. *The Other Bostonians.* Cambridge, Mass.: Harvard Univer- sity Press.

Thernstrom, Stephan and Richard Sennett (eds.). 1969. *Nineteenth Century Cities.* New Haven, Conn.: Yale University Press.

Thompson, Carl D. 1925. *Public Ownership: A Survey of Public Enterprises.* New York: Crowell.

Thompson, Carl D. 1930. "Why the Traction Ordinance Should Not Pass." Chicago: Committee Against the Traction Ordinance.

Tideman, S. N. 1939. Transit Issues, draft. Chicago: Douglas Aldermanic Papers. Chicago: Chicago Historical Society.

Transportation Advisory Group. 1965. The Proposed Chicago Crosstown Express- way. Chicago: Chicago Historical Society, Mimeo.

Transportation Workers Union of America. 1939. Convention Proceedings, New York.

U.S. Bureau of the Census, Department of Commerce and Labor. 1905. Special Re-

# References

ports: Street and Electrical Railways, 1902. Washington, D.C.: Government Printing Office.

1908. *Special Reports: Statistics on Cities.* Washington, D.C.: Government Printing Office.

1912. *Thirteenth Census of the United States,* Vol. IX, *Manufacturers, 1909.* Washington, D.C.: Government Printing Office.

1972. *Census of Manufacturers,* Vol. 2. Washington, D.C.: Government Printing Office.

1972. *County and City Data Book.* Washington, D.C.: Government Printing Office.

1976. *Historical Statistics of the United States,* Part 2. Washington D.C.: Government Printing Office.

1978. "Social and Economic Characteristics of the Metropolitan and Non-Metropolitan Population: 1977–1978." Current Population Reports, SER-P-23, No. 75. Washington, D.C.: Government Printing Office.

1978. *Statistical Abstract of the United States.* Washington, D.C.: Government Printing Office.

U.S. Department of Transportation (DOT). 1972. National Transportation Survey.

1976. Urban System Study. Washington, D.C.

1976. Annual Budget. Washington, D.C., Mimeo.

1976. *Innovation in Public Transportation: A Directory of Research, Development, and Demonstration Projects.* Washington, D.C.: Urban Mass Transportation Administration.

1976. Urban Mass Transportation Act of 1964 and Related Laws. Washington, D.C.: Government Printing Office.

1976. *Increasing Transit Ridership: The Experience of Seven Cities.* Washington, D.C.: Urban Mass Transportation Administration, Office of Policy and Program Development.

1976. *Urban Systems Study.* Washington, D.C.

U.S. Federal Highway Administration. 1975. *Highway Statistics.* Washington, D.C.

U.S. Housing Corporation. 1918. Chicago Southeastern District and Indiana Steel Towns Housing Survey, December 21.

U.S. National Resource Committee. 1940. *Urban Government,* Vol. 1: *Supplementary Report of the Urbanism Committee.* Washington, D.C.: Government Printing Office.

U.S. Senate Committee on Public Works. 1955. Hearings on the National Highway Program, February–June.

Varrentrap, Adolph. 1915. *Drei Oberbürgermeister von Frankfurt/Main.* Frankfurt/Main: Knauer.

Vatter, Harold G. 1952. "Closure of Entry in the American Automobile Industry," *Oxford Economic Papers,* 4 (October):213–34.

Verband der Automobilindustrie. 1973. *Mit dem Auto in die Zukunft.* Frankfurt/Main.

Vickers, Leslie. 1934. Fare Structures in Transit Industry, New York. Unpublished Ph.D. thesis. Department of Political Science, Columbia University.

Vogel, Walter and Christoph Weisz. 1976. *Akten zur Vorgeschichte der BRD.* Munich: R. Oldenburg.

Vorhees, Alan M. and Bellomo, Salvatore. 1970. "Urban Travel and City Structure," *Highway Research Record,* 322:121–35.

Vorlaufer, Karl. 1975. *Bodeneigentumsverhältnisse und Bodeneigentümergruppen im Cityerweiterungsgebiet Frankfurt/M-Westend.* Selbstverlag des Seminars für Wirtschaftsgeographie. Frankfurt/Main: J. W. Goethe Universität.

Vorwig. W. R. 1970. *Die deutsche Automobilindustrie und ihre Verbände.* Frankfurt/Main: Verband der Automobilindustrie.

# References

Wagner, Carl. 1889. *Denkschrift zu einem generellen Ringbahn-Projekt.* Frankfurt/Main: Baist.

Wallich, Henry C. 1955. *Mainsprings of German Revival.* New Haven, Conn.: Yale University Press.

Walther, Rudolf. 1943. *Der grossstädtische Verkehr im Rahmen des Siedlungsproblems.* Stuttgart: Kohlhammer.

Ward, David. 1971. *Cities and Immigrants: A Geography of Change in Nineteenth Century America.* New York: Oxford University Press.

Warner, Sam Bass, Jr. 1968. *The Private City: Philadelphia in Three Periods of Growth.* Philadelphia: University of Pennsylvania Press.

Warner, Sam Bass, Jr. 1975. *The Urban Wilderness.* New York: Harper & Row.

Warner, Sam Bass, Jr. 1976. *Streetcar Suburbs.* New York: Atheneum.

Wascoe, Dan. 1979. "The Interstate Fund Shuffle," *Mass Transit,* (June):56.

Webber, Melvin. 1976. *The BART Experience: What Have We Learned?* Berkeley: Institute of Urban Regional Development, Monograph 6.

Weber, Alfred. 1928 (1909). *Alfred Weber's Theory of the Location of Industries,* trans. by C. J. Friedrich. Chicago: University of Chicago Press.

Weber, Richard D. 1971. Rationalizers and Reformers: Chicago Local Transportation in the Nineteenth Century. Unpublished Ph.D. dissertation. Department of History, University of Wisconsin-Madison.

Weger, Wolfgang. 1976. *Die Autobiographie.* Frankfurt/Main: Verband der Automobilindustrie.

Weil, Reinhold. 1952. *Der Kraftomnibus-Linienverkehr in Westdeutschland.* Düsseldorf: Fischer.

Weiss, Leonard. 1962. *Economics and American Industry.* New York: Wiley.

Weiss, Lothar. 1904. "Die Tarife der deutschen Strassenbahnen," *Volkswirtschaftliche Abhandlungen der Bädischen Hochschulen,* Vol. II.

Weisser, Michael. 1975. "Arbeiterkolonien-Über die Motive zum Bau von Arbeitersiedlungen durch industrielle Unternehmen im 19. und frühen, 20. Jahrhundert in Deutschland," in Joachim Petsch (ed.), *Architektur und Städtebau im 19. Jahrhundert.* Berlin: Verlag für das Studium der Arbeiterbewegung.

Weitzel, A. 1924. "Siedlung und Verkehr Gross-Frankfurt am Main," in *Der Rhein/Mainische Städtekranz.* Frankfurt/Main: Heuerdruck.

Wenzel, Axel et al (eds.). 1974. *Frankfurt-Terror-Folter.* Frankfurt/Main: MEGA Flugschrift.

Werner, R. 1974. *Interdependenzen zwischen Städtebau-Konzeptionen und Verkehrssystem.* Gottingen: Vandenhoeck and Ruprecht.

Wiedenbauer, Anton and Hans-Jürgen Hoyer. 1968. *Fahrt in die Zukunft: Die Geschichte der Frankfurter Strassenbahn.* Frankfurt/Main: Kramer.

Wiersch, Bernd. 1974. *Die Vorbereitung des Volkswagens.* Hannover: Technische Hochschule.

Wiese, Arthur E. 1979. "Public Opinion: A Mixed Bag for Transit," *Mass Transit,* 5/9 (September):24–34.

Willeke, Rainer. 1975. *Verkehr und Stattshaushalt.* Frankfurt/Main: Verband der Automobilindustrie.

Whitt, J. Allen. 1975. Means of Movement: The Politics of Modern Transportation Systems. Unpublished Ph.D. thesis. Department of Sociology, University of California, Santa Barbara.

Wilbur Smith and Associates. 1968. *Patterns of Car Ownership, Trip Generation and Trip*

# References

*Sharing in Urbanized Areas*. Washington, D.C.: Bureau of Public Roads, U.S. Department of Transportation.

Wilcox, Delos F. 1919. "Solving the Traction Problem from the Public Point of View." An address at the 10th Anniversary of the New York State Conference of Mayors and City Officials, Schenectady, N.Y., June.

Wilcox, Delos F. 1921. *Analysis of the Electrical Railway Problem*. New York: D. F. Wilcox.

Wilcox, Delos F. 1925. *Why the Utilities Win: Sidelights of the Denver Tramway Case*. Grand Rapids, Mich: Public Service.

Wonnacott, R. J. and T. H. Wonnacott. 1970. *Econometrics*. New York: Wiley.

Wünschmann, Peter. 1972. *Stellungsnahme zum Gesamtverkehrsplan, Frankfurt/Main*. Frankfurt/Main: Frankfurter Forum für Stadtentwicklung.

Yago, Glenn. 1978. "Current U.S. Transportation Politics," *International Journal of Urban and Regional Research*, 2/3 (July):351–9.

Yago, Glenn. 1979. "What's Good for General Motors is Good for General Motors," *These Times*, (April 18–24):12–14.

Yago, Glenn. 1980. "Corporate Power and Urban Transportation," in M. Zeitlin (ed.), *Classes, Class Conflict, and the State*, Cambridge: Winthrop.

Yago, Glenn. 1982. "Class, Politics, Mass Transit, and the City," *Comparative Social Research*, 5:299–338.

Yago, Glenn. 1983. "The Sociology of Transportation," *Annual Review of Sociology*, 9:173–90.

Zapf, Wolfgang. 1965. *Wandlungen der deutschen Elite: Ein Zirkulationsmodell deutscher Führungsgruppen 1919–1961*. Munich: Piper.

Zwerling, Stephen. 1974. *Mass Transit and the Politics of Technology: A Study of BART and the San Francisco Bay Area*. New York: Praeger.


## Archival References

*National Archives (NA), Washington, D.C.*
  Record Group 3, U.S. Housing Corporation, Boxes 406–407.
  Record Group 30, Bureau of Public Roads, Boxes 420, 3469.
  Record Group 48, National Resources Planning Board, Boxes 56–70.
  Record Group 10, Department of Justice, File Nos. 60-107-09 to 60-107-27
*National Archives (NA) Chicago, Ill.*
  Court Records of the U.S. vs. NCL et al., Criminal and Civil Actions
*American Public Transit Association, Washington, D.C.*
  File No 900.01, various cities
  File No. 308.01
*Chicago Historical Society (CHS) Chicago, Ill.*
  Roewade Papers, Lobdell Papers, Sheridan Papers, Douglas Aldermanic Papers, Dean Papers, Durand Papers, Richberg Papers, Larned Papers, Moore Papers.
*Wisconsin Historical Society, Madison*
  Blaine Papers
*Highway Action Coalition, Environmental Action, Washington, D.C.*
  Files of various highway construction fights.

# References

*General Motors Public Affairs Library, Detroit, Mich.*
  GM Files R-89, G-230, G-250
*Federal Highway Administration, U.S. Department of Transportation, Washington, D.C.*
  Chicago Case Study File, Urban System Study
*Frankfurter Stadtarchiv (FSA), Frankfurt/Main, Federal Republic of Germany*
  File Reference Nos.: R1770, R1743, R1797/IV, R34/No.4d, R1711, R1797/IV,
    4117/1/Bd.1, 1233/14–26/Bd.1, 3461/Bd.1–2
*Bundesarchiv, Koblenz, Federal Republic of Germany*
  File Reference Nos.: R42/753, R4311/748, R11/1542, R7/3288, R78/1542, R43/1468,
    R4311/748, R43/753, R4311/753, R11/1542, R11/1540, R4311/749a, R58/170, R58/172,
    R11/1516, R4311/748, R11/1540, R431/749a, R4311/753, NS24/145, R4311/747

# Index

# Index

# Index

# Index

Liberal Club of Chicago, 161
Liberty League, 39
Lindley, William, 89
Lingnau, Dr. Robert, 111, 116
Linsenhoff, H., 117
Lobdell, E.L., 151, 159
local economic activities, 18, 19
Local Transportation Committee, 141, 145, 146
Lortz, Rudolph, 121
Lubbert, Erich, 37, 44

Mack Manufacturing, 60
Mallough, Charles, 158
Maltbie, Milo, 145
Massachusetts Bay Transit Administration (MBTA), 207
Master Plan, 119
Master Plan of Residential Land Use in Chicago, 167
May, Ernst, 97, 98, 99, 103, 107, 118, 251n11
mechanization, 29–30
Mellon, Andrew, 53
Merchants Club, 151, 153
Merck-Finck Bank, 127
Merriam, Charles H., 149
Merzbach, S., 85
Metropolitan Atlanta Regional Transit Authority, 202
metropolitan growth, 19
military importance of motorization, 241n14
Miguel, Johannes von, 85, 86, 180, 185
Mobil Oil, 199
Möller, Walther, 122, 124
monopolization of transit, 136
Mooney, James, 31, 38–9, 40
Mor, Martin, 90
Moses, Robert, 203
motorization, 35, 36–45, 68
Motor Transit Corporation, 59
Mueller Certificates, 149, 150, 254n13
Mueller Law, 146, 147
Municipal Architectural Commission, 121
Municipal Department IV for Planning and Construction, 121
Municipal Electrical and Rail Office (SEBA), 93
Municipal Government Act of 1935, 241n16
"municipal industrialization," 11, 32, 90, 178
municipalization of transit, 34

Municipal Ownership Delegate Convention, 146
Municipal Transportation Office, 95, 116–17
Municipal Voters League, 140

*Nahverkehrsverbände*, 187
Nash, Charles W., 57
National Advisory Commission for a National Highway Policy, 72
National Automobile Chamber of Commerce, 57, 72
National City Lines (NCL), 24, 58, 59–61, 63, 65
National Civic Federation (NCF), 54
National Committee on Urban Transportation, 73
National Highway Users Conference (NHUC), 72, 73, 170
nationalization of rail transit, 31–4, 185
National League of Cities, 203
National Resource Planning Board (NRPB), 70–1, 166
Nationalsozialistische Deutsche Arbeiterpartei (NSDAP), 43
Nationalsozialistisches Kraftfahrkorps (NSKK), 40, 43
National Trailways Bus Company, 172
national transit policy, x, 33, 182
National Transportation Policy Study Commission, 203
National Transportation Report, 200
Nehring, Oberstleutenant Walther, 37
Neue Heimat, 122
New Deal highway policy, 70
Niemayer, Rheinhold, 107, 110
Nitzling, Erich, 121
Nixon, Richard, 198
Non-Partisan Citizens' Traction Ordinance Committee, 161
Nordhoff, Heinz, 46
North Chicago City Railway, 135
Northeastern Illinois Regional Planning Commission, 171
Norton, Charles D., 151, 254n14
Null Tarifbewegung, 126

Oakland Study, 64
Office of Technology Assessment, 203
Omnibus Corporation, 58, 158
"One City–One Fare," 145
Opel AG, 30, 31, 35, 48, 103, 105
Osborne, Cyrus R., 38, 172

# Index

technology, transit, 2, 55
tertiary employment, 17, 178
Thomazewski, Otto, 121
Thompson, Bill, 158, 160
Thyssen Steel, 207
Todt, Dr. Fritz, 42, 105, 107, 110
"traction settlement ordinances," 147–50
Tractions and Subway Commission, 158
traffic regulations, 71, 256n31
Transbus, 203
"transit trust," 136
Transportation Advisory Group, 174
Transportation Advisory Office, 116
Transportation Office, 99, 102
Transport Workers Union-Congress of Industrial Organizations (TWU-CIO), 65

U-Bahn, 124, 125, 126, 243n23
United Cities Motor Transit (UCMT), 59
urban centrality, 16–18, 214
urban industrial structure, 18–21
urbanization, 1, 12–16, 179, 182, 183; German, 221–2, 225, 230–1; U.S., 223–4, 232–3
urbanization index, 215
Urban Mass Transportation Administration (UMTA), 199, 200, 208
U.S. Construction Company, 137
U.S. Housing Corporation (USHC), 159
U.S. Manufacturers Export Association, 38

Verband der Automobil-industrie (VDA), 45–6; see also Reichverband der Automobilindustrie

Verein für Gesundheitspflege, 85
Verein für Vorbereitung der Autobahn Hansastädte–Frankfurt–Basel (HAFRABA), 41–2, 103–5, 107, 109, 117; see also Gesellschaft zur Vorbereitung der Reichsautobahn
Verein für Wohnungsreform, 88
Volksauto, 41

Wacker, Charles H., 151, 153
Walker, W.R., 151
Warren, Fletcher, 38
Washington Metropolitan Transit Authority, 202
Ways and Freytag, 126
Weikel, A., 116
Weiman, W., 85
Weintraut, J., 85
Werno, Charles, 149
Westinghouse, 63
West Side Alliance, 162
Widener, George, 137
Wilcox, Delos, 49
Wilson, Woodrow, 72
Winter, Eduard, 38–9
Wirtschafsgruppe Fahrzeugindustrie, 45
Workers' and Soldiers' Council, 94, 95
Wörner, Anton, 42
Wrigley, William, 158

Yellow Truck and Coach, 58, 59
Yerkes, Charles T., 53, 136, 137, 141, 145, 150, 151, 190

Zoning Act of 1891, 88